British
Social and Economic History

from 1760 to the present day

Peter Lane

Oxford University Press

Dedicated to Anthony Paul

Oxford University Press, Walton Street, Oxford OX2 6DP

Oxford London Glasgow
New York Toronto Melbourne Wellington
Kuala Lumpur Singapore Jakarta Hong Kong Tokyo
Delhi Bombay Calcutta Madras Karachi
Nairobi Dar es Salaam Cape Town

Printed in Great Britain by
Spottiswoode Ballantyne Limited, Colchester.

Contents

Preface

In preparing this volume I have had three purposes in mind. The first is to present information to the increasing number of pupils who study this subject for their examinations. The second aim, which does not conflict with the first, is to give the pupils a taste of 'history' and 'the historian at work' by a plentiful use of original material in the Documents section which appears at the end of each chapter and as captions to the numerous illustrations which have themselves been carefully integrated with the text. The third aim has been to help the pupils to acquire a number of skills — by asking them to write, research, compare, criticise, draw and paint. I have provided a wide variety of questions in each chapter in the hope that pupils of different interests and at different stages of development will be able to find enough that is interesting and challenging. It is hoped that the glossary at the end of the book will be found useful. Words that appear in the glossary are picked out in the text in italic. Quotations appearing in the text are preceded by an asterisk.

I would like to acknowledge in particular the debt I owe to the editors of the many collections of documents which have appeared in the recent past. While I have used their collections in preparing this volume, I hope that in turn this volume will lead pupils to a deeper study of the original material available in these collections.

Neither the text nor the suggestions for further study and work are in any way exhaustive. The nature of the subject is such that no one book could cover everything, but I hope that this text will act as a launching pad from which students may 'take-off' into a study of topics and subjects which interest them.

Unit One

Economic changes 1760–1850

Revolution or evolution?

You may have heard the term 'the industrial revolution' used to describe the great changes that have taken place over the last two hundred years or so. The words were first used in the 1880s by Professor Arnold Toynbee to describe the changes that had taken place between 1760 and 1830. He suggested that before 1760 little or no change had taken place, but that after 1760 there was a rapid and complete transformation of society.

Because of the work of many historians we now know that this is a false picture and that there had been many changes in British industry before 1760. Indeed, one professor writes about the 'industrial revolution of the thirteenth century' while another writes about the 'industrial revolution of the sixteenth century'. In fact, over many years there had been a gradual process of changes which we call evolutionary rather than revolutionary.

However, the rate of change (or evolution) was much greater after 1760 than it had been before. By 1850 Britain was quite a different country to what it had been in 1750. Huge factories in large towns and cities (Unit 2), housing massive machines powered by steam-engines, were producing enormous quantities of goods of various sorts. Britain had become 'The Workshop of the World' by the middle of the nineteenth century and many of its people enjoyed a standard of life that had previously been the privilege of a very few.

In this Unit we will examine the industrial and agricultural changes that took place between 1760 and 1850. While making this study and learning about various inventions remember that these changes made Britain a much richer country than it had been. Each year the working people of the country, using whatever machinery was available to them, produced many and different kinds of goods – wheat, bricks, glass, beer, clothes and so on. In 1688 the total value of the goods produced was £48m; in 1801 the total value was £232m and in 1901 this had risen to £1,642m.

British agriculture and industry was producing more wealth each year and each British workman was producing more than his father or his grandfather had done – because of the improved machinery that he was using.

(Opposite) The pride in the achievements of the nineteenth century captured in the cover of the *Illustrated London News*.

3

Chapter 1   Before the great changes

Population

As historians we have to try 'to see' the past in our mind's eye. In the case of Britain before 1760 this is very difficult. Although the towns and counties have familiar names, Britain was very different from the country in which we live.

In 1700 the population of England and Wales was about $5\frac{1}{2}$ million, less than the population of London today, and only about 1 million more than the population had been in 1600. Although most mothers had many babies, few of these lived beyond the age of five, and few baby girls lived to become mothers themselves. So, there was only a slow rise in the size of population.

In the graph you can see that in 1730 more people died than were born. The population therefore actually went down that year. However, you can also see that from 1733 the death rate fell, so although the birth rate did not rise very much after that date, the final result was an increase in population.

One major reason for this fall in the death rate was that there were many very good harvests between the years 1690–1740. This led to a fall in the price of bread, the main food of the people. There was also a high demand for workers to get the harvest in. This meant that wages rose and that there was full employment.

So people had money to spend on better food including the potato which had been brought from America at the end of the sixteenth century but did not become part of ordinary people's diet until the eighteenth century. Today we know

A view of Manchester across the River Irwell in 1745 by which time it had grown from the town described by Celia Fiennes in 1698:

* Manchester looks exceedingly well at the entrance, very substantial buildings, the houses mostly of brick and stone, the old houses are timber work. There is a very large church all stone which stands so high that walking round the churchyard you see the whole town and also the other town that lies below, called Salford, which is divided from this by the river Irwell.
(Fiennes, *The Great Journeys* 1698.)

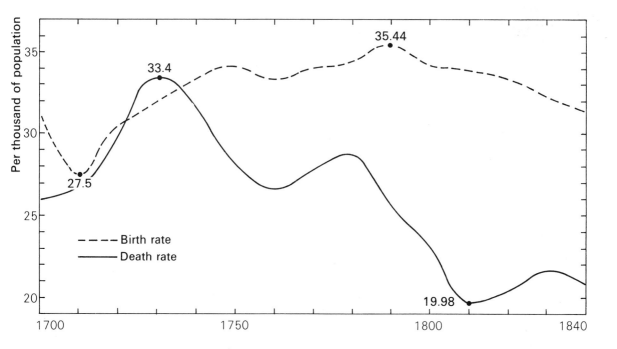

Changes in the birth-rate and death-rate from 1700 to 1840. Between 1728 and 1730 there were bad harvests. How can you tell this from looking at the graph?

that the potato is a most valuable food. There can be little doubt that its introduction had a good deal to do with the fall in the death rate.

Towns and villages

Before the industrial revolution most British people lived in small villages. Nowadays most of us live in large towns or cities.

In the eighteenth century London had a population of 500,000, which would make it a big town even today, but Bristol and Norwich, the next largest towns, had populations of only 30,000 in 1730. In 1700 Liverpool had a population of only 6,000.

Occupations

Most people worked in agriculture — using fairly primitive tools to get a living from the land. There were, of course, a number of other industries and trades. Since 1300 coal had been mined in the North East, some to be sold in London. Copper, tin and lead were also mined. There were iron foundries (see Chapter 3). There were brewing and milling firms in which men had long ago learned to use the water-wheel to provide power.

Water-wheels and machines worked by horses (the most common type of power) were primitive. The eighteenth century workman produced little compared with today's workman. He received very poor wages and had a low standard of living.

Before the steam-engine was developed and in places where water power was not readily available, horsepower was used to drive grinding and crushing wheels.

Harvesting was a laborious task. While one man cut the wheat with a sickle (right centre), a girl made bonds from straw, which a man on her right used to bind the sheaves together. A third man (on the left) put the sheaves into stooks.

Domestic industry

Most people lived in simple cottages with one or two rooms downstairs and one or two bedrooms upstairs. In many of these cottages people worked in the woollen industry.

British woollen goods had been bought and sold throughout the world for centuries. The wool was sold by the farmer to the wool merchant, who employed people in one or other of the various jobs to be done to turn the wool into cloth. The greasy, dirty fleece off the sheep's back had to be:

a) sorted – the long wool being separated from the short;

b) washed in a stream to get rid of the dirt;

c) *carded* – combed so that all the fibres lay in the right direction;

d) spun – by a 'spinner' or 'spinster' using either a distaff (a short stick with a V-shaped top) and a spindle or a spinning wheel. The fine thread which resulted from spinning was then handed to

e) a weaver who wove the thread on a loom, making a piece of cloth.

All these tasks were carried out by people in cottages.

Cottage hand-spinning in the eighteenth century. This was the downstairs room of the cottage. The spinning wheels would be pushed into a corner when the family wanted to eat. Their food was cooked over the open fire.

1 *Why was this system of production known as the 'domestic' system?*
2 *What sort of lighting did the cottages have?*
3 *Suggest some disadvantages of this system.*
4 *Where might the men be working?*

The merchant then gave the cloth to the *fuller*. A mixture of fuller's earth and water was used to thicken the cloth which was then stretched on frames called *tenters* (hence the word 'tenterhooks') until it was dry. The dried, thickened cloth was then brushed with teasles to bring any loose ends to the surface. It was then given to the cropper who used a large pair of shears or scissors to get rid of loose ends and so give the cloth a smooth finish.

These tasks could not be done in the cottage, so small mills or workshops grew up under the control of the merchants. They also employed dyers who used plants grown in Britain or imported from abroad to make the dyes which gave each cloth its special colour.

Local industry

Most trades were carried out in this way, in peoples' homes or nearby. Other domestic industries included blacksmithing, nail making, and other metal trades. Most small towns also had their own carpenter, baker, brewer and candle or soap manufacturer. Most peoples' needs were satisfied by local tradesmen and craftsmen.

One reason why goods were not traded more widely was because transport was so slow. Until railways were developed it was not possible to sell something throughout the country. A Cornish dairy farmer, for example, could not sell his milk in London. It would have turned sour long before it arrived!

Changing society

So we have a picture of a thinly populated country in which most people lived in small villages or towns. They worked in

7

A Birmingham forge, 1784, when there were hundreds of forges, attached to such hovels, within a few miles of the expanding town. In such places were made the millions of nails used in industry and building. The whole family helped at the forge and for very little reward for the hard, brutalising work.

agriculture, and the woollen industry (and other 'domestic' industries) from which they gained enough to provide themselves with a low standard of living.

However, it was a changing society. Towns like Liverpool were growing because of an increased volume of trade with other countries.

An important point to note is that people in Britain were free to move to growing cities like Liverpool. In some European countries (like France and Russia) people were not so free because they were forced to stay with the landowner. This mobility gave the British an advantage over their rivals in trade and industry. A British industrialist could get people to come and work for him. New ports, towns and industrial centres developed where these people worked.

Also, it was a society which was *socially mobile*. If a man made a lot of money, he could buy land, get a title (like Earl or Viscount) or become a member of the House of Commons. In a short time he would be an accepted member of the upper class. In France and several other European countries there was no such movement between classes. The aristocracy looked down on tradesmen and industrialists and would not mix with them. They thought that it was wrong to earn money by manufacturing. In Britain it was different. English

This shows part of the Brighton-Henfield road as it went past the ruins of the medieval manor of Poynings (on the right). Such paths were muddy (or in the summer, dusty), often flooded and deeply-rutted.

Most of the early machinery was made from wood by carpenters, wheelwrights and millwrights. But there was a long-established use of iron and steel parts for some machines. The skills and tools of the metalworkers (smiths, braziers and clockmakers) were used to make the machine parts. The clock-makers in this picture are using wheel-cutting engines to cut gear-wheels. The power was supplied by the labourer turning a wheel (centre of picture) which, through rope-drives, pulleys and shafts, operated the milled cutting wheel used by the skilled craftsman.

[Wheel-cutting Engine.]

landowners were quite willing to become part-owners of mines when coal was discovered on their estates. In fact, most of our English aristocracy is descended from people who made their money in trade or industry.

When the need arose for money to build factories and buy machines, the early industrialists of the late eighteenth century were able to borrow from the aristocracy. They could depend on the local Earl, Lord or squire to invest some of his money in the hope of getting a profit on it. French, German and Russian landowners were less likely to invest in this way, and foreign industrialists often found it difficult to raise money.

Britain had another advantage in her skilled craftsmen. Men such as the blacksmith, wheel turner, millwright, carpenter, metal turner and others were an essential base on which the industrial revolution was founded. Why do many under-developed countries today find it difficult to become industrialized? One reason is that they do not have the skilled workmen needed to build, maintain and work the machinery of a modern industrialized society.

When the early industrialists looked for people to build the first machinery, they found enough among the existing craftworkers. Without these men the industrial revolution would not have got under way.

Documents

Was life better in pre-industrial Britain?

a) **The clothier tries to cheat the domestic worker**

We'll make the poor weavers work at a low rate,
We'll find fault where there is none, and so we will
  bate *(pay less)*,
If trading goes dead, we will presently show it,
But if it grows good, they shall never know it;
We'll tell them that cloth beyond sea will not go,
We care not whether we keep clothing or no;
By poor people's labour we fill up our purse,
Although we do get it with many a curse.
(from J. Burnley, *History of Wool and Woolcombing*
1883)

b) **A low standard of living is normal**

Where the poor are full of work they are never empty
of wages; they eat while the others starve, and have a
tolerable plenty; while in the unemployed counties it
goes hard with them. And whence is all this? Look to
the lands, and consequently to the estates of the
gentry; the manufacturing counties are calculated for
business, the unemployed for pleasure; the first are
thronged with villages and great towns, the last with
parks and great forests; the first are stored with people,
the last with game. The reason of the thing answers
for itself; a poor labouring man that goes abroad to his
day's work and husbandry, hedging, ditching, threshing,
carting, etc, and brings home to his wife his week's
wages, suppose at eightpence to twelvepence a day or
in some counties less, if he has a wife and three or four
children to feed, and get little or nothing for themselves,
must fare hard and live poorly: 'tis easy to suppose it
must be so.
(Daniel Defoe, *A Plan of English Commerce* 1728)

c) **Cruelty to child workers**

A most unhappy practice prevails in most places to
apprentice poor children, no matter to what master
provided he lives out of the parish; if the child serves
the first forty days we are rid of him for ever. The master
may be a tiger in cruelty; he may beat, abuse, strip
naked, starve, or do what he will to the poor innocent
lad. I knew a poor old weaver who some time ago took
a poor apprentice from another parish; he covenanted,
as is usual, to teach him his trade, to provide and allow
him meat, drink, apparel, etc and indemnify the parish
whence he took him, and to give him two good new
suits of wearing apparel at the end of his apprenticeship.
This master has several times been convicted of theft,
and had then actually left off his trade through
weakness and old age, and as soon as the money he had
with the boy was spent, threw himself, apprentice and
all, upon the parish.
(from an Enquiry into the causes of the Increase of
the Poor 1738)

1 *Make a list of the ways in which the clothier cheated
the domestic worker (a). Why did these workers not
form trade unions?*

2 *What evidence is there in (b) that 1728 was a 'bad
year'? Look at the table on p.5 and say why 1728 was
not typical of the period 1690–1740. What effect did
the bad harvest have on the death rate? Can you
suggest why this was so in 1728–30 and would not
be so today?*

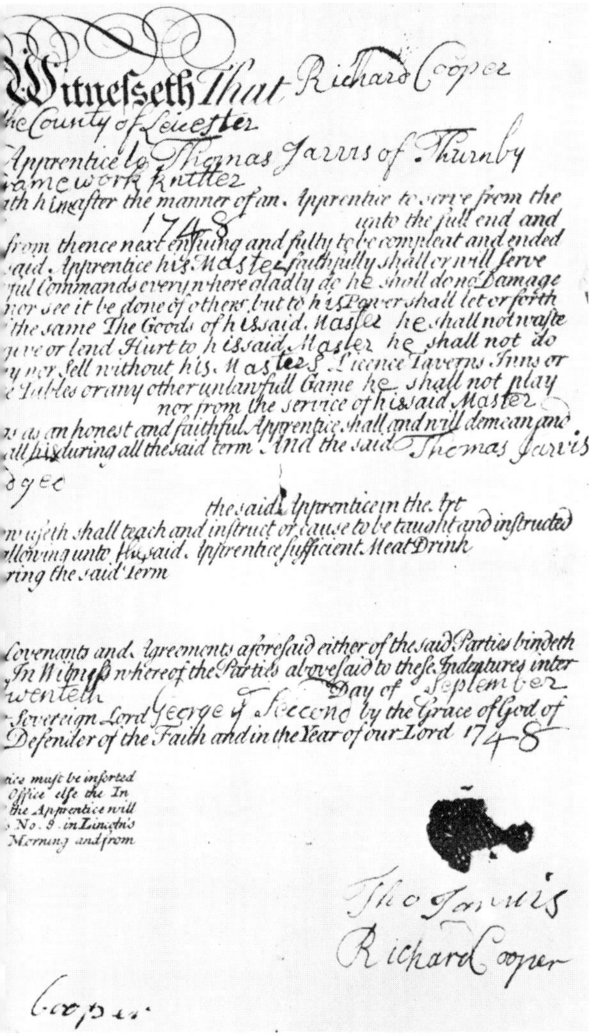
Witnesseth That Richard Cooper
the County of Leicester
Apprentice to Thomas Jarvis of Thurnby
ame work knitter
ith him after the manner of an Apprentice to serve from the
1748 unto the full end and
from thence next ensuing and fully to be compleat and ended
said Apprentice his Master faithfully shall or will serve
ful Commands every where gladly do he shall do no Damage
nor see it be done of others, but to his Power shall let or forth
the same The Goods of his said Master he shall not waste
give or lend Hurt to his said Master he shall not do
y nor sell without his Masters Licence Taverns Inns or
Tables or any other unlawfull Game he shall not play
nor from the service of his said Master
as an honest and faithful Apprentice shall and will demean and
all his during all the said term And the said Thomas Jarvis
the said Apprentice in the Art
useth shall teach and instruct or cause to be taught and instructed
allowing unto his said Apprentice sufficient Meat Drink
ring the said Term
Covenants and Agreements aforesaid either of the said Parties bindeth
In Witness whereof the Parties abovesaid to these Indentures inter
twentieth Day of September
Sovereign Lord George the Second by the Grace of God of
Defender of the Faith and in the Year of our Lord 1748
ice must be inserted
Office else the In
the Apprentice will
No. 9 in
Morning and from
Tho Jarvis
Richard Cooper
Cooper

d) The indenture of Richard Cooper.

3 *Look at (d). Who had looked after Richard Cooper before this document was signed? Why, do you think, did they want to sign him into an apprenticeship? What was the name and occupation of the master who signed him on? Why is it, do you think, that such young children could not work in a modern factory?*

4 *Look at document (c) and (d). Make a list of the duties owed by 'the master' to his apprentice. How might a master become 'a tiger in cruelty'?*

5 *Make a five- or six-word newspaper headline for each of these documents. A collage of these might be used to illustrate the theme, 'The eighteenth century'.*

Questions on Chapter One

1 *Liverpool was one of the ports which were growing rapidly during the early eighteenth century. Can you say why it was growing, and why this growth was a sign of economic development? What, do you think, were the occupations of some of the Liverpool rich? How did such people help the early industrialists?*

2 *What evidence is there in this Chapter that there were a number of skilled craftsmen in pre-industrial Britain?*

3 *What evidence is there that the majority of the British people were engaged in agriculture as well as in some sort of industry? Do you think this was a good thing? What are some of the advantages and some of the disadvantages of the domestic system?*

4 *Can you show* how and why, *most villages and small towns were more or less self-supporting? Why would this indicate that most people put up with a fairly low standard of living?*

5 *What forms of power were used to work machinery in Britain before 1760? Why did the workers in these industries produce less per hour than workers in modern industry? How did this affect the level of wages and the standard of living enjoyed by the workpeople?*

6 *Write a letter from a child in a pre-industrial village on 'Life in 1760'. Consult the Documents and the Pictures in the Chapter.*

7 *Paint or draw any scene from 'Life in pre-industrial Britain'. You might choose a cottage interior, an agricultural worker, a spinning wheel or a village street. The class might wish to construct a frieze – which could be linked to other friezes – to make a display of 'British social and economic development since 1760'.*

Chapter 2 Agricultural revolution

This cartoon by Cruikshank in 1835 made fun of the merchants and factory owners who bought farms with the newly-made wealth. Such people often became 'improving' farmers and landowners. They were thus able to make a good profit on their investment and also provide the country with the extra food required by the growing population.

Demand for changes

We have seen that the population doubled between 1700 and 1801. It was 12·6 million in 1811 and 14·4 million in 1821. This increase was not spread evenly throughout the country. The most rapid growth was in towns and cities. By the early nineteenth century there was a sizeable urban, industrial population. This urban population had to be fed. But the old methods of farming, which had been able to supply enough food for $5\frac{1}{2}$ million people were unable to provide enough for more than double that number.

Alongside the growth of towns there was a rise in the number of rich men buying farms and estates. These men had made their fortunes out of industry or trade. They used their business sense to try to make a profit out of their newly-acquired property. This led them to look for ways of changing the old, wasteful system.

This is a page from a survey book of Strettington, Sussex, made in 1781. The survey shows the numbered strips in various furlongs in the open field system. On another page the names of the owners of these strips were given. Surveys such as this had to be made by Enclosure Commissioners so that they could find out what land was owned by each person and then determine how much 'compact' land was to be awarded to each.

1 *How can you explain the name given to each of the 'furlongs' in the open field?*

2 *Why did it seem 'fair' to allocate each farmer some land in each of these furlongs rather than create a compact farm?*

3 *Imagine that you are the owner of strip numbered 2 in each furlong. Write your own criticism of this system of farming.*

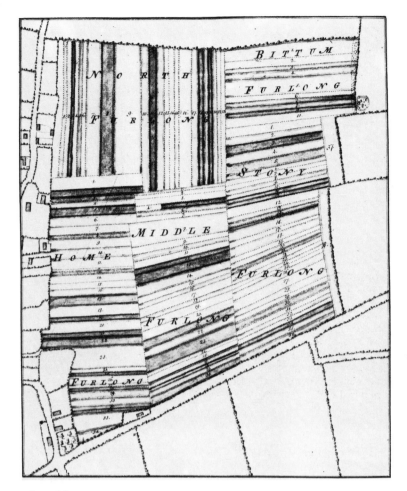

The old system

In 1700 throughout the Midlands and Eastern England there was a system of *open fields*. Each village or an estate would have on average three main fields. One farmer would have a strip or a number of strips in each of these fields. There would also be a *common* or waste ground which was not divided up. In fact, it was never ploughed at all. It was used as grazing ground for each farmer's animals and as the source of firewood, fencing, pig food and so on.

This system had provided enough food for the smaller population of 1700. But by the middle of the century there was a demand for a change in this system.

Enclosures

From about 1760 onwards a movement grew up for turning the separate strips into compact holdings, each enclosed behind its own hedge. Those who led this movement believed that *enclosure* would save land and time, and allow the farmer to experiment. Those who supported the enclosing of the open fields also wanted to divide up the commons and wastes so that those too might become part of compact and separate farms.

Enclosure Acts

Sometimes the reallocation was done by agreement between all the people concerned.

But if the more important landowners could not persuade the less well-off tenants to agree to a change, they went to Parliament. There they paid £5,000–£7,000 for a private *Act of Parliament*. When this Act was passed it would legalize the enclosure of the fields and commons of their villages. But first they had to get the agreement of the owners of three-quarters of the land involved. This would not be difficult where one or two people owned most of the land. They then had to fix a notice on the local church door for three Sundays, telling the rest of the villagers of their intentions. Having done so they then presented their Bill to a Committee of the House of Commons which was allowed to hear evidence for and against the scheme. When this Committee was satisfied with the proposals the Bill went before the whole House and, in due course, became law. Then the Commons appointed between three and seven Enclosure Commissioners to carry out the proposals in the new Act.

This painting shows John Cotes, MP for Shropshire and a smaller landowner, with his steward. They are watching a workman adjusting a new type of plough, known as a Rotherham plough. This had a triangular frame, unlike the older ploughs which had a four-sided frame. The new plough could be pulled by horses whereas the older, more cumbersome ploughs had to be pulled by the slower oxen.

These Commissioners had to map out the land, check everyone's claim to a share, divide the land and settle all the arguments about fencing, pasture rights and ownership of woods. Enclosure caused hardship for many people and anti-enclosing riots were common.

But in spite of such opposition 1,355 Enclosure Acts were passed between 1760 and 1793 and 1,934 between 1793 and 1815. Indeed the demand for Private Acts had risen so sharply by 1801 that parliament passed a *General Enclosure Act*. Thousands of enclosures took place under the terms of this Act alone. By 1850 nearly all the land in the country was enclosed.

Gainers from enclosure

And so the face of the countryside was changed and in place of the open fields there were the hedged-in farms that we see today. Not everyone welcomed this change in Britain's major industry. But there were many people who gained from it. The enterprising landowner was now able to go ahead with some of the experiments that had proved successful elsewhere. He could try to rear healthier and bigger animals.

The majority of British farmers, however, were not landowners but tenants. Some of these gained from enclosure as their landlords agreed to give them long leases (say 21 years or more). This gave the more enterprising tenants the time to try out some of the new ideas. They could spend money on drainage and soil improvement, knowing that if they were successful they had a long time in which to make a profit before handing back the land to the landlord.

And the British people in general gained. More and cheaper food for the growing population led to a reduction in the death rate. This then led to a demand for even more food from the growing population.

Not all the tenants were successful in their new compact farms. Some of them were unable to produce food at the prices charged by the more efficient farmers. These then sold their farms (if they were owners) or leases, which allowed the successful to get their hands on even larger farms.

The flight of these 'farming failures' has given rise to the idea that there was a depopulation of the countryside after 1760 as enclosures drove people away. While some people were badly affected by enclosures and did lose their rights, many of them still remained as labourers on the larger farms. These people worked as shepherds, ploughmen and dairymen, so that the population of the countryside showed little signs of declining. It did not rise, however, as quickly as the population of the urban centres.

Who lost from enclosure?

While many tenants had leases from their landlords, there were some whose families had farmed the same strips for many years, even centuries, without ever having had a written agreement or lease. These customary holders (as distinct from leaseholders) could not prove to the Enclosure Commissioners that they had any right to their strips and so they did not share in the reallocation of the land. These were forced to become wage-earning labourers or to go into the industrial towns. There were also the many thousands of *squatters* who lived alongside the common land, keeping a pig or two, living in a hovel. These recent arrivals had no legal claim to any landholding and also lost out when the land awards were made.

New machinery

Once they became owners or tenants of enclosed farms men began to think up ways of making those farms pay. One was by the introduction of many and varied machines to make the work of the farmer both easier and more productive.

These new machines included a series of ploughs (such as the Rotherham plough), reapers and threshing machines.

Two important machines were invented by Jethro Tull, a Berkshire farmer. He is best remembered for his drill which he invented in 1701. This enabled the farmer to sow a regular number of seeds in rows, which would make hoeing, weeding and watering much easier. His horse-hoe, which was described in his book *Horse-Hoeing Husbandry* in 1731 was intended to improve the soil and promote growth by breaking it up much more finely than had been done before.

These developments, including Tull's, were slow to catch on, however, and it took many years before they became popular.

Jethro Tull advocated the use of the horse-drawn drill and hoe. But little use was made of his suggestion until the end of the eighteenth century when lighter but stronger machines were produced in the new iron foundries. Here you can see men using a hand-driven wheeled hoe between the rows of growing plants which must have been planted by farmers using a drill or a hand dibble.

Crops

During this period the system of *rotation of crops* became popular. By rotation is meant the growing of different crops year by year on the same piece of land. This meant that the soil was kept fertile and did not have to be left without any crop for a year (or 'laid fallow') in order to rest it.

One system of rotation was the Norfolk four-course

rotation. The crops used here were turnips, barley, clover and wheat. It was grasses, like clover, and root crops, like swedes, that helped the soil in this way, and new kinds were introduced into England from overseas — often from Holland. Many crops that had been in Britain for some time became more widely used. These included the pea and the turnip.

The Earl of Leicester, better known as Thomas Coke of Holkham, inspecting some of his Southdown flock. This was one of the purer, improved breeds of sheep developed in the eighteenth century to produce more meat from healthier animals.

Animal breeding

In the days of the open field the winter feeding of animals was a major problem. But on the enclosed farm, with the wider use of root crops as part of continuous use of fields, there was a greater supply of winter fodder. This meant that animals did not have to be slaughtered off as autumn approached and people did not have to rely on salted meat for winter food. This had a good effect on the health of the people.

At the same time as more and better food for livestock became available some people tried to improve the livestock itself. This led to experiments with stock breeding. Robert Bakewell, the Colling Brothers and Thomas Coke, of Holkham Hall, were the most notable of the stock breeders. They mated the best of the females in their flocks with the best of the males and improved the quality of their stock. The animals were heavier, and provided more meat. In the case of cattle, they produced more milk as well as more meat. Bakewell, the Collings and other breeders hired out their animals to neighbouring farmers so that their stock could be improved. Bakewell earned, on average, £1,200 a year from hiring out three rams.

Spreading the new ideas

News of the success of the experimenters and pioneers was spread in various ways. There was the work of Arthur Young, who had failed as a farmer but who was able to appreciate the success of others. He travelled throughout the country ('above four thousand miles' he claimed) and wrote articles and books on the improvements that were being made in the better farms. He claimed that 'the subsequent improvements that have been made originated with my journeys and writings'.

There were other ways in which ideas were spread. There were local Agricultural Societies, the first of which was set up in Brecknock in 1755. There were larger Societies such as the Bath and West (1777) which ran shows, set up experimental farms and published their findings in farmers' journals. The Royal Agricultural Society, set up in 1838, promoted much larger, national, shows. At such meetings farmers saw the latest machines, heard about the latest experiments and met people who had successfully tried out new ideas. In this way they were educated into experimenting for themselves.

The Duke of Bedford made his home, Woburn, a centre of agricultural interest. He held an annual sheep-shearing to which people came from all over the country. This engraving shows the scene in 1804. Although the smaller farmers were unable to afford the high fees charged by the famous stockbreeders, they could learn some lessons from the work done by Bedford, Coke and the rest.

The Napoleonic Wars

The increase in population provided a ready market for the produce of the more efficient farms and for imported food. Once Britain had started the war with France (1793) which later became the Napoleonic Wars, the population was better off. This was because there was fuller employment and higher wages were being paid by industrialists eager to supply the army and navy with what they needed. There was a demand for more food. And none of that food could be brought from the Continent.

This led to a vast increase in prices after 1793, which in turn led to farmers receiving much higher incomes. This encouraged some to rent land which previously had been considered not worth developing. They paid high rents for this land.

In 1815 all this was threatened with the onset of peace. If food was imported from Europe again the price in Britain would fall. As a result some tenant-farmers would be unable to pay the high rents and the aristocratic landowners would receive a lower income.

The upper class landowners controlled parliament. In 1815 they passed the *Corn Laws* which stated that no foreign corn was to be imported until the price of British corn had reached £4.00 a quarter (28 lbs) – a very high price. This has been called a 'naked piece of class legislation'. It led many industrialists, who had not previously been involved, to join one or other of the societies which demanded the reform of the parliamentary system.

After 1815 the farmers speeded up their improvements with even better and more efficient machines. This led to a decline in the demand for labour and so to unemployment. It also enabled farmers to recruit the labour force they wanted, for lower wages. In 1830–31 the resentment of the farm labourers spilled over and, led by a mythical Captain Swing, there was an outbreak of violence against farm machinery, hay and wheat stacks, animals and farmers. The Whig government in which Lord Melbourne was the Home Secretary took drastic action to curb this labourers' uprising and by 1832 the countryside was peaceful again.

DESCRIPTION of TWO MEN detected in the act of SETTING FIRE to a STACK of OATS in the Parish of PAMPISFORD, in the County of Cambridge, about Eight o'clock in the evening of MONDAY the 6th of December, 1830.

One a tall Man, about 5 feet 10 in. high, sandy whiskers, large red nose, apparently between 50 and 60 years of age. Wore at the time a snuff-colored straight coat, light-colored pantaloons, and low shoes.

The other Man was apparently about 5 feet 4 inches, and between 30 and 40 years of age; had large black full whiskers, extending under the chin. He wore a blue straight coat, light colored breeches, and boots with cloth overall-tops.

Both the Men were seen at Pampisford at half-past twelve at noon on Monday, coming from Babraham, and probably from the Newmarket road.

Notice issued by Cambridgeshire magistrates, December 1830

This notice was typical of hundreds put up by magistrates in the South and East of England during the agricultural riots of 1830–32.

A 'Captain Swing' letter sent out by rioters.

19

Documents

a) Arthus Young versus enclosure

What is it to the poor man to be told that the Houses of Parliament are extremely tender of property, while the father of the family is forced to sell his cow and his land, and being deprived of the only motive to industry, squanders the money, contracts bad habits, enlists for a soldier, and leaves his wife and children to the parish? The poor in these parishes may say, and with truth: 'Parliament may be tender of property; all I know is that I had a cow and an Act of Parliament has taken it from me.'

(A. Young, *A six-month Tour through the North of England* 1770)

1 *Where had the 'father' pastured 'his cow' before enclosure? Why could he not do so after enclosure?*

2 *What is meant by the reference to 'an Act of Parliament'?*

3 *Why were some tenants not allocated any land by the Enclosure Commisioners? Why might some who had small plots allocated to them be unable to afford to run an enclosed farm?*

4 *Was enclosure to blame if the man squandered his money? What might he have done with it to benefit himself and his family?*

b) The House of Commons on enclosure, 1797

The commoners and other persons entitled to the right of common, or land intended to be enclosed, will be deprived of an estimable privilege, which they now enjoy, of turning a certain number of their cows, calves and sheep, on and over the said land; a privilege that enables them to maintain themselves and their families in the depth of winter. In addition they can now supply the grazier with young and lean stock at reasonable price. A more ruinous effect of the enclosure will be the almost total depopulation of their towns, now filled with bold and hardy husbandmen driving them from want and necessity into the manufacturing towns, where the very nature of their employment, over the loom or the forge, soon wastes their strength.

1 *Make a list of the benefits which farmers enjoyed on the commons.*

2 *Why were the commons the first lands to be enclosed?*

3 *Why were animals better fed in winter time after enclosure than before? Who gained from this improvement?*

4 *Why did enclosing the commons lead to an increase in the demand for agricultural workers?*

c) The poacher in a man-trap.

1 *Where, in the open field system, might a man have caught rabbits?*

2 *Why did the families of the less well-off hunt rabbits?*

3 *Why and how did enclosure turn rabbit catching into a crime?*

4 *Look at document (a). How might a 'Parliament tender of property' make it unlawful to hunt for rabbits?*

5 *This poacher has been caught in a man-trap. Explain (i) who laid the trap and why; (ii) what injury the poacher might suffer and (iii) how he might be further punished by the local magistrates.*

Extracts

Dividing up common land

. . . that about 80 acres of High Common shall be allotted to the Lord and another part allotted for the use of the poor of Little Baddow and that the rest of the Common (about 57 acres) and all other pieces of waste ground belonging to the Manor shall be allotted to each of the tenants in equal proportion, and shall be enclosed by each of them at their own expense.

(An agreement between the Lord of the Manor of Baddow Hall, Essex, and his tenants 1773)

A farmer remembers

As for the sheep, they hadn't such food as they have now. In winter there was little to eat, except what God Almighty sent for them, and when the snow was thick on the ground, they died off.

(from A. Toynbee, *The Industrial Revolution* 1884)

Questions on Chapter Two

1 *Why did the old method of strip farming have to be abandoned? How did the development of the Agrarian Revolution help the progress of the Industrial Revolution?*

2 *Your local librarian will be able to help you to find out from the local archives office whether there were any Enclosure Acts dealing with your area. If there were any, spend some time examining the Acts and trace out the enclosure on a modern map of your area.*

3 *Find out more about the work of Tull, Bakewell, the Colling Brothers, Young, Coke of Holkham.*

4 *How do you explain the rise of the movement led by the mythical Captain Swing?*

5 *Arrange a debate on the good and bad aspects of the enclosure movement.*

6 *Make a collage of newspaper headlines which might have appeared above articles dealing with (i) Bakewell's work, (ii) an enclosure, (iii) Tull's machinery, (iv) Young's publications.*

Chapter 3   Industrial revolution

Iron

There has been an iron industry in Britain for many centuries. In 1700 iron and steel was produced in iron works and foundries where skilled workmen worked at blast furnaces and moulding plants. With this iron and steel other craftsmen made a variety of goods — from pots and pans to plough-shares and swords. The fuel used to smelt the iron was charcoal, obtained by burning wood from the forests which once covered a good deal of the countryside. This industry was centred on the heavily wooded areas of the country such as the Weald of Kent and Sussex and the Forest of Dean. But charcoal became increasingly scarce and expensive. For many years men had tried to replace it with coal. They could not do this as coal contained too much sulphur, which made the iron brittle. It was not until 1709 that Abraham Darby succeeded in doing so by developing 'coke'.

A seventeenth century engraving of charcoal burning, showing the different stages of the process. Wood to be burned was placed around a pole (centre) to a height of about 2·5 metres. This was covered with straw, fern and turf (left of picture). This pole being removed, burning charcoal was dropped down into the stack which then burnt for five or six days.

1 *Why was the English iron industry first concentrated in the Weald of Kent and Sussex?*
2 *Explain why charcoal became (i) scarcer and (ii) more expensive during the eighteenth century.*
3 *Why were charcoal-fired furnaces smaller than later furnaces which used coke or coal?*

As with the invention of agricultural machinery, it took fifty years or so for Darby's discovery to be widely accepted. Even at the end of the nineteenth century there was still a charcoal-fired blast furnace operating at Backbarrow in the Lake District.

In 1767 Darby's firm at Coalbrookdale built the first iron bridge. Darby's firm produced mainly *pig iron* and *cast iron*

in his coke-burning furnaces. The more refined *wrought* (or bar) iron could not be made with coke as fuel until Henry Cort developed his puddling process. In this process carbon was extracted from the pig iron in a coke-fired reverberatory furnace. Other people invented new methods of rolling the hot iron into bars which saved time and fuel in hammering.

The older iron works needed to be near forests (for fuel) and rivers. Water-wheels supplied the power which drove the bellows used in the blast furnaces. The invention of the *rotary steam engine* in 1782 which could work the bellows enabled the ironfounders to build large works away from the riverside. This led to the shift of the industry from its old centres in the Weald and the Forest of Dean to the coalfields of Scotland, Yorkshire and South Wales. In South Wales the families of Crawshay and Guest made Merthyr one of the world's industrial centres. The Carron works founded by John Roebuck in Scotland were also very large.

Coal

The growth of new, large foundries increased the demand for coal. So did the increasing numbers of steam engines and textile machines being produced by these foundries.

The coal industry was another ancient one which had to be developed if the industrial revolution was to proceed. Men had to go deeper into the earth to get out the increased

The Darby factory had its own coal mine. Here you can see the mouth of the shaft, the great horse-driven wheel which raised and lowered the workers and brought up the coal. There are also tracks along which carts took the coal away. These were originally made of wood, but they were soon converted to iron, even in the pre-railway age.

amount of coal required. But flooding was a danger in deep mines. There was therefore a demand for better methods of pit-drainage. This led to the demand for a more efficient steam-engine (or pump).

As mines became deeper there was also increasing danger from the gas 'fire-damp'. When this gas came into contact with the naked light of the candle stuck into the miner's hat, it exploded. Unfortunately, candles were the only form of underground lighting they knew. In 1812 a particularly serious mine disaster in Sunderland roused public interest. Sir Humphrey Davy was a Cornishman who had known Cornish tin-miners when he was young. By 1812 he was a famous scientist, the first professor of chemistry at the Royal Institute and already well-known for his work on chlorine, electricity and laughing-gas. The mine disaster led Davy to invent a new miners' lamp. Men could now work in the deeper gas-ridden mines with some degree of safety.

In 1814 this was the exterior of the Soho Foundry of Peel and Williams, the Manchester engineering firm. This was one of many engineering firms established to produce textile machinery, water-wheels, steam engines, boilers, gearing, water pipes, fire grates, fences and other iron goods. Notice the canal in the foreground. How else were heavy goods to be carried before the coming of railways? Why was a transport revolution needed before industrialization could really get under way?

The steam-engine
Here we have another example of steady improvements being made as the demand for better steam-engines grew. In 1698 Thomas Savery had invented a steam-engine which was used to pump water out of tin and copper mines. A Cornish blacksmith, Thomas Newcomen, improved on Savery's work and in 1709 produced a more efficient engine. It was this engine that was used by the Darbys at Coalbrookdale and by 1770 there were over 170 of them in use in various industries. James Watt's first experiment with a steam-engine was concerned with an attempt to mend a Newcomen engine. This led him to design a more efficient one in 1765. He entered into a partnership later on with Matthew Boulton. Watt and Boulton used Wilkinson, a famous ironmaster, to make the cylinders for their engines and between 1775 and 1800 they built over 500 of them.

An engraving made in 1798 of the Soho, Birmingham, factory, built in 1796 by Boulton and Watt to produce their steam-engines. Before this date their cylinders had been made by Wilkinson, and other parts by local iron masters. From 1796 the partnership not only produced designs and erected engines; it also made engines. Notice the rural setting.

Up to 1780 all steam-engines had really been simple pumps — with a to-and-fro motion. This was suitable for pumping water out of a mine or into an iron foundry. It was only in 1781 that Watt invented an engine which produced rotary motion. This had a system of cogs and wheels which Watt called a 'sun and planet' system, which could be used to drive a machine or number of machines. By the end of the century this engine was being used in textile factories, ironworks, coal mines, breweries, flour mills, potteries and other industries. Watt's *rotary steam-engine* made a new source of power available to a great range of industries.

Watt's rotary steam-engine, 1788. Savery, Newcomen and others had invented or improved on simple steam pumps which had only a to-and-fro action. Watt's able assistant, William Murdock, showed him how to develop a system of cogs and gearing wheels which translated the pumping motion into a rotary motion so that the steam-engine could be used to drive machinery.

Textiles

In 1700 the woollen industry was Britain's largest industry (other than agriculture) and British woollen goods were sold throughout the known world by merchants and traders. The growth in population and the increased demand for goods from Britain's expanding Empire sparked off a series of inventions in the textile industry. But it was cotton and not wool which adopted the new ways. Why was wool so slow to modernize itself? First, the old wool industry had a plentiful supply of workpeople whereas the new cotton industry had no such traditional labour force. It was compelled to go in for machinery if it wished to expand. Second, the supply of cotton increased in the late eighteenth century, especially from America, India and Egypt. It was more difficult to increase the supply of wool. As you can see from the graph the woollen industry had to wait for the development of Australian sheep-farming in the nineteenth century before the supply of wool was greatly increased. Finally, there were a number of groups in the woollen industry which resisted change. There were the merchant *guilds* and the workers of the *journeymen's* guilds. These used their power and influence to block attempts to use new machinery in the industry. The cotton industry was relatively free from this organized resistance.

Graphs showing the progress of the cotton and woollen industries.

1 *What evidence is there that the output of English wool rose slowly? Can you suggest why this was so?*

2 *When did the amount of imported wool exceed the amount produced by English sheep? From which country did most of this wool come? Why was it not imported before 1790?*

3 *What evidence is there that the export of cotton exceeded the export of wool during the nineteenth century? Explain why the demand for cotton goods was higher than the demand for woollen goods in India and other parts of the British Empire.*

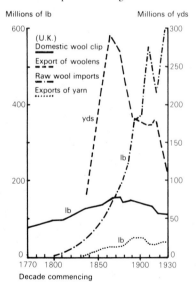

Export of wool goods

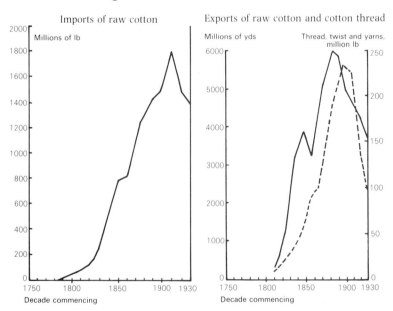

Imports of raw cotton

Exports of raw cotton and cotton thread

Spinning

One weaver was able to use the yarn provided by as many as ten spinners. It is not surprising then that most of the early inventions were made by men anxious to increase the amount of spun yarn.

In 1764 a Lancashire carpenter and weaver, James Hargreaves, made a machine which could work a number of spindles at once. He called the machine a *Spinning Jenny* after his wife, and patented it in 1770. This was a simple, wooden machine which could be used in the cottage. It worked on the same principle as the old spinning wheel. The first machine worked eight spindles, but by 1775 there were machines that had 120 spindles. One spinner could now provide more yarn than any weaver could use.

Hargreaves's Jenny, named after his wife. It was made of wood and small enough to be installed in the workers' cottages.

In 1769 a Lancashire wig-maker, Richard Arkwright, saw a new machine. He had the good business sense to claim it as his own and patented it in that year under the name of the 'water-frame'. This was a spinning machine driven by a water-wheel. This machine could not be used in the cottage but had to be housed in a factory. In 1771 Arkwright opened the first cotton-spinning mill at Cromford in Derbyshire. The River Derwent provided the power and the word 'mill' as in 'water mill' has been used for cotton factories ever since.

In 1775 Arkwright patented another machine, a carding engine which combed out the cotton or wool fibres. Other owners who wanted to use his machines had to pay him a good deal of money. He also made a lot of money from his mills at Cromford and Belper and from another which he opened at New Lanark in 1784. Arkwright became a very rich man, was made Sir Richard and enjoyed the sort of life that up till then only the landed gentry had led.

In 1779 Samuel Crompton, a weaver from Bolton, invented a new spinning-machine which was a cross between the jenny and the water-frame. This earned it the name of the 'mule'. It could spin thread as fine as that produced on the jenny and as strong as that produced on the frame. At first it was hand-driven and used in the workers' cottages. By 1790 it was converted into a power-operated machine, driven first by water and later by steam.

Weaving

In 1733 John Kay, a weaver, patented his fly-shuttle. This new kind of shuttle could be pulled across the loom by a system of springs and strings instead of passing it across by hand. This speeded up weaving. But weavers could already use as much yarn as ten spinners could provide and Kay's invention was largely ignored until improvements had been made on the spinning side of the industry.

In the 1770s, with the increased supply of yarn from the power-operated spinning machines, the hand-loom weavers had more than they could cope with. They were able

New Lanark Mills. This was established in 1784 by Arkwright in partnership with a Glasgow merchant, David Dale. The River Clyde provided the power for this new mill, around which there had to be built houses, to accommodate the mill workers.

Samuel Crompton's Mule, which combined features of the Spinning Jenny and the water-frame.

to demand high wages from merchants anxious to have their yarn woven.

In 1785 the Reverend Edmund Cartwright invented a power-loom. At first merchants were reluctant to adopt this large, power-driven machine. Hand-loom weavers continued to earn high wages even though their output was only a fraction of that of the machine-minder in the power-loom factory. But gradually the power-loom became more widely used. As it did, the price of cloth fell and so did the earnings of the hand-loom weavers. Even as late as 1850, however, there were still thousands of them trying to make a living in an industry now dominated by the power-loom.

Other processes in the textile trade also became increasingly mechanized or otherwise improved. Dyeing, once a domestic chore, now became factory-centred. The croppers who put the final finish onto woollen cloth by clipping it with shears were replaced by shearing machines in the 1800s. These once highly-paid and skilled men were now replaced by cheaper machine-minders — and the unemployed croppers became leaders among the Yorkshire Luddites.

Other industries
Coal, iron, steel, cotton and wool were not the only industries to be affected by the development of new techniques. There were also brewing, glass making and, above all, pottery in

which the Wedgwood family led the way.

Josiah Wedgwood employed high quality artists to design his famous Wedgwood ware. He also sent out salesmen to all the capitals of Europe and sold his goods to Emperors, Tsars, Kings, Queens, Dukes and Duchesses — and then advertised his goods 'As bought by . . .' which attracted the attention of the upper classes everywhere.

He used china clay from Devonshire and Cornwall and flints, for grinding, from the Thames valley. One major problem faced him — the unmade roads of the time. They could not carry the loads of heavy clay he used, nor was it safe to transport his delicate china over them as waggons often tipped over on the rutted roads. He was one of the industrialists who played a part in the development of the canal system, which we will examine in the next chapter.

Effects of changes

One obvious effect of these changes was that there was a vast increase in the output of goods — coal, iron, cotton and woollen goods. This increase in the nation's income made many people very rich. It enabled some of them to spend large sums of money on even more industrial development. Another effect was the move of the population from older, traditional areas of domestic industry to new centres based mainly on the coalfields. These new towns provided their own problems, which we will examine in Chapters 5 and 6. A third effect was that a new method of transport had to be discovered to replace the slow horse-driven waggons and coaches. This was necessary if all the raw materials and manufactured goods, building materials and food, were to be taken into and away from the enlarged industrial towns.

Documents

a) The prosperous hand-loom weaver, 1780

The hand-loom weavers might be truly said to be placed in a higher state of 'wealth, peace and godliness', by the great demand for, and high price of, their labour, than they had ever before experienced. Their dwellings and small gardens clean and neat, and all the family well clad, the men with each a watch in his pocket, and the women dressed to their own fancy; the church crowded to excess every Sunday; each house well furnished with a clock in elegant mahogany or fancy case; handsome tea-services in Staffordshire ware, with silver or plated sugar-tongs and spoons; Birmingham, Potteries and Sheffield wares for necessary use and ornament, wherever a corner cupboard could be placed to show them off. Many cottage families had their cow, paying so much for the summer's grass, and about an acre of land laid out for them in some croft or corner, from which they got hay for the winter. As before observed, I was intimately acquainted with the familes I am speaking of in my youth, and though they were then in my employ, yet, when they brought in their work, a sort of familiarity continued to exist between us, which in those days was the case between all masters and men.

(W. Radcliffe, *Origin of the New System of Manufacture* 1828)

b) The decline of the hand-loom weaver, 1835

A very great number of the weavers are unable to provide for themselves and their families a sufficiency of food of the plainest and cheapest kind. They are clothed in rags, and indisposed on this account to go to any place of worship or to send their children to the Sunday schools. They have scarcely anything like furniture in their houses. Their beds and bedding are of the most wretched description and many of them sleep upon straw. Notwithstanding their want of food, clothing, furniture and bedding, they, for the most part, have full employment.

(Report of the Hand-loom Weavers' Committee 1835)

c)

d)

1 *What inventions in the spinning industry had been responsible for 'the great demand for and high price of their labour'?*

2 *In 1780 the hand-loom weavers enjoyed a high standard of living. Compare their homes and clothes with those of the weavers in 1835.*

What evidence is there in (a) that the hand-loom weavers worked at home? What were some of the advantages they enjoyed from the domestic system?

4 *Why were employers anxious to find a cheaper method of weaving after 1780? What machine was invented to satisfy their demand?*

5 *Why was the power-loom worker able to produce more cloth per hour than the handloom weaver? How does this help to explain a fall in the price of cloth? Why was this fall welcomed by (i) housewives and (ii) exporters of cloth?*

6 *What happened to the earnings of the hand-loom weavers as the price of cloth fell? Why did thousands of them continue to work on the hand-loom rather than move to the factory towns?*

7 *Why was spinning done by women while hand-loom weaving was done by men (as in (c))? Why could women and children manage the power-loom (as in (d))?*

Extracts

From a shareholder of the Carron Ironworks

It is undoubtedly right to begin our works in a situation that looks the most favourable on account of its nearness to the Firth of Forth and Glasgow and where exceptionally fine coal can be had always at moderate expense; and charcoal can be delivered cheaper from the Highlands as well as from woods that are now near it. The land in the neighbourhood might be rented for us to plant large woods for the supply of our works.
(Samuel Garbett, a Birmingham merchant, to William Cadwell, a Scottish shipowner, 1759)

This letter mentions the closeness of good coal and woods for charcoal. Which of the sources of fuel became the more important in the nineteenth century?

The earliest engineers were skilled craftsmen from the pre-industrial era

Wanted immediately, two trained clock-makers or others that understand tooth and pinion making; also a smith that can forge and file, two wood turners that are used to wheel-making, spoke-turning etc.
(Cromford cotton mill, 10 December 1771)

The Staffordshire potteries

I had the pleasure of viewing the Staffordshire potteries at Burslem. There are 300 houses, which employ twenty hands each, or 6,000 in the whole; but of all the people that work in the preparation for the immediate manufactures, the total number cannot be much short of 10,000 and it is increasing every day. The earnings of the people are various: Grinders 7 shillings per week (1s = 5p). Washers and breakers 8 shillings. Throwers 9 shillings to 12 shillings. Engine lath men, 10 shillings to 12 shillings.
(A. Young, *A Six-month tour through the North of England* 1770)

Questions on Chapter Three

1 *Why were the changes in the coal and iron industries so important a part of the industrial revolution? Do you think that they were more or less important than the changes that took place in the textile industry?*

2 *Find out more about the work of the Darby family, Cort, Huntsman, Wilkinson and Roebuck.*

3 *Trace the stages (between 1698 and 1785) by which the steam pump became an engine able to drive machinery. Use this as an argument to prove that there was 'an evolution in the textile industry'.*

4 *Was Richard Arkwright the 'father of the factory system'? Why?*

5 *Find out more about the work of Arkwright, Cartwright, Hargreaves and Crompton.*

6 *Arrange a debate on the good and bad aspects of the factory system.*

7 *Make a collage of newspaper headlines which might have appeared above articles dealing with (i) the opening of Arkwright's first mill, (ii) the patenting of Watt's first rotary steam-engine (iii) the Darby family's use of coal as a fuel in the iron industry.*

Chapter 4   Transport revolution

Pre-industrial transport

We have already seen that the majority of people once lived in small villages and towns in which they made most of the goods that they needed for themselves. The volume of goods being transported, either between British towns or from towns to ports for export, was very small.

Goods were carried on horseback or on horse-drawn waggons. Packhorses were used to carry coal, wool, clay and other products along roads where waggons could not go. Waggons drawn by one, two, four or more horses carried china, cloth, iron and other goods along what roads there were. This slow and difficult movement was suitable for a pre-industrialised country – but only just. Carts and carriages frequently overturned. When this happened goods were spoilt and, in the case of fragile items such as china or pottery, smashed.

To try to prevent the cutting up of the poor road surfaces, Parliament passed a number of Broadwheel Acts in the eighteenth century. The Act of 1773 ordered 16-inch rims; hence the wheels of this cart. The last Broadwheel Act was passed in 1822.

1 *Why did poorly-surfaced roads become badly pitted? Why was this a danger to (i) travellers and to (ii) carriers of fragile goods?*
2 *Suggest some words that might have been used to describe the condition of the roads in (i) very wet winters, (ii) very dry summers.*
3 *How might the broader wheels have helped lessen the damage to the road surface?*

Roads and road bridges

The Romans had left Britain with a system of roads linking up the main centres of population. By 1700 little had been added to this system and each parish was responsible for maintaining these roads. But the parish authorities were

Eighteenth century roadmenders. Although road-mending was supposed to be a duty to the parish and the community, few people wanted to perform it. Thus we read:

* When a man is called to perform statute work, he goes reluctantly; his servants and his horses seem to partake of his laziness. The surveyor cannot rouse them and the work done is less than half what it ought to be. (A Survey of Somerset, 1798.)

usually unwilling to ask their inhabitants to go to work on roads which were used most often by strangers and not by the parishioners.

Turnpike trusts

In the 1660s the government had encouraged rich people to set up companies which were allowed to build and maintain roads near London. The company would employ men to do this work and would get the money back from the money paid by the passengers, waggoners or farmers passing through toll-gates. In the eighteenth century a number of such companies, or *turnpike* trusts were formed, each being responsible for a stretch of road.

A stage coach passing through a turnpike gate at night.

Road and bridge builders

The trusts employed road engineers to supervise the building of the roads and bridges on their particular stretch. The four most famous were:

John Metcalf (1717–1810) who had been blind since he was six. He had done a number of unskilled jobs before he became the road engineer for the Harrogate-Boroughbridge Turnpike Trust in 1765. During the next thirty years he supervised the building of roads in Yorkshire, Lancashire, Cheshire and Derbyshire. He made his road-builders dig deep ditches on either side of the proposed roadway. The earth from the ditches was put on to the roadway, beaten down and covered with stones. The earth and stones were piled highest in the middle of the road so that the road sloped down towards each of the ditches. This meant that any rain would run down off the road.

Thomas Telford (1757–1834) who had had little education before becoming a stone mason. He read a great deal and became one of the most famous engineers of all times. He built canals, in Britain and abroad, and many famous bridges, including the Menai Bridge which links Anglesey with the Welsh mainland. He also built huge *aqueducts* which carried canals over valleys. One of his most famous aqueducts was the one at Pontcysyllte.

Telford was a better road engineer than Metcalf. He planned his roads so that there were no steep hills on them; the maximum gradient on his roads was one in thirty. He laid drains under the foundations of his roads to carry off rainwater into ditches alongside the roads. Telford made his roadbuilders lay a curved foundation, the centre being about four inches above the level of the sides. On this he placed stones, each seven inches high and cut so that they were narrower at the top than at the bottom. He packed the spaces between these stones with even smaller stones, then had broken stones laid over these to a depth of six inches. On top of this he placed a layer of gravel, over one inch thick. It is not surprising that Telford's roads were noted for being firm, dry and that they rarely needed repairing.

John Rennie (1761–1821) was another engineer of roads and canals, best remembered now for his bridges. He built three across the Thames – Waterloo (demolished in 1937), London (demolished in the 1970s) and Southwark, which is still in use. He and Telford were lucky because the new ironworks were producing more, stronger cast-iron which Telford used for the trough carrying the water at Pontcysyllte. The improved wrought-iron invented by Cort was three times as strong as cast-iron so that Telford was

A section of Thomas Telford's Anglesey road.

able to give his Menai bridge much wider spans than had been possible at Pontcysyllte and in earlier bridges.

John Macadam (1756–1836) was a successful business man who took an amateur's interest in road engineering. He used some of the ideas of Metcalf (raising the road above the level of the nearby ground, making a curved surface so that water drained off). He also borrowed ideas from Telford (using foundations of stone which, he wrote, 'must be so prepared and laid as to unite into a firm body'). He also devised his own idea for the road surface. He put down a surface of very small stones, so small that they became bound together by the mixture of rain-water, dust and the pressure from the traffic. Today the 'tarmac' or 'tar-Macadam' road surface gets this effect by mixing small flints with tar which is then rolled in.

A section of a Macadam road.

Stage coaches

Stage coaches were so called because each journey was broken up into stages. Each stage normally ended at a coaching inn where both passengers and horses rested and ate. The work of the road engineers provided good surfaces along which the stage coaches could travel at speeds varying from 5 to 10 miles an hour. The specially designed Royal Mail coaches were the fastest. They did not pay tolls and other traffic had to make way for them. Passengers in the mail or other coaches had a very unpleasant time, in spite of the improved roads. In 1812 two froze to death on the London-Bath coach, and in 1836 the London-Exeter coach was lost in the snow five times on a single journey. It was also expensive to travel. Passengers had to pay not only the coach-owner, but pay their share of the tolls as well. They also had to buy meals at the coaching inns and pay for an overnight stay if the journey was long. Sir Walter Scott, the novelist, travelled from Edinburgh to London in the 1790s and paid and spent almost £50. This was when workers were paid about 8/- (or 40p) per week.

Canals

But not even the best road system could have carried the traffic created by industrialisation and the growth of towns. Building materials and raw materials were required for the factories and workshops. Food was needed for the growing population. Canals were the earliest solution. In the past a good deal of trade had always taken place along navigable rivers and along the coast. Wedgwood's china clay came from Cornwall in coastal vessels as far as Liverpool and then by pack horse from there.

The West of England Mail Coach services, c. 1830.

1 *How long did it take to go by post coach from (i) London to Bath, (ii) Brighton to Bath?*

2 *Why did the development of such coach-services only take place after the work of the great road engineers had been completed?*

3 *Why did the coming of the railways in the 1830s and 1840s bring the 'golden age of coaching' to an end?*

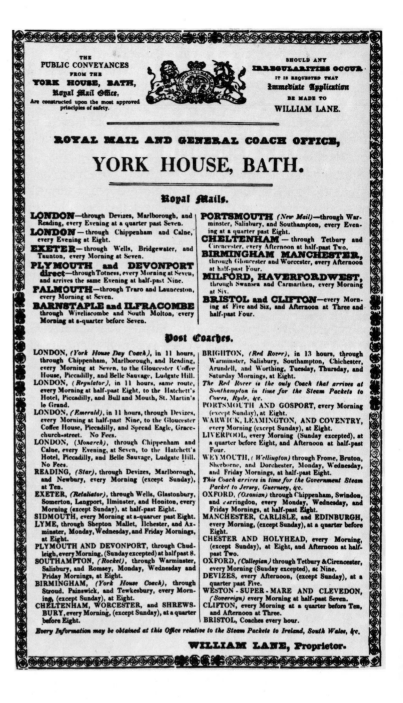

THE
PUBLIC CONVEYANCES
FROM THE
YORK HOUSE, BATH,
Royal Mail Office,
Are constructed upon the most approved principles of safety.

SHOULD ANY
IRREGULARITIES OCCUR
IT IS REQUESTED THAT
Immediate Application
BE MADE TO
WILLIAM LANE.

ROYAL MAIL AND GENERAL COACH OFFICE,
YORK HOUSE, BATH.

Royal Mails.

LONDON—through Devizes, Marlborough, and Reading, every Evening at a quarter past Seven.
LONDON—through Chippenham and Calne, every Evening at Eight.
EXETER—through Wells, Bridgewater, and Taunton, every Morning at Seven.
PLYMOUTH and DEVONPORT direct—through Totness, every Morning at Seven, and arrives the same Evening at half-past Nine.
FALMOUTH—through Truro and Launceston, every Morning at Seven.
BARNSTAPLE and ILFRACOMBE through Wiveliscombe and South Molton, every Morning at a-quarter before Seven.

PORTSMOUTH (*New Mail*)—through Warminster, Salisbury, and Southampton, every Evening at a quarter past Eight.
CHELTENHAM—through Tetbury and Cirencester, every Afternoon at half-past Two.
BIRMINGHAM MANCHESTER, through Gloucester and Worcester, every Afternoon at half-past Four.
MILFORD, HAVERFORDWEST, through Swansea and Carmarthen, every Morning at Six.
BRISTOL and CLIFTON—every Morning at Five and Six, and Afternoon at Three and half-past Four.

Post Coaches.

LONDON, (*York House Day Coach*), in 11 hours, through Chippenham, Marlborough, and Reading, every Morning at Seven, to the Gloucester Coffee House, Piccadilly, and Belle Sauvage, Ludgate Hill.
LONDON, (*Regulator*), in 11 hours, same route, every Morning at half-past Eight, to the Hatchett's Hotel, Piccadilly, and Bull and Mouth, St. Martin's le Grand.
LONDON, (*Emerald*), in 11 hours, through Devizes, every Morning at half-past Nine, to the Gloucester Coffee House, Piccadilly, and Spread Eagle, Gracechurch-street. No Fees.
LONDON, (*Monarch*), through Chippenham and Calne, every Evening, at Seven, to the Hatchett's Hotel, Piccadilly, and Belle Sauvage, Ludgate Hill. No Fees.
READING, (*Star*), through Devizes, Marlborough, and Newbury, every Morning (except Sunday), at Ten.
EXETER, (*Retaliator*), through Wells, Glastonbury, Somerton, Langport, Ilminster, and Honiton, every Morning (except Sunday), at half-past Eight.
SIDMOUTH, every Morning at a-quarter past Eight.
LYME, through Shepton Mallet, Ilchester, and Axminster, Monday, Wednesday, and Friday Mornings, at Eight.
PLYMOUTH AND DEVONPORT, through Chudleigh, every Morning, (Sunday excepted) at half past 8.
SOUTHAMPTON, (*Rocket*), through Warminster, Salisbury, and Romsey, Monday, Wednesday and Friday Mornings, at Eight.
BIRMINGHAM, (*York House Coach*), through Stroud, Painswick, and Tewkesbury, every Morning, (except Sunday), at Eight.
CHELTENHAM, WORCESTER, and SHREWSBURY, every Morning, (except Sunday), at a quarter before Eight.

BRIGHTON, (*Red Rover*), in 13 hours, through Warminster, Salisbury, Southampton, Chichester, Arundell, and Worthing, Tuesday, Thursday, and Saturday Mornings, at Eight.
The Red Rover is the only Coach that arrives at Southampton in time for the Steam Packets to Cowes, Ryde, &c.
PORTSMOUTH AND GOSPORT, every Morning (except Sunday), at Eight.
WARWICK, LEAMINGTON, AND COVENTRY, every Morning (except Sunday), at Eight.
LIVERPOOL, every Morning (Sunday excepted), at a quarter before Eight, and Afternoon at half-past Four.
WEYMOUTH, (*Wellington*) through Frome, Bruton, Sherborne, and Dorchester, Monday, Wednesday, and Friday Mornings, at half-past Eight.
This Coach arrives in time for the Government Steam Packet to Jersey, Guernsey, &c.
OXFORD, (*Oxonian*) through Chippenham, Swindon, and Farringdon, every Monday, Wednesday, and Friday Mornings, at half-past Eight.
MANCHESTER, CARLISLE, and EDINBURGH, every Morning, (except Sunday), at a quarter before Eight.
CHESTER AND HOLYHEAD, every Morning, (except Sunday), at Eight, and Afternoon at half-past Two.
OXFORD, (*Collegian*) through Tetbury & Cirencester, every Morning (Sunday excepted), at Nine.
DEVIZES, every Afternoon, (except Sunday), at a quarter past Five.
WESTON-SUPER-MARE AND CLEVEDON, (*Sovereign*) every Morning at half-past Seven.
CLIFTON, every Morning at a quarter before Ten, and Afternoon at Three.
BRISTOL, Coaches every hour.

Every Information may be obtained at this Office relative to the Steam Packets to Ireland, South Wales, &c.

WILLIAM LANE, Proprietor.

The Dutch had built canals in the sixteenth century and the English had improved their own river navigation by widening or diverting rivers around awkward places such as waterfalls. However, the first important canal was built for the Duke of Bridgewater. He owned coal mines at Worsley, about ten miles from Manchester and he wanted a quick and cheap method of bringing this coal into the growing town.

He employed a millwright, James Brindley, to design and supervise the building of his canal. Brindley had to plan the building of tunnels to carry the canal through hillsides. He had to devise a method of 'puddling' the bottom of the canal with heavy clay to stop the water draining away. He had to design and help build the first canal *aqueduct* which carried the canal across the River Irwell, which divided Manchester from Salford.

The canal was regarded as one of the wonders of the age. And, which is more important, it was a great financial success. The price of coal in Manchester fell from 60p a ton to 30p, so that the industrialists and other coal-consumers benefited. The Duke, who sold his coal and carried other people's goods on his canal, became an even richer man and other industrialists were encouraged to build other canals. Josiah Wedgwood financed the building of a canal from Liverpool to the Potteries so that heavy clay could be carried quickly and cheaply while the fragile pottery would be carried away safely. Before long this canal was linked with Bridgewater's and with about twenty new canals being built each year from 1780 to 1810, the industrial Midlands, Lancashire, and Yorkshire was soon covered by a network of linked canals.

Bridgewater and Wedgwood had paid for their own canals; but not everyone was so rich. Most canals were paid for by groups of rich men joining forces to form a *Joint Stock Company* (in which many people joined together to provide the money required). Some, especially those in the south, did not make any profit. But many did because they had been built in the industrial heartland.

The Duke of Bridgewater pointing to the Barton aqueduct over the River Irwell.

The Trent and Mersey (also known as the Grand Trunk) Canal passing the pottery works owned by Josiah Wedgwood. He had organised the formation of the company which provided the money for Brindley to build this canal which brought the china clay, shipped from Cornwall to Liverpool, to the potteries district.

1 *Barges were pulled by horses, sailing boats or humans. Explain why one horse can pull a heavier load on a canal barge than six horses could pull in a waggon on a road.*

2 *Explain Wedgwood's keen interest in canal building.*

3 *Suggest some of the difficulties that faced the canal builders.*

The Pontcysyllte aqueduct on the Ellesmere Canal, designed by Thomas Telford. This was merely one of the hundreds of aqueducts built to carry canals across valleys or roads. The first stone was laid in 1795 and it was finished in 1803. The iron trough, carrying the canal, is over 300 metres long and 'floats' 40 metres above the valley so that it was called 'the stream in the sky' and regarded as one of the boldest ventures of the age.

It is worth noting that although Brindley was a semi-literate millwright and Telford a self-educated stone-mason, the building of canals led to the development of a new profession — that of civil engineer. Bridges had to be built, tunnels dug out and aqueducts constructed to carry water across roads and rivers. In 1820 the men who designed these great works banded together to form the Institution of Civil Engineers, and invited Telford to become the first President.

In spite of their success at the time, canals had a number of drawbacks. This meant that when railways were developed they quickly replaced canals in popularity.

Firstly, canal builders and owners had shown too little foresight in their work. Each company had built a canal to suit itself, with its own width and depth. As a result it was impossible for barges to move from one canal to another. If the barge was right for a canal with lock gates of 5 feet, it was too big for the canals whose locks were only 3 feet wide. The railway designers learned from this lesson and came to an agreement over a common width, or gauge, of track.

Secondly, factory owners and industrialists had built their businesses and warehouses along the canal banks. This meant that it was too expensive to widen the canals to compete with the railways in the 1840s. To make matters worse, railway companies sometimes bought up small sections of the canal system and imposed very high charges for the use of their section. This drove business off the canals and onto the railways. Other sections owned by the railway companies were allowed to fall into decay. With one vital section out of action, the rest of the system was of less value to the potential users.

Railways

Railways made of wooden rails along which heavy waggons could be pulled by horses had been built near British collieries in the sixteenth century. At Coalbrookdale the Darby family had constructed the first iron railroad in 1767. The use of a steam engine to replace the horse as the motive power had been suggested by Richard Trevithick in 1804 when he built up the first successful steam locomotive for use at the Penydarren colliery in South Wales. By 1812 goods were being carried from Middleton to Leeds on the world's first regular steam railway.

However, the public attention was really captured by the opening of the Stockton to Darlington railway in 1825. This showed that goods and passengers could be carried much more quickly than had ever been thought possible. A group of businessmen then formed a joint stock company (a lesson learned from the canal builders) and paid for the construction of the Liverpool to Manchester Railway (1826–30). This railway involved the building of sixty-three bridges, a two-mile long cutting over eighty feet deep, a tunnel over two thousand yards long and the laying of a line across the black muddy bog of Chat Moss. And all this was supervised by George Stephenson, another uneducated man who had taught himself to be an engineer at various Durham collieries.

In 1833 another company began the building of an even greater line from London to Birmingham. This was over one hundred miles long and was the greatest job of work ever done in Britain up to that time. It took twenty thousand men using shovels and wheelbarrows over five years to build this gigantic work with its tunnels and bridges. But by 1838 the Midlands was connected with the capital by trains travelling at over 40 miles an hour. This was a revolutionary speed compared with the leisurely progress of the packhorse or the canal barge.

The Derby Canal Tramroad. Horse-drawn tramroads were commonplace in the eighteenth century, particularly near coal mines and at approaches to canal quays.

A sketch of the opening of the Stockton-Darlington Railway made on 27 September 1825 by John Dobbin. There were thirty-two waggons in the train which, pulled by the engine *Locomotion*, moved at about 10 miles per hour. A man on horseback rode in front of the engine and there were twenty-four horse drawn waggons following it.

Effects

The coming of the railway speeded up the whole industrial system. The rapid growth of the British coal and iron industries was the result of the building of the railways. Coal was needed to operate the engines and as fuel to produce the iron and steel needed for railway construction. There was the growth of a number of new professions, mechanical engineering, surveying and accountancy, because of the railway development. And there were hundreds of thousands of people employed on the railways as drivers and porters, clerks and managers. These people had well-paid jobs and became the leaders among the prosperous working class of mid-Victorian Britain.

British farmers gained as they were now able to sell their products over a wider area. British workers gained since a wider variety of cheaper food became available than there had been before. By the end of the century there was a well-established system of national chain stores – the first owned by Thomas Lipton, another owned by the chemist, Boots. Everywhere in Britain one could now get a standard branded article in place of the locally-produced but dearer article.

And, socially, there were great benefits flowing from the development of a railway system. The growing number of middle class parents used the system to send their children away to boarding schools. Middle and working class people used the system to get away from the towns to the countryside and seaside for a day or two. Into the towns poured not only cheap food and building materials but national papers as well as organised theatrical companies and music-hall groups. Britain after the railways was no longer a country of isolated villages but a closely-knit community in which life was lived at a much greater pace than it had been before.

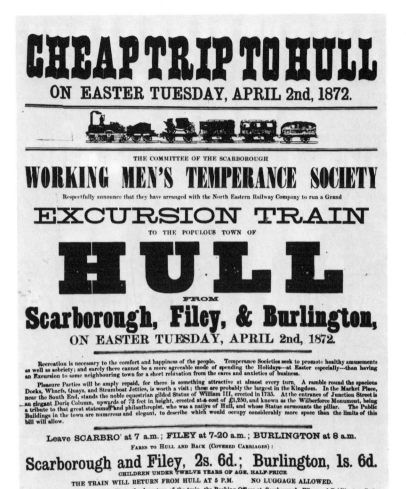

An excursion handbill of 1872.

1 *Why was it easier for people to travel in 1872 than it had been in 1772?*
2 *What evidence does this handbill offer for the argument that workingmen's lives improved during the nineteenth century?*
3 *What was a temperance society? Why were such societies formed?*

Documents

a) Railways versus canals, 1840s

Your Committee have stated in their former Report, that there are about 32 Bills before Parliament in which power is sought to effect the amalgamation of Canals with Railways. These may be classed under the following heads:

First, bills for the amalgamation by lease, purchase, or otherwise, of entire lines of Canal with competing lines of Railway.

Second, bills for the amalgamation of some Canal forming a link in a chain of water communication with a line of Railway competing with the whole chain.

In the introduction of Railways, and in the early period of their development, competition with the Canals checked any great abuse of their powers. As the Railway extended itself, improvements in its organisation placed a check upon Canals, and the competition reduced the cost of transport to one-seventh of their former amount; and there are now few parts of the country which have not derived material advantage from the competition between Railways and Canals.

One great impediment has been found to exist, in the present disjointed state of the Canal interests and the varying systems under which they carry on their operations. Some of the existing Companies, possessing lines of Canal which form central links in a great chain, take advantage of their position, and establish a rate of charges so high as to secure to themselves a large return for their capital, even upon a small amount of traffic. This practice, while it obliges the other Companies not so advantageously situated, to reduce their rates to such an extent that they are unable to conduct their business with a profit, at the same time prevents such a reduction in the general charges.

(*Second Report of the Select Committee on the Amalgamation of Railways and Canals* 1846)

1 *Pick out one sentence in (a) which shows that the cost of transport fell following the development of the railway system. How would this affect the price of (i) coal for industrialists, (ii) final costs of manufactured textiles, (iii) food, (iv) building materials?*

2 *What does document (a) mean when it talks of canals being 'linked' together? Why could the owner of one link in a chain of canals 'take advantage' of his position? How would his decision to increase charges affect the owners of other canals in the chain? Why did some railway companies try to buy only one canal chain?*

3 *What would be the effect on the chain of canals if the railway company allowed its one canal to fall into disrepair?*

4 *Pick out and name two jobs being done be men in 1837 in (b) which are done by machines today?*

b) The building of Tring cutting, 1837.

c) Helicopter and bulldozer at the building of the M1.

5 *Over 200 men were required to build a mile of railway in 1837; only 70 men are required to build a mile of motorway today (as in (c)). Explain the fall in numbers.*

6 *Why does the building of a motorway lead to the formation of large construction firms? On what do these spend their money? How far does this help to explain the formation, in the past, of companies for the building of (i) roads, (ii) canals and (iii) railways?*

7 *Why does the modern road engineer sometimes use a helicopter? How did Stephenson supervise the building of his railways?*

Extracts

Even well-to-do passengers suffered on eighteenth century roads

If you love good roads, conveniences, good inns, plenty of postillions and horses, be so kind as never to go into Sussex. We thought ourselves in the northest part of England. We were forced to drop our post-chaise, in which we were thrice over-turned, and hire a machine that resembled a baker's cart.

(Letter from Horace Walpole to George Montagu, 1749)

Effects of canal building

It will be found that canals are chiefly useful for the following purposes; first, for conveying the produce of mines to the sea-shore; second, conveying fuel and raw materials to some manufacturing towns and districts and exporting the manufactured goods; third, conveying groceries and merchant goods for the consumption of the district through which the canal passes, fourth, conveying fuel for domestic purposes; manure for the purposes of agriculture; transporting the produce of the districts through which the canal passes, to the different markets; and promoting agricultural purposes in general.

(Thomas Telford, *Survey and Reports of the Proposed Extension of the Union Canal* 1804)

Questions on Chapter Four

1 *A pack horse could carry about five hundredweight (about 250 kilograms). If there had been no improvement in transport systems how would this have affected (i) the building of towns and factories, (ii) the distribution of raw materials and finished products?*

2 *What were the disadvantages of the horse-drawn waggon? How does this help to explain (i) the small number of people who travelled and (ii) the demand for coastal shipping?*

3 *Write a letter explaining why you are willing to become a member of a turnpike trust. You have chosen a road between two large towns. Why? How do you hope to gain from your investment?*

4 *What advantages did the canal system bring to (i) a mill owner in Manchester, (ii) housewives, (iii) Wedgwood and other industrialists?*

5 *Why were (i) canals and (ii) railways, regarded as 'wonders of the age'?*

6 *Find out more about the work of Brunel, the Stephensons, and George Hudson, the Railway King.*

7 *Summarize the advantages which the railway system brought to (i) farmers. (ii) mine owners, (iii) the iron and steel industry, (iv) inhabitants of seaside towns.*

8 *Find and name four local public houses whose names link them with the transport system (eg Coach and Horses, Railway Inn).*

9 *Make a collage of headlines which might have appeared above articles dealing with (i) the building of the Bridgewater canal, (ii) the opening of a new railway line, (iii) Thomas Cook's first organized excursion.*

Unit Two   Social changes 1760–1850

Rich and poor. *Punch's* view in 1843 of the way in which many worked, and suffered, for the few.

The great changes in the methods of production which have been outlined in Unit 1 were responsible for the growth of Britain's industrial towns (Chapter 5). In the pre-industrial society the majority of the population lived in villages or small towns. By 1851 over half the population lived in factory towns, most of them situated on one or other of Britain's coalfields.

These new towns with their factories, businesses, ports and warehouses were the sources of the great wealth which flowed into the pockets of the new industrial middle classes.

But the majority of the inhabitants of these early

industrial towns were members of the working classes. At first, most of these lived in appalling conditions (Chapter 7), as builders and factory owners put up houses as rapidly and as cheaply as possible.

They also suffered from frequent unemployment and total loss of income (Chapter 7) unless their children went out to work. The employment of children and women as machine minders (Chapter 8) allowed the employers to offer low wages to men workers as well as to the women and children. This low income was one reason for the poor quality of the workers' houses. What could they afford for rent, and what could they get for that small rent? It was also the reason for the poor quality of their general standard of living. This was evident from their food, health, education, clothing, furniture and entertainment.

The country was getting richer at an increasingly rapid rate. By 1851 Britain was already the 'Workshop of the World'. But the increased wealth was not shared out in an equal fashion. Some groups (in the middle classes) got a high proportion of the increase while the rest, the majority, got a very small share. But even the well-off were not entirely satisfied. They complained that parliament in 1830 was still elected as though Britain was an agricultural country. Large towns such as Manchester sent no one to represent their larger population – despite the taxes now paid by the wealthy middle classes. It was these people who led the demand for parliamentary reform (Chapter 9). Many members of the working classes supported this campaign in the hope that a reformed parliament would turn its attention to their appalling working and living conditions. But their hopes were disappointed. The self-made businessmen were not willing to pass laws to share out the nation's wealth more fairly. Not until the beginning of the present century (Unit 4) were laws passed to provide for compulsory full-time education, medical care, old age pensions, national insurance and supplementary benefits.

Chapter 5

Towns – their growth and government

A new industrial society

Today we can look around Britain and see a number of New Towns that have been created by the government since 1945. These New Towns were planned. They were built with roads, hospitals, shopping centres, parks, libraries, schools and museums as well as factories and workshops. Each of these towns had, from the very start, a local council which has to carry out Acts of Parliament. These Acts ensure that the new councils maintain certain standards in housing, education and other social services, as does every other council in the country.

It was not like this between 1760 and 1850 during the first stage of the industrial revolution. The industrial towns of that new society grew up without any guidance from parliament and, until the late 1830s, without local councils.

Pre-industrial towns

In 1760 about three quarters of the British people lived in small villages. However, even then, there were a number of small towns. There were ports such as Bristol, towns such as Oxford, which grew up at river crossings, and those such as Exeter, which acted as market towns for the surrounding area. Originally these towns had been part of the landed estates of some feudal lord. But between 1300 and 1700 about 170 of these small towns had bought their freedom from their feudal lords and had obtained from parliament a *charter* which spelt out the legal freedom of the town and its inhabitants. This charter often named the citizens who were to govern the town – a mayor, aldermen (or elderman), and burgesses (or free citizens). It also allowed this council to make laws for the town.

The chartered towns

These chartered towns were also known as *corporate boroughs* because their charters gave the richer citizens the right to elect a corporation or town council.

It is not surprising that the majority of these chartered towns or boroughs were in the South and South West of the country. These were the main centres for the agricultural and woollen industries and where the majority of people lived.

We know a great deal about the ways in which these

The right to charge tolls at the gates of the walled town was one of the privileges granted to most self-governing chartered towns. This was one source of the moneys which the members of the corporation could spend as they wished.

TOLLS PAYABLE IN THE CITY OF CARLISLE

FOR GOODS BROUGHT INTO THE CITY

Grain	per cart load 1^d
Fresh Butter & Cheese	per basket 1^d
Potatoes	per cart load 1^d
Onions, Fruit & Other Garden Stuff	per barrow or basket 1^d
do. do. do.	per cart load 2^d
Meat, Flour, Malt, Fish, Butchers Meat Bacon Pork, Hay, Straw, Earthenware	
Guano & all Artificial Manures & all Other Goods Wares & Merchandise	per cart load 2^d per horse load
do. do. do.	or under 1^d

FOR GOODS CARRIED OUT OF THE CITY

Potatoes & Grain bought in the Market & Carried out for Sale	per cart load 2^d per horse load
do. do. do.	or under 1^d
Pigs bought in the Market & Carried out for Sale	each 1^d
All other Goods Wares & Merchandise carried out per cart load 2^d	
do. do. do.	

Carts & Public Coaches drawn by more than one horse are to Be charged the entire Toll for each horse
Tolls Payable on Horses Cattle or Sheep sold in the City & Suburbs thereof or on Carlisle Sands and take out of or Brought into or through the City.

Horses	Each	4^d
Cattle	,,	1^d
Sheep	,,	¼^d

During the time of Fairs-Commencing 26TH August & Continued For fifteen days following—Double Tolls are payable.

EXEMPTIONS

The following Articles are Exempt from Tolls—Eggs Poultry Wild Fowl, Coals, Peat & other Fuel brought into the City Provisions & other Articles bought in the City & Carried out For Home Consumption & not for Sale.

Renewed	R. Wilson.
Aug. 1977	Chief Executive & Clerk.

councils behaved because of a *Royal Commission* which examined the chartered boroughs in 1834–35. This Commission proved that in most boroughs the richer citizens had managed to control affairs for their own benefit. *Rates* and other taxes were spent on great feasts for the small number who controlled the town. These men were also guilty of paying themselves or their relations very large salaries for unimportant jobs – Chief Cup Bearer to the Mayor for example. When money was spent on a new building or on repairing the town's walls, the contracts were usually given to one of the corporation or to a relation. This person was then allowed to make a very high charge for the work done, sharing out the money with his friends on the corporation.

The Commission also found out that few of these

The Severn Bridge at Worcester. This was built in 1780 and paid for by private subscription. The river embankments were also tidied up making them useful, safe and neat. This was typical of the work done by Improvement Commissioners.

corporations bothered about such social problems as housing, street cleansing and refuse collection. Attempts to cope with these problems and to try to make towns healthier had been the work of groups of rich citizens. These people paid for a private Act of Parliament which allowed the setting up of a number of *Improvement Commissioners* elected by the rate-payers. But the Improvement Commissioners had powers to deal with only specific problems. So in some towns there was one group of Improvement Commissioners looking after street cleansing, another looking after street lighting and perhaps a third looking after street widening.

Newer towns

The chartered or corporate boroughs needed reform and this came in 1835. But the Commission of 1834–35 did not look at the conditions inside the new, growing towns being built on the coalfields of the North East, the Midlands, the North West and South Wales. Most of these had been thinly populated before 1760 and the towns grew up around what had been villages (as in the case of Manchester) or, more commonly, in previously uninhabited areas.

And these centres grew very rapidly as can be seen from the case of Manchester:

Year	Population
1700	6,000
1788	50,000
1800	96,000
1844	350,000

The government of the new towns

The corporate boroughs had some sort of government, even if it was corrupt and inefficient. Some new and rapidly expanding towns were governed by one or more authorities

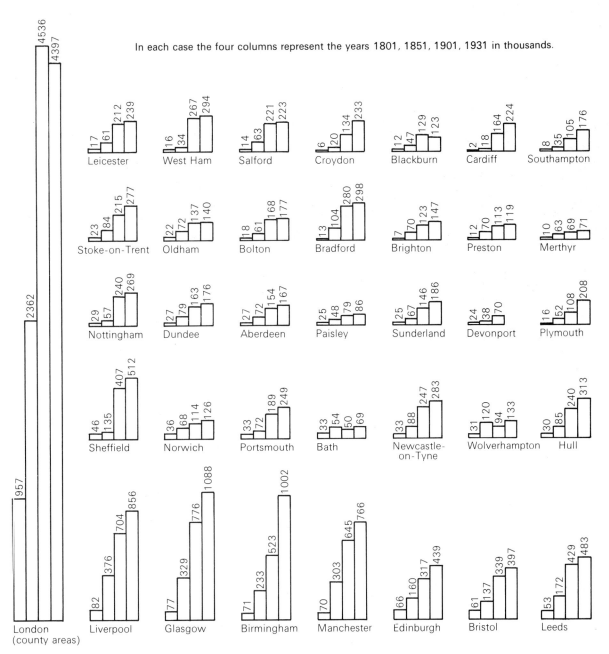

In each case the four columns represent the years 1801, 1851, 1901, 1931 in thousands.

Leicester — 17, 61, 212, 239
West Ham — 16, 34, 267, 294
Salford — 14, 63, 221, 223
Croydon — 6, 20, 134, 233
Blackburn — 12, 47, 129, 123
Cardiff — 2, 18, 164, 224
Southampton — 8, 35, 105, 176

Stoke-on-Trent — 23, 84, 215, 277
Oldham — 22, 72, 137, 140
Bolton — 18, 61, 168, 177
Bradford — 13, 104, 280, 298
Brighton — 7, 70, 123, 147
Preston — 12, 70, 113, 119
Merthyr — 10, 63, 69, 71

Nottingham — 29, 57, 240, 269
Dundee — 27, 79, 163, 176
Aberdeen — 27, 72, 154, 167
Paisley — 25, 48, 79, 86
Sunderland — 25, 67, 146, 186
Devonport — 24, 38, 70
Plymouth — 16, 52, 108, 208

Sheffield — 46, 135, 407, 512
Norwich — 36, 68, 114, 126
Portsmouth — 33, 72, 189, 249
Bath — 33, 54, 50, 69
Newcastle-on-Tyne — 33, 88, 247, 283
Wolverhampton — 31, 120, 94, 133
Hull — 30, 85, 240, 313

London (county areas) — 957, 2362, 4536, 4397
Liverpool — 82, 376, 704, 856
Glasgow — 77, 329, 776, 1088
Birmingham — 71, 233, 523, 1002
Manchester — 70, 303, 645, 766
Edinburgh — 66, 160, 317, 439
Bristol — 61, 137, 339, 397
Leeds — 53, 172, 429, 483

which had once been set up to deal with a thinly-populated rural countryside. In some places the local *magistrates* governed whole counties or large sections of counties. For example, when South Wales contained only a scattering of fishing villages this system may have worked. But when huge new towns grew up in Merthyr, Cardiff and Swansea and when dozens of large mining villages grew up in separate valleys, the handful of magistrates were obviously unable to govern their district properly.

Graphs showing the growth of towns, 1801–1931. Mark the growing towns on a map. How do these bar graphs show the movement of population which was a feature of the industrial revolution?

A sketch of cottages in Preston, taken from the First Report of the Health of Towns Commission, 1844. The narrow space between the privies in the backyards of each row of cottages was a cesspool which was emptied only twice a year.

(Below) The standpipe in Fryingpan Alley. Clerkenwell, London, 1864. The artist wrote:

* In the afternoon you will find that there are about 30 people, with bottles, pails, tubs, tea-kettles, broken jugs and other vessels waiting for the man to turn on the water from the main. It is essential to be in time because there are many to be supplied and the water is only turned on for 20 minutes. (Godwin, *Another Blow for Life* 1864.)

1 *How often and for how long was the water turned on at this standpipe?*
2 *Why might some people get (i) less water than they really needed or, (ii) no water at all?*
3 *How does this picture help you to understand the dirtiness of many homes and people in nineteenth century Britain?*

In some places the new town grew up around an ancient manor and the officers of the manor were responsible for the running of affairs. This was the case in Manchester where, even as late as 1837, the problems of housing, cleansing, refuse collection and so on were supposed to be handled by three officials from the Moseley manor-court. These officials were obviously not qualified to handle the many problems of a huge new town nor were there enough of them to even try to tackle these problems.

In other places the only form of government was the local parish council. This was the case in Bradford where, in May 1798, the parish officers sent out the town crier to warn the people that if any pigs were found wandering in the street their owners would be arrested by the town constable. The catching of wandering pigs may have been an important part of the work of the council of a small parish; it was hardly what was needed in the growing towns of industrial England.

Parliament and the industrial towns
Apart from having no local councils, the new towns had no MPs in parliament to represent them. As a result no laws were passed to improve matters. Parliament, in 1760, was composed largely of MPs from the South and South West and they had no experience of what was happening in the new industrial towns which had no MP to speak for them.

Today, with TV, radio and national papers, we would expect MPs to know what was going on. In the eighteenth century there were none of these methods of communication.

However, even if the government had known what was happening, it is unlikely that it would have done very much. It was not felt that the government should concern itself with poverty (at least until 1834), health (until 1848) or housing (until the 1860s). It was thought that these things and the development of factories and workshops were best left to private enterprise.

And of course private enterprise did work. The industrialists did build factories, docks, railways and canals. But they built these in the hope that they would make a profit. For example, the Crawshays who took such pride in their profitable ironworks had little concern for the state of things in the town of Merthyr which grew up alongside the expanding works. The same was true of most industrialists. They lacked a 'civic conscience'. If they had applied only one-tenth of the energy and skill they showed in business to the question of town development, we would not have had the massive slums which were created in Victorian Britain.

A cellar dwelling, Manchester, 1844. There were thousands of such cellar-dwellings in the industrial towns and the poverty of the people can be seen from the flooring, furniture, clothing and general appearance.

But the industrialists might defend themselves in a number of ways. They could well argue that they broke no laws since there were no laws to break. They could argue that they were in business and should not be expected to be social workers as well. They might also have argued that economics required them to do what they did.

Rent and housing

The industrialist and house developer did build houses for the workpeople. But he built with his profit in mind. How much rent could a working man afford out of his 75p which he earned? Maybe 15p a week. The builder then provided a house for which he could charge a rent of 15p and still make a profit. All that could be provided were small houses, closely packed together, with none of the amenities which we expect in a house today.

An open society

In spite of the poor living and working conditions of the worker in the industrial town, certain important social changes were taking place. In 1700 Britain had been a country in which the bulk of the population lived in small villages. In these villages there was a recognisable *social hierarchy*, each person knowing exactly his or her place in the order of things. As the prayer went:

'God bless the squire and his relations
And keep us all in our proper stations.'

This was a fairly 'closed' society. Although men could get on and move out of their 'stations', most people remained where God had put them. The industrial town created a new set of attitudes to employers, authority and society. This led in time to the development of an 'open' society in which more and more people claimed the right to equal opportunity with others. This was a society in which 'Jack is as good as his master'.

Reforming society

It should also be noted that while the industrial towns had their origins in dirt and squalor, it was this very dirt and squalor which sparked off the demand for social reform in the mid and late nineteenth century. Today we expect to have a water supply, street cleansing and refuse collection. We expect to have libraries and parks, museums and schools, buses and houses. If it had not been for the gigantic problems presented by the early industrial towns, it is unlikely that we would have had the reforming movements which have brought about these changes. And, as we have seen, without the wealth produced in the industrial towns we would not have had the money to carry out the reforms.

Municipal Corporations Reform, 1835

In 1835 the Whigs (the political party in power) passed the Municipal Corporations Reform Act, which immediately affected the 178 existing chartered boroughs. This Act created a more democratic and uniform system of election to the corporations (or councils): every man over the age of twenty-one who paid rates on a shop or a house was allowed to take part in the election of councillors. These had to elect the aldermen who were to be one third of the number of councillors. The

An early type of water closet, designed in the 1770s. This was a very expensive item, largely because of its many and complicated valves and other moving parts. In 1870 Twyfords invented a simple fireclay basin which had no moving parts so that it could be made in one piece and so was much cheaper.

Memorandum

On Saturday the 26th day of December 1835 the election of Councillors for this Borough, under the Act of 5th & 6th Wm 4th c. 76. took place and on Monday the 28th day of the said Month of December at one o'clock in the afternoon Richard Rawson, Esquire Mayor published and declared the names of the Councillors elected pursuant to the directions of the said Act of Parliament Whereupon and by virtue of the 38th section of the said Act this Corporation which had existed from time immemorial was doomed to final

Dissolution

Nevertheless God save the King and all that are put in authority under him —

The last entry in the Hall Book of the unreformed Leicester Corporation. It was written on 26 December 1835 by Thomas Burbidge, Town Clerk of Leicester, 1813—35. He had led the opposition to the Municipal Reform Act, 1835, organised the distribution of the corporation's funds when reform was inevitable and obtained a large sum of money as compensation for the loss of his job in which he had been the leader of the corrupt council.

1 *When were the first elections held under the terms of the 1835 Act? Who voted in these elections?*
2 *What was 'doomed to final dissolution' on 28 December 1835?*

whole body of councillors and aldermen had to elect a mayor. The democratically-elected council was compelled by the 1835 Act to 'elect a number of their own body, called the Watch Committee which shall appoint a number of men to act as Constables for preserving the peace by day and night'. The Act did not compel the council to concern itself with housing, health, water supply or other social problems. In 1835 parliament was concerned only with safeguarding property and with trying to prevent the recurrence of the riots which had taken place during the struggle over the Reform Act of 1832.

The Act also had a clause by which other towns, which had previously not had councils, could apply to become chartered or incorporated towns so that the terms of the Act would apply to them. This was the opportunity for the new industrial towns. Manchester, for example, became 'incorporated' in 1839 and from that time on had its own elected council. Other towns followed this example although in some towns, such as Merthyr, the industrialists prevented this happening until the 1880s.

Document

a) The state of affairs in Merthyr, 1845

Drainage and Cleansing – in these respects this town is in a sad state of neglect. With the exception of some little care in the main streets, and regulations about removing ashes before the doors in Dowlais, all else is in a miserable condition. Because the poorer inhabitants, who constitute the mass of the population, throw all slops and refuse into the nearest open gutter before their houses; because of the impeded course of such channels, and the scarcity of privies, some parts of the town are complete networks of filth, emitting noxious exhalations.

There is no local Act for drainage and cleansing. In some localities, a privy was found common to 40 or 50 persons, and even up to 100 persons and more. As an illustration of the habits of the poorer classes, it may be stated, from the information of the clergymen at Dowlais, (about three miles away) that when the schools at Dowlais were first built, holding 150 boys and 150 girls, the children did not know how to make use of the privies, and were obliged to be taught.

The greater proportion of the houses in Merthyr is occupied by those who are employed in the iron works, either in smelting the iron itself, in the subsequent processes, or in procuring the necessary coal and ironstone.

A large number of these cottages consist of only two rooms, the upper being the sleeping-apartment for the family, and usually, ill-ventilated. Mr Davies, superintendent of the Merthyr police, states that in these two-roomed houses, occupied by workmen, there are generally three beds in the sleeping apartment, containing five or six persons. These cottages are often very small, 8 feet by 10 feet, and 8 feet by 12 feet being not uncommon. Some are of less dimensions. The average rent of these houses is about 6 shillings (30p) per month (of four weeks) – a high rent apparently for such tenements. Another kind of cottage, of a better kind, consisting of a kitchen, pantry and sleeping room on the ground floor, and two sleeping rooms above, is not uncommon, the rent for which varies from 8 shillings (40p) to 12 shillings (60p) and 13 shillings (65p) per month. The proportion that these rents bear to the wages of the workmen may be estimated by the following rates of pay, stated to be about the average at present received: Colliers 17 shillings (85p) per week; Miners 14 shillings (70p); Labourers 12 shillings (60p); Masons 14 shillings (70p); Firemen and Puddlers 20 shillings (100p).

(Health of Towns Commission, *Report on State of Large Towns* 1845)

b) While the workers of Merthyr lived in the conditions described opposite, the local industrialist, William Crawshay, was able to give the Ball shown above to celebrate his son's marriage.

1 *Why were 'some parts of the town complete networks of filth'?*

2 *The older, pre-industrial villages had no form of refuse collection. Why was this less of a problem than was the case in an industrial town such as Merthyr?*

3 *What authority provides your area with its system of (i) street cleansing, (ii) refuse collection, (iii) drainage? How are these services paid for? Do you consider that such services should be provided?*

4 *The 'immigrants' into Merthyr did not know how to use a privy (toilet). What does this tell you of their previous experiences and homes? Can you suggest why their grandchildren (in say 1880) expected much more from life than had these first industrial workers?*

5 *What percentage of a collier's wage would be spent on renting (i) the poorer cottage, (ii) the better cottage? Why were the unskilled and lower paid workers forced to live in overcrowded houses?*

6 *Why was there a high death rate among the working classes of industrial towns such as Merthyr? Can you say why a child living in these conditions would have found it very difficult to study?*

Extract

A report of poverty

To show what was the state of the poor, he would refer
to Liverpool. In 1839 there were 7,860 cellars in that
city, which were dark, damp, confined, ill-ventilated
and dirty. 39,000 people inhabited them, being one
seventh of the whole population of the town, and one
fifth of the working class.

In Bury the population of which is 20,000 the
dwellings of 3,000 families of working men were
visited. In 773 of them the familes slept three and four
in a bed; in 209, four and five slept in a bed; in 67 five
and six slept in a bed, and in 15, six and seven slept in
a bed. (see p. 51).
(Parliamentary Debates [Third Series, LI, cols 1225–6])

Questions on Chapter Five

1 *Find out when your borough received its charter and
first had an elected council. What is the name of the
ward in which you live? Who are your ward
councillors?*

2 *Name five of the services which are provided by your
local council. Explain why (i) these are beneficial to
you, (ii) many people were opposed to them when they
were first introduced.*

3 *Compare life in towns in the early nineteenth century
with life in a modern town or city. Why is the death
rate lower now than then? (Note that the development
of local government is only one of the reasons for this
change).*

4 *Imagine you were a house builder in the 1840s.
Explain why you cannot provide good housing which
the poorly paid could afford.*

5 *Write a letter from an opponent of increasing activity
by local councils in the nineteenth century. (You might
want to mention laisser faire, self-help, taxation,
busybody officials.)*

6 *Examine, then draw, the coat of arms used by your
local council or county council. Can you explain its
make-up?*

7 *Find out when your local council has a meeting which
is open to the public. Go to a meeting and write a
report.*

Chapter 6   Housing and health

Profits and services

In building the early industrial towns, as we have seen, men were guided only by the profit motive. Would a venture make a profit? If the answer was 'yes' then someone would provide whatever was asked for. So, for example, there was an adequate supply of good houses provided for the richer middle class of the industrial towns who could afford them. They could also afford to have their streets drained and cleaned. Sometimes the streets of the less well-off were not cleaned or drained because the people living there were unable to pay someone to do the job. Sometimes there was no one to clean the streets because the area lay outside the boundaries within which the Improvement Commissioners were allowed to work. However, even when some of these Commissioners had powers, they did not always use them. This was largely because the money required would have to come from the ratepayers, and the Commissioners did not want to take it from them.

Poverty, dirt and disease

We have seen that housebuilders provided houses to rent for those people who could pay sufficient rent to allow the builder or owner to make a profit. Because of the low wages earned in most early industrial towns, the majority of the population could afford only a low rent and so they were provided with poor quality houses. With limited water supply and no proper drainage, these houses quickly became places where

In 1867 the architect, Edward Pugin, designed this house – Meanwood Towers – for Mr Thomas Kennedy of Leeds. There are thousands of such large houses on the outskirts of the industrial towns whose factories, mines and workshops provided a few people with a great deal of wealth and comfort.

This picture was drawn by Cruikshank in 1840. There were no laws about the age at which children could buy strong drink, nor were there any fixed hours during which such ale houses had to close. The poor used these places as an escape from the conditions in which they lived and worked.

1 *Find two things which show evidence of poverty.*

2 *Why did such poor people spend their pennies on drink and not on clothes or food?*

3 *Why were such places a possible source of disease? (Think of glasses, dirt, spitting and so on).*

disease could flourish. It is not surprising that 57 per cent of the children born in Manchester died before reaching the age of five. Many of them were the victims of their squalid environment.

And if over half the children in towns died at an early age, there was an even higher proportion of such infant mortality among the children living in the poorer districts of those towns. In 1842 a report of a Royal Commission noted the differences in the average ages of death of people in different areas of Manchester and compared these with the age of death of people in a country district:

Average age of death	*In Manchester*	*In Rutland*
Professional persons, gentry and families	38	52
Tradesmen and their families	20	41
Mechanics, labourers and families	17	38

There were thousands of lodging houses such as this one. In the crowded, squalid conditions, the already badly-fed and ill-clothed helped to spread infection and disease.

The Report went on to show that conditions were even worse in Liverpool where 62 per cent of children died before reaching the age of five.

Today, we have a much longer life expectancy than people had in the nineteenth century. Why is this so? Even then people in rural Rutland had a longer life than even the wealthiest people in industrial Manchester. Why was this so? The answer to both those questions is the better environment in nineteenth century Rutland and today's industrial towns than in nineteenth century Manchester.

Cost of death and disease

It was by appealing to the profit-motive that Edwin Chadwick and other sanitary reformers attempted to make Britain a healthier country. Their aim was to appeal to middle class politicians and councillors to provide some, at least, of the services which we expect from our modern local authorities.

Chadwick was the Secretary of the Poor Law Commission. It was Chadwick and the Commission which set up groups to study the effects of insanitary conditions, and it was Chadwick and his friends who first proved the link between environment and the death rate. They also showed that death and disease were costly to the state. They pointed out the continued rise in Poor Rates — which had to be paid by the middle class ratepayer. The Poor Law authorities had to look after the orphan children when parents died from cholera or

The Thames was the source from which most Londoners got their inadequate water supply. The sewers and street drains poured their filth into the Thames and so provided not only a stinking river but a major source of infection and disease.

PUNCH, OR THE LONDON CHARIVARI, JULY 10, 1858.

THE "SILENT HIGHWAY"-MAN.
"Your MONEY or your LIFE!"

some other contagious disease. It was the Poor Law authority which had to take in the mother and children when the father died, or when the father was unable to work because of some disease or sickness. The wage earner who came from one of the insanitary slums was likely to be off work very frequently through illness because of the unhealthy conditions in which he lived. During such times the Poor Law authorities were expected to contribute towards the upkeep of his family, to provide some sort of medical service and to bury him when he died.

Local effort

A good deal of this expense might be saved, Chadwick argued, if people lived in healthier conditions. In addition, the nation's wealth would increase more rapidly if men were not so frequently off sick, and worked more efficiently because they were healthier. All this was calculated to appeal to the economically-minded middle class. They were also forced to consider the effects of allowing disease to run riot through the working class districts. It was from these districts that there came their servants, delivery boys and men, shop assistants and van drivers. Contact with these people would spread the disease from the working class to the middle class areas.

For a variety of motives, then, the middle class were

driven to take an interest in sanitary reform. Manchester got itself a number of Private Acts of Parliament which allowed it to build a corporation-owned water supply. In 1847, Liverpool began a scheme to provide the city with an adequate water supply. In 1846 the Liverpool Council got an Act of Parliament to allow it to provide drainage, paving, sewerage systems and a street cleansing system for the growing town. It also appointed the very first-ever Medical Officer of Health (William Duncan). London appointed John Simon as its Medical Officer in 1848 and, slowly, other towns followed their example.

Central control

All these actions in Liverpool, London and Manchester were due to local people. They forced parliament to give them certain powers which allowed them to lay down laws about

PUNCH, OR THE LONDON CHARIVARI.—March 27, 1875.

"HAPPY HAMPSTEAD!"

(A SUBURBAN PLAY(GUE) GROUND.)

Sunday-Outer. "HA, MY DEAR! NOW THIS IS WHAT I CALL PLEASANT AND SALOOBRIOUS! DO THE YOUNG 'UNS NO END O' GOOD. LET'S GET ON TO THE 'EATH."

Smallpox killed off 40,000 people in 1871. Other killer-diseases were diphtheria, influenza, typhoid, measles, scarlet fever and tuberculosis. While the poor were the main sufferers from these and other diseases, the better-off were also exposed to them.

1 *Why was a middle class family in less immediate danger from fever than a poor family?*
2 *Suggest four ways in which the better-off came into daily contact with the poor.*
3 *In what ways, apart from personal contact might disease be spread from the poor to the better-off?*
4 *Why were some middle class people anxious to provide a healthier environment for the poor? Why did some oppose this?*

One of the many notices put up
during the cholera outbreak in
1832.

street cleansing, refuse collections and drainage. However,
there were many towns where no one acted to force
parliament's hands and the towns remained dirty and disease-
ridden.

In 1848 there was a fresh outbreak of cholera. The
disease was brought into the country by a sailor coming from
the Far East. Within months it had spread throughout the
country, killing thousands of people and leaving thousands of
families without a father to bring in the family income.

There was a widespread demand from the more educated
people for parliament to take some action. The cholera germ,
like other germs was at home in the overcrowded, undrained
and badly-ventilated homes of the poor. In 1848 parliament
passed the first ever Public Health Act. As a result a Board
of Health was set up in London. The three original members
of this were Lord Morpeth, Lord Shaftesbury and Edwin
Chadwick. This central Board was to supervise the work of
Local Boards of Health. These could be set up whenever 10
per cent of the ratepayers asked the central Board to set one
up or when the death rate in a town was greater than 2·3
per cent of the population in a year. In such a case the
Central Board could force local ratepayers to set up a Local
Board.

While the cholera epidemic was still raging people from
about 300 towns wrote asking the Central Board to help them
set up Local Boards of Health. These were then given power
to organise systems for refuse collection and street cleansing.
To pay for this and for laying down decent water and drainage
systems they were given the power to collect rates.

SITTING OF THE BOARD OF HEALTH, GWYDYR HOUSE, WHITEHALL

A meeting of the General Board of Health, 1849. The energetic but unpopular Edwin Chadwick is seated (reading) on the right.

Opposition

However, it would be a mistake to think that this interference by a central authority was welcomed, even though the aim of that interference was to make towns healthier. The cholera epidemic died out in 1849 and memories of its horror quickly faded. The better-off then began to complain about the rise in their rates. They objected to the way in which officials from the Local Board of Health forced them, as house-owners, to make the homes of the poor better places in which to live.

It was unfortunate for the future of Public Health legislation that Chadwick was so important a figure in the first Central Board. He was stubborn, and very determined to get his way. He was not willing to persuade people gently. He preferred to use the powers given him by parliament to force people to carry out the terms of the 1848 Act. This roused a great deal of opposition from many people in towns which badly needed to be made healthier places. These people, many of them newly entitled to vote by the 1832 Reform Act, did not welcome the idea of having to pay high rates. Chadwick's ambition to make England, and their town, a healthier place mattered less to them.

Many of his opponents used their influence with MPs, a number of whom were also annoyed by the way in which the energetic Chadwick went about his work. In 1854 the opposition was able to get parliament to dismiss Chadwick from his post at the Central Board. As a result of Chadwick's departure and of the strength of opposition to its work, the Board became weaker.

In 1858 the Board itself was abolished. Its medical duties were handed over to the *Privy Council* which appointed John Simon as its first Officer of Health. However, as we shall see, the task of making the industrial towns much healthier went on. Chadwick's work did not end with his departure because the need for that work did not end. Indeed, the pressure for a healthier environment grew rather than diminished as the century went on.

Documents

a) Lord Shaftesbury opposes government interference, 1883

If the State is to be asked not only to provide houses for the labouring classes, but also to supply them at nominal rents, it will, while doing something on behalf of their physical condition, destroy their moral energies. It will, in fact, be an official proclamation that, without any efforts of their own, certain poor people shall enter into the enjoyment of many good things at the expense of others. The State is bound, in such a case as this, to give every facility by law; but the work itself should be founded on voluntary effort, for which there is in the country an adequate amount of wealth, zeal and intelligence.

Should private zeal be insufficient, it might then be necessary for the Government to use the money of the State for the improvement of the housing conditions of the labouring classes by placing them in new homes at subsidised rents; but this must not take place until every effort has been made and indisputable proof given that, if the State does not do the work, it will never be done at all.

The mischief of it would be very serious. It would, besides being a kind of legal pauperization, give a heavy blow and great discouragement to the spirit of healthy thrift now rising among the people. The statements of the last few years show an improvement that is almost marvellous in the habits of the population. The wise and considerate measures to give facilities for the investment of savings, specially those introduced at the Post Office by Mr Fawcett and his predecessors, are greatly changing the character of the English nation, generally regarded, hitherto, as that of the most wasteful in Europe. But much of the old spirit still remains, and under the influence of bad example it would regain its ascendancy. 'My money is mine, and I've a right to spend it as I like, and if the worst comes to the worst, there's the workhouse.' This sentiment, it is feared, is still the sentiment of thousands in this country; nor will it be expelled or modified by the gigantic hints, given in speeches and pamphlets, of the depth and extent of State benevolence. It is a melancholy system that tends to debase a large mass of the people to the conditions of a nursery, where the children look to the father and mother, and do nothing for themselves.

(The Earl of Shaftesbury in the magazine *The Nineteenth Century* 1883)

1 Pick out the three ways in which, according to Shaftesbury, good housing might be provided by or for the people.

2 Shaftesbury wrote about 'subsidised rents' and, earlier, of 'nominal rents'. If rents have to be subsidised who pays the subsidy? Do you believe that this is a good thing or not? Which services do you enjoy which are paid for, partly or wholly, in this way?

3 If adequate housing was to be built by 'voluntary effort' who would pay the builder? What voluntary efforts are made today to help people who have housing difficulties?

4 Find out what 'facilities for the investment of savings' had been set up 'at the Post Office' in 1861.

5 Why were so many people unable to practice what Shaftesbury called 'healthy thrift'?

6 Do you agree that state social security has tended to 'debase the large mass of the people'?

b) The neglected poor

While systematic efforts have been made to widen the streets, to remove obstructions to the circulation of free currents of air, to extend and perfect the drainage and sewerage where the wealthier class reside, nothing whatever has been done to improve the conditions of districts inhabited by the poor. These neglected places are out of view, and are not thought of; their condition is known only to the parish officers and the medical men whose duties oblige them to visit the inhabitants to relieve their necessities and to attend to the sick.

(Dr S. Smith, *On the Prevalence of Fever in Twenty Metropolitan Parishes and Unions* 1839)

1 What names were given to the groups which made 'systematic efforts' to improve conditions in the industrial towns?

2 If such a body were set up in Manchester in, say, 1801, why might it not be able to deal with the problems of a much larger Manchester in, say, 1841?

3 What evidence was there in 1839 that sickness and death were (i) more common among the poor than among the rich: (ii) the cause of an increase in the level of the Poor Rate?

c) A slum in Stockton

Each house contains two rooms, namely a house place and a sleeping room above. Each room is about three yards wide and four yards long. In one of these houses there are nine people belonging to one family. There are 44 houses and 22 cellars all of the same size. The cellars are let off as separate dwellings; these are dark, damp and very low, not more than six feet between floor and ceiling.

(*Report on the Sanitary Conditions of the Labouring Population* 1842)

1 Explain briefly why the poor lived in such squalor. Were they to blame for their conditions?

2 Can you suggest three reasons why the workmen in Rutlandshire had as high an expectation of life as the gentry in Manchester? (see p. 57).

Extract

The link between poverty and ignorance

Often, in discussion of sanitary subjects the filthy habits of the lower classes are cited as an explanation of the inefficiency of measures designed for their advantage.

It is constantly urged, that to bring improved domestic arrangements within the reach of such persons is a waste, that if you give them a coal scuttle, a washing basin and a water closet, these several utensils will be applied indifferently to the purpose of each other; and that people will remain in the same unredeemed lowness and misery as before. But the task of interfering in behalf of these classes begins at length to be recognised as an obligation of society.

(Dr J. Simon, *City Medical Reports* 1849)

Questions on Chapter Six

1 *Write a letter which might have been written by a middle-class child who has visited a poor home.*

2 *Write a letter which might have been written by a poor child who has gone to work as servant at the home of a wealthy person.*

3 *Why were so many deaths described as 'preventable'? How could they have been prevented?*

4 *Draw up a petition which might have been written by ratepayers asking that a local Board of Health be set up in their town.*

5 *'Cleanliness is next to godliness'. Why was this possible only for the well-to-do?*

6 *Make a collage of newspaper headlines which might have appeared above articles dealing with (i) the announcement of the Manchester death rate in the 1840s, (ii) the setting up of a local Board of Health.*

7 *Find out more about the work of Chadwick.*

d) A back street in Glasgow, 1868. By this time many improvements had been made; the street is paved and has gas lighting; there are pipes to carry the rainwater from the roofs and a gutter for surface drainage. But the problem remained that too many lived in overcrowded houses which lacked lavatories, water supplies and sufficient ventilation.

Why were so many people unable to afford the full rent for a decent home? What effects did poor housing have on their physical condition?

Chapter 7   The problem of poverty

The Cottage Lunch, a painting by G. Moreland. This was intended to give a romantic view of the 'good life' led by the agricultural worker and his family. As you can see they had little furniture, a poor diet and rough clothing. In such an under-developed country few people had a decent standard of living.

1 *Look again at Chapter One and then say who you think made the furniture in this cottage.*
2 *What food and drink did these cottagers have for lunch? How does this help you to explain the decisions made at Speenhamland? (Opposite.)*
3 *Why do you think the cottagers were unable to afford better food (e.g. meat), furniture (e.g. more chairs) and clothing?*

What is poverty?

'If the income of a family is too low to allow that family to buy the necessities of life, then that family is living in poverty.' This is what one social worker wrote. But this simple definition does not tell us what is meant by the 'necessities of life'. Some people might think that a large house was a necessity; poor people might think a washing machine a great luxury. In the eighteenth century many people thought that simple furniture and food were good enough. Today we expect more from life. Our ideas of the necessities are different from those of our grandparents.

Causes of poverty

It may be difficult to define poverty. It is fairly simple to make a list of its causes. The old, the sick, the unemployed or those who can get work for only a day or two (the under-employed) as well as people working in poorly-paid jobs are all people without enough income to enable them to buy all that they need. Large families which depend on one person's wages are also likely to suffer poverty.

All these causes of poverty have always existed. But during the late eighteenth and nineteenth centuries more people than ever before suffered from some or all of the causes of poverty.

William Cobbett spent many years travelling around England during the period 1790–1820. He saw some of the effects of the changes brought about by the industrial revolution. Cobbett believed that the poverty which he saw was due to industrialisation which had destroyed the old domestic system. It had made men slaves to the new machines.

Poverty before the industrial revolution

Cobbett did not mention that there was a great deal of poverty even before the new machines were invented. From Tudor times onwards it had been the duty of the local parish to look after its own poor. Overseers were appointed, with powers to collect poor rates from the parishioners. They also built work-houses where the poor could be housed and where orphans could be brought up. In order to keep rates as low as possible, each parish tried to make sure that it looked after only its own people. So wandering beggars and vagrants were hustled from parish to parish with no one accepting them. In 1662

William Cobbett giving money to 'the deserving poor' by which the famous writer meant the people who tried to find work. Cobbett believed that industrialisation had led to the end of the domestic system and so to a fall in the income of the families of agricultural workers.

an Act of Settlement was passed which gave parish authorities the right to send any such vagrant beggars back to the parish which was judged to be 'theirs'.

Speenhamland (see p. 73)

With the coming of the industrial machinery there was, as we have seen, a fall in the wages of some handworkers. They were also affected by the changes in agriculture, particularly the enclosing of common land. After 1793 Britain was engaged first in wars against the French revolutionary government and then against Napoleon. One effect of these wars was to make it more difficult to import food from abroad. Therefore the price of home-grown food rose. The poor, who already had lower incomes than they had once enjoyed, now faced a period of rising prices which made their lives even harder. Even men who were working found it difficult to make ends meet and were forced to ask the Poor Law authorities for help. This help was provided locally and not by the national government.

In 1795 the magistrates at Speenhamland in Berkshire decided to give wage earners some 'dole' or hand-out from parish rates to help them meet the increased cost of living.

The Beadle. This was the man appointed by the parish authorities to see to the running of the workhouse. In *Oliver Twist* Charles Dickens showed how cruel some of these men could be.

Opposition to Speenhamland

The Speenhamland method (or system) of dealing with the problem caused by low wages and high prices was quickly followed by parish authorities in other parts of Southern England. This led to a rise in the level of poor rates. The Rev. Thomas Malthus was an Anglican clergyman who wrote a number of important books on the question of population. He was opposed to the Speenhamland system. He argued that it encouraged earlier marriages – since a man could get his 'dole' from the parish to help him support his wife. The system also encouraged people to have more children – who would be brought up on the 'dole' handed out by the authorities. This, said Malthus, would lead to an ever-rising poor rate. It would also mean that there was less food available for the hard-working people who decided not to get married and did not apply for help to the parish authorities. Malthus argued that if a man could not support a family then he ought not to get married. The Speenhamland system encouraged him to get married, to have children, who would also marry and have more children until, Malthus argued, there would be so many people that there would not be enough food to go round. The result would be starvation. Better, he said, not to help the poor in the first place. Some would die because they would not have enough to eat. But the number of such deaths would be smaller than if the poor were given a 'dole' and enabled to have children of their own.

The Poor Law Amendment Act, 1834
The Whigs came to power in 1830 and reformed the corrupt parliamentary system. They then reformed a number of other British institutions. They reformed the system of local government, abolished slavery in the British Empire, set up a tidy

The Whitechapel Poor House, 1840. Notice the straw for bedding, the notice about smoking and the flooring. Some people are queuing for food (centre and right); others sit and lie around in an attitude of hopelessness. The authorities believed:

* In the giving of relief, the public should impose such conditions as will help the individual and the country at large. Every penny given that helps to make the position of the pauper more eligible (better) than that of the other workmen will encourage laziness.
(From Report of the Commissioners inquiring into the Administration of the Poor Laws, 1834.)

The dining hall at St Pancras Workhouse, 1900. By 1900 there had been many improvements in the working of the Poor Law, but as this photograph shows, there was still the sense of being in a prison-like building where the imates had to do as they were told. Notice, too, that the women are still separated from their husbands and children. Charlie Chaplin tells of his early life in such a workhouse in the first chapters of his *Autobiography*.

method of registering births, marriages and deaths, passed the first effective Factory Act – and also reformed the Poor Law system.

Instead of allowing each separate parish to deal as it wished with its own poor, the Whig Amendment Act set up a uniform pattern for the whole country. A parish, or more usually, a number of parishes uniting in a Union, had to build a workhouse, staffed by paid officials. The ratepayers were to elect a Board of Guardians of the Poor who were to supervise the work of the officials, organise the collection of a poor rate and see that the new regulations were carried out.

These regulations, laid down in the 1834 Act, were to be issued by a Central Board of three Commissioners with an office in London. The Secretary to these Commissioners was Edwin Chadwick. One of the regulations that the Commissioners had to apply was that no fit (or 'able bodied') man was to be given any money (or 'relief') from the poor rates. If such a man asked for help he and his family were to be forced to live in the workhouse. In order to make this as unattractive as possible, conditions in the workhouse had to be made worse (or 'less eligible' in the words of the 1834 Act) than the conditions endured by the lowest paid workman outside the workhouse. On entering the workhouse, the family was split up. The men went to one section, the women to another and the children to a special children's section. The Commissioners issued a set of diet sheets to each workhouse to make sure that the inmates of workhouses were given only the very bare essentials.

Factory children scrambling for food in a pig-trough. It was not only the inmates of the Andover Workhouse (see extract p. 73) who had too little to eat; the low wages paid to many workpeople meant that they, too, could not afford to buy enough food.

The Andover scandal 1845—46

Many of the Boards of Guardians tried to observe the letter of the Commissioners' laws; others went beyond even that harsh limit so that the inhabitants of the workhouses were treated inhumanly. In 1845 there was a public outcry when it was learned that the poor in the Andover workhouse had been driven by hunger to eat rotting bone marrow.

Opposition

But even before this scandal had come to light there was a good deal of opposition to the new system. Critics called the workhouses, 'Bastilles' — the name of the prison where the French Kings had once housed their enemies. John Fielden, a cotton manufacturer of Todmorden was only one of many who tried to prevent the authorities setting up a workhouse. Clergymen up and down the country preached about the new system's inhumanity to the poor. Richard Oastler, a woollen manufacturer from Huddersfield, toured the country to try to rouse the people against the new system. He urged them to fight and there were a large number of riots against the harsh system and its officials.

The Chartist movement grew in strength as working people realised that the Poor Law system was not meant to find the causes of poverty nor to help find remedies for it but was meant only to punish the poor.

Changes

The Commissioners based in London soon found that the new system could not cope with the massive unemployment following a fall in trade. They were forced to change their rules to allow Guardians to give money to unemployed workers and their families. This, after all, was cheaper than trying to build workhouses to take in many thousands of people. This happened during the so-called 'Hungry Forties' when many people were temporarily thrown out of work.

In 1847 a new Poor Law Board was set up to replace the three Commissioners and in 1871 this Board was united with the Public Health Board to form the Local Government Board. This advised the Guardians to treat the poor more kindly. In 1867 and 1884 some working class men were given the right to vote in parliamentary elections. Some of them and some women were also allowed to stand for election to the Boards of Guardians. Working men and women demanded that the poor be better treated; they were allowed to visit friends outside the workhouse, their condition was improved — men being allowed a ration of tobacco while

women were given a small allowance of tea. But it was not until the twentieth century that politicians started to solve the problem of the causes of poverty.

An attack on the Workhouse at Stockport, 1842. As you can see, many well-dressed and, presumably, respectable people joined in such attacks which Oastler, Fielden and other employees called for. The army had to be called in to put down this riot and other riots elsewhere. It is not surprising that many people were afraid that there might be a general revolutionary uprising in the 1840s. Oastler declared:

* The country ought to be one blaze of fire which only the blood of all who support the Poor Law will be able to put out.
(From a speech by Richard Oastler in Newcastle, 1842.)

Documents

a) Joseph Fielden against the Poor Law, 1836—8

In Todmorden Union, immediately on the introduction of the new system, an attempt was made by the partners of the manufactory, as stated in our last Report, to prevent the peaceful operation of the law, by throwing the whole of their workpeople at once out of employment, and closing their works. This attempt to intimidate the guardians by endangering the peace of the neighbourhood, having been defeated by the promptitude of the magistrates, and the steady determination of the guardians, Messrs Fielden, on the 16th day of July re-opened their works.

On the guardians proceeding to assume the administration of relief, and to demand from the overseers of the several townships the sums necessary for this purpose, the overseers of Todmorden and Langfield (the townships in which Messrs Fielden's works are chiefly situate) adopted a course of passive resistance and disobedience to the law, in which they have persevered up to the present time. The overseers of the other townships having supplied the necessary funds, the guardians at once assumed the administration of relief to the poor of those townships; but the poor of Todmorden and Langfield have not been relieved by the Board of Guardians for want of necessary funds.

In the meantime the powers of the law have been exerted against the overseers of the two townships making default. The overseers of Todmorden have been convicted of a first and second offence on the 98th section of the Poor Law Amendment Act, and the fines of £5 in the first instance and of £20 in the second, have been levied by distress upon the goods of one of them.

On the 16th November last two constables from Halifax, who were employed in executing a warrant of distress upon the overseer of Langfield, were violently assaulted and overpowered by a concourse of persons, the first assembling of which was accompanied by the ringing of a bell in one of Messrs Fielden's factories, from which a large number of workpeople issued, and took part in a riot which ensued. The two officers were stripped of their clothes, and otherwise brutally treated, and had great difficulty in escaping with their lives into the adjoining township of Stanfield; and here a further riot took place, accompanied by some destruction of property and an attack upon the building in which the guardians were accustomed to meet.

Such was the state of excitement and alarm occasioned by these unfortunate proceedings, that the magistrates, in their subsequent active exertions to apprehend the rioters, deemed it expedient on two occasions to call out a military force in support of the constables while engaged in making prisoners of some of the workmen in Messrs Fielden's mills. It has also appeared essential to the security of the neighbourhood that a combined force of infantry and cavalry should be stationed at Todmorden for the present.

(*Fifth Annual Report of the Poor Law Commissioners 1838*)

1 *What is 'a Union'? Who were to supervise the treatment of the poor within a Union?*

2 *Why did Fielden and some other manufacturers throw people out of work? When and why might they re-employ these same people?*

3 *What is meant by 'passive resistance and disobedience'? What did Fielden hope would be the result of this behaviour? How might the government try to bring an end to such behaviour?*

4 *Why were the constables attacked on 16 November?*

5 *Did opposition to the new system come mainly from the poor or from the better-off? Why?*

Cullompton, May 14th, 1847.

At a Meeting held at the White Hart Inn, on Thursday, for the purpose of taking into consideration the distress of the Poor of this Parish, and the best means of providing for them—

It was resolved, "That it is the opinion of this Meeting that the actual wants of the Poor, more particularly in Bread Food are great, and require our sympathy and attention, to alleviate to the extent of our means; but at the same time, this Meeting deprecates the illegal and violent conduct of certain persons, in attacking the Houses of Mr. TROOD, Mr. JUSTICE, and Mr. SELLWOOD. If any repetition of violence occur, the energies of the Subscribers will be checked, the intended relief will be discontinued, and the persons requiring it, will be left to the ordinary course of the Poor Laws."

FROST, PRINTER, (CIRCULATING LIBRARY,) CULLOMPTON.

---

b) The magistrates at Cullompton had experienced some of the unrest advocated by Oastler. They threatened to make the Poor Law work if the people did not behave.

Where is Cullompton? Why was there poverty in the aaricultural areas of the country? What evidence is there in (b) that the Poor Law system was unable to cope with the problem of poverty? What evidence is there that the unrest was widespread?

c) **The Speenhamland system**
The Magistrates will make the following allowances for the relief of all industrious men and their families:
When the 4lb loaf shall cost 1 shilling (5p), then every man shall have, for his own support, 3 shillings (15p) weekly, either from his wages or an allowance from the poor rates; for the support of his wife and every other member of his family he shall have 1s 6d (7½p). When the loaf shall cost 1s 4d (7p) then he shall have 4 shillings (20p) for his own support and 1s 10d (9p) for the support of each member of his family.
(The Reading 'Mercury', 11 May 1795)

1 *Why were workers unable to afford to buy as much bread in 1795 as they had bought before the outbreak of war against France in 1793?*

2 *Why did this system (i) make it possible for workpeople to have more children (ii) tempt employers to pay even lower wages?*

3 *Why did this system lead to an increase in the Poor Rates?*

Extracts

The Andover Scandal – Evidence of Charles Lewis, labourer:
What work were you employed about when you were in the workhouse? — I was employed breaking bones.
Were other men engaged in the same work? — Yes.
Was that the only employment you had? — That was the only employment I had at the time I was there.
Was the smell very bad? — Very bad.
How did you break them? — We had a large bar to break them with.
During the time you were so employed, did you ever see any men gnaw anything or eat anything from those bones? — I have seen them eat marrow out of the bones.
Have you often seen them eat the marrow? — I have.
Did they state why they did it? — I really believe they were hungry.
Did you see any of the men gnaw the meat from the bones? — Yes.
Did they used to steal the bones and hide them away? — Yes.
And when a fresh set of bones came in, did they keep a sharp look-out for the best? — Yes.
Was that a regular thing? — While I was there.
(*Report from the Select Committee on the Andover Union 1846*)

Questions on Chapter Seven

1 *Down one side of a page make a list of the causes of poverty. Suggest briefly how each may be tackled.*

2 *Do you agree that industrialization was a cause of poverty?*

3 *Write a letter from someone who was getting help under the Speenhamland system. (He might write about his family, wages, prices, meeting with the poor law authorities, etc.)*

4 *Why did the Poor Law Commissioners insist on the principles of less-eligibility? Give some examples of ways in which they ensured that conditions in workhouses were very harsh.*

5 *Why could the workhouse authorities not cope with the large-scale unemployment which accompanied a slump in trade? How did this affect the working of the Poor Law Amendment Act?*

6 *Make a collage of headlines which might have appeared above articles on: (i) the rising cost of poor relief in the early nineteenth century, (ii) the opening of a workhouse in the late 1830s, (iii) the Andover scandal.*

7 *Find out more about the work and importance of (i) Oastler, (ii) Cobbett, (iii) Malthus.*

Chapter 8   Factories and factory reform

Why build factories?

Before the so-called industrial revolution men, women and children worked on simple machines to produce the clothes and other things that they needed. The spinning-wheels and weaving-looms were small so that they could be used in the two-roomed cottages in which most people lived.

However, even in that pre-industrial period there were some machines that were driven by water-power. This was not readily available at the workers' cottages. Businessmen built factories alongside a river or stream and used the current from the river to drive their machines. The first factory of this kind was built in 1717 by Thomas Lombe and his brother John. They had stolen the designs for machinery from an Italian factory. They built a silk-throwing factory on an island in the River Derwent in Derbyshire. Within a few years John Lombe was poisoned by some jealous Italian silk makers and the business declined.

We have seen that Arkwright invented a water-frame. As its name suggests, this machine was driven by water-power so that it had to be housed in buildings on river banks. Once Boulton and Watt had solved the problem of making a rotary steam-engine this, and other machines such as the 'mule', were driven by steam power. When Watt's engine became widely known and used by manufacturers there was an increase in the number and size of factories and a fall in the number of handworkers.

The Lombe brothers' mill, Derby. This was the first factory in Britain and was built to house the water-driven machinery which John Lombe built from designs which he smuggled from Italy where such machines were used in the silk-making industry.

The advantages of the factory system

In the domestic system the worker pleased himself when and for how long he worked. In the factory the worker was under the eye of the owner. Rules and regulations could be made to force the people to work regular hours or face dismissal. The first machines were easy to operate – so easy that children could do most of the work. Employers liked this because they were able to pay low wages to children and could get child labour from the Poor Law authorities.

In the domestic system people had worked and lived in the same place – the cottage. In the factory system they lived in a house and worked in a factory. It could be argued that it was healthier to separate the place of work from the home. There was less dust and dirt in the home once the work of spinning and weaving had been taken into the factory.

There is no doubt that the country as a whole became richer as a result of the spread of the factory system. From the new, mechanised textile mills and iron foundries, potteries and engineering works, there came an increasing flow of goods. A new, wealthy, middle class appeared, some of whose members became extremely rich. This class led the demand for a reform of the parliamentary system (Chapter 9). Although at first this reform benefited only the middle class, in time there were other reforms which gave the working class the right to vote and the chance to form their own working class political party.

While at first much of the wealth went into the pockets of a small number of people, in time the mass of the population came to have a fairer share of that wealth. Industrialisation has provided the wealth which enables us, today, to have a high standard of living and a well-developed welfare state.

Opposition to the new machines

It is easy for us to see that modern Britain is much wealthier than pre-industrial Britain and that modern workmen have a higher standard of living than workmen in the eighteenth century. It is also easy to show that this improvement is due to the way in which machines pour out goods which can be sold for money, some of which is paid as wages and some of which is paid as taxes to the government which provides the welfare services.

But even today people are frightened of machines which might make them unemployed. Dockers try to stop the building of modern docks and modern equipment. Steel-workers oppose schemes to cut down the number of men needed in steel works and, I suppose, teachers would try to prevent the introduction of robots or machines which might

Children winding cotton in an early textile mill. Children had worked in the domestic system and it seemed natural that they should work in the early factories. Their 'nimble fingers' were able to cope with the work on the simple machines, but as machines became larger and more complicated there were many accidents and this led to a demand that children should not be allowed to work in textile mills.
The poet, Southey, visited a factory in 1811:

* The owner told me that nothing could be so useful to a country as factories. 'You see these children, sir,' said he. 'In most parts of England poor children are a burden to parents and poor rates; here the Parish is freed for that expense. The children earn their bread from the time they can walk. They come at five in the morning and leave at six in the evening and another lot take over for the night; the wheels never stand still.' (The poet Robert Southey, *Espriella's Letters from England*.)

RULES AND REGULATIONS

AGREED TO, AND TO BE

STRICTLY OBSERVED BY THE WORKMEN

EMPLOYED BY

T. RICHARDSON & SONS.

I.

FOR WORKING HOURS, the bell will ring at 6 o'clock in the Morning, and 6 o'clock in the Evening, for a day's work, throughout the year; except during the months of November, December, and January, when the work-hours will be from half-past 6 in the Morning till 6 in the Evening. On Saturdays, the day's work will end at 4 o'clock.

II.

THE HOUR FOR DINNER to be from 12 to 1, throughout the year—the half-hour for Breakfast, from half-past 8 to 9, during November, December, and January; and from 8 to half-past 8, during the remainder of the year. The first quarter-day shall end at Breakfast-time—the second at 12 o'clock—the third at 3—and the last at 6 o'clock; throughout the year.

III.

The aforesaid Rules to apply to every man employed in the Works. If engaged in any job away from the Works, the day's work to be, in summer, from 6 to 6, and, in winter, from light to dark, without any half-hour allowed for Breakfast. The day's-work to end, on Saturdays, at 4 o'clock. If engaged at a greater distance than 3 miles from the Works, lodgings to be allowed, at the rate of 1s. 6d. per week; and an hour, on Saturday afternoons, for every 3 miles distance up to 12 miles, when the day's-work will end at noon.

IV.

OVER-TIME to be reckoned at the rate of 8 hours for a day's-work both in and out of the Works.

V.

Each Workman to be provided with a Drawer, with Lock and Key, for his Tools. The Drawer, Key, and Tools, to be marked with the same number, and lettered "T. R. & S.," and the Key to be left in the Office, or Storehouse, every night. Each man to be accountable for his Tools, when leaving his employment; and in case of loss, the amount to be deducted from his wages.

VI.

NO TIME WILL BE ALLOWED to any man neglecting to take out and give in his own Time-Board; on which must be written his time, the name of the article he has been working at during the day, and what purpose it is for. Any man, either giving in or taking out any Board but his own, to be fined 1s.

VII.

Any Workman neglecting to leave the Key of his Drawer in the Office or Storehouse, on leaving work, to be fined 1s.

VIII.

Any Workman leaving his Candle burning, or neglecting to shut his Gas-Cock, to be fined 1s.

IX.

Any Workman opening the Drawer of another, or taking his tools, without leave, to be fined 1s.

X.

Any person not returning Taps and Dies, or any other general Tools, to the person who has charge of them, to be fined 1s.

XI.

Any Workman interfering with, or injuring, any Machinery or Tool, to pay the cost of repairing the damage, and to be fined 1s.

XII.

Any Workman making preparation for leaving Work before the Bell rings, to be fined 1s.

XIII.

Any Workman smoking, during working-hours, to be fined 1s.

XIV.

Any Workman using oil to clean his hands, or for any other improper purpose, to be fined 2s. 6d.

XV.

Any Workman giving in more time than he has worked, to be fined 2s. 6d.

XVI.

Any Workman taking strangers into the Works, without leave, or talking to such as may go in, to be fined 1s.

XVII.

No Workman to leave his employment without giving a fortnight's notice, and the same to be given by T. R. & Sons, except in cases of misconduct.

XVIII.

Wages to be paid once a fortnight. Any Workman dismissed for misconduct, not to be entitled to the Wages he may have earned previously, until the next following pay-day.

XIX.

Any Workman wilfully or negligently damaging or spoiling any Work committed to his charge, to have the amount or value thereof deducted from his Wages, at the next and regular following pay-days.

XX.

Any Workman defacing or damaging any Drawings, Plans, or Copies of these Rules, to be fined 1s.

No Beer, or Spirits, allowed to be taken into the Works without leave.

ALL FINES TO GO TO THE SICK FUND.

I _____

agree to abide by the above Rules and Regulations, as witness my hand this _____

day of _____ 18

J. PROCTER, PRINTER, UNION PLACE, HIGH STREET, HARTLEPOOL.

Luddites attack a mill. In different parts of England the Luddite movement had different aims. The Yorkshire croppers tried to prevent the introduction of shearing machines. In Nottingham the frameknitters argued that the law forbade the use of machines in their industry. In 1811–13 Britain was engaged in a desperate struggle against Napoleon, Emperor of France. It is not surprising that the ruling class thought that the Luddites were dangerous revolutionaries.

* The attack on Daniel Burton's power loom mill in Middleton was made by a crowd of several thousands armed with stones and a body of men consisting of from one to two hundred, some armed with muskets with fixed bayonets and others with colliers' picks who marched into the village and joined the rioters. At the head of these armed bandits a Man of Straw was carried, representing the renowned General Ludd whose standard-bearer waved a sort of red flag. (The *Leeds Mercury*, April 1812)

(Opposite) In the domestic system the women had spun in the time that they were not cooking or doing some other housework and the men had helped out when they were free from working in the fields. This casual approach to work had to be stopped if factories were to work efficiently and workpeople forced to realise that strict time-keeping was essential.

1 *Read Rules I and II carefully. Make a time-table showing the way in which the working day was divided up. How many hours were worked (i) daily and (ii) weekly for 9 months in the year? Why and by how much was the working day shorter from November to January?*
2 *How often were the workpeople paid?*

replace them. It is not surprising then that the workmen of the eighteenth and early nineteenth centuries, faced with the immediate effects of the first machines, were violently opposed to them. After all, for many of them it would mean the loss of a job or a lowering of wages. This helps us to understand the attacks made by men on the first machines even in the 1760s and 1770s.

The most violent and best-remembered opposition to the new machines came from the workmen called the Luddites. In 1811 workmen in different parts of the country banded together to try to stop the introduction of machinery. In Nottingham the handworkers in the lace-making industry argued that the old laws of the land gave them the right to smash new, labour-saving machines. In Yorkshire the movement was led by the croppers, men who used the huge shearing scissors in the final process of cloth-making. They were against the introduction of the steam-driven shearing machines which were larger, more efficient and labour-saving. Using huge hammers (which they called 'Great Enochs'), they tried to smash the new machines.

But the Luddites were unable to halt the increasing use of machinery. Later on, workpeople learned to take advantage of the new wealth pouring from the machines to demand higher wages for themselves.

Factory reform
The first 'immigrants' into the new industrial towns were, in one sense, 'slaves' to the machines. From a very early age they worked very long hours and for low wages.

Many of the first factories were overcrowded, badly-lit and poorly ventilated. Accidents were common, and the crippled or maimed child or adult was dismissed by his employer to become a beggar or an inmate of a workhouse. We have seen that Richard Oastler was one of those who had campaigned against the Poor Law after 1834. He was also one of those who campaigned for factory reform. Oastler argued that the conditions in which children and adults had to work in British factories were worse than conditions in which slaves lived and worked on plantations in the West Indies. Oastler asked why British MPs were working for the abolition of slavery in the British Empire while they ignored what he called the 'Yorkshire Slavery' in which the workers in woollen mills worked.

In 1802 and 1819 Sir Robert Peel and Robert Owen persuaded parliament to pass Factory Acts which were meant to improve the conditions of the pauper apprentices sent to the factories by the Poor Law authorities. In 1833 an Act was passed: it said, among other things —

> 'It shall not be lawful to employ in any factory as aforesaid, except in mills for the manufacture of silk, any child who shall not have completed his or her ninth year. It shall be lawful for His Majesty to appoint four Inspectors of factories where children and young persons under eighteen years of age are employed. The Inspectors shall have power to make such rules as may be necessary for the execution of this act, binding on all persons subject to the provisions of this Act.'

This Act, which also limited the number of hours which could be worked by older children and by women, was the

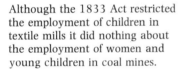

Although the 1833 Act restricted the employment of children in textile mills it did nothing about the employment of women and young children in coal mines.

first effective Act because of the appointment of these Inspectors. Previous Acts had relied on the reports of clergymen or local JPs. These men were too often related to or friendly with the factory owners they were supposed to check on. Now, after 1833, there were a small group of independent *Civil Servants* whose task it was to check on conditions in textile mills.

However, the Act was a very limited one. It said nothing of the hours of work for male workers. It did not deal with conditions in the masses of workshops, engineering shops and iron foundries. Above all, it did not deal with conditions in the mines – to which parents sent their children after 1833 in increasing numbers.

But the Act was a start and it encouraged reformers and leaders of trade unions to campaign for a shorter working day, improved conditions for male workers and an end to the employment of young children.

In 1844, 1847 and 1850 Factory Acts were passed by

Children carrying wet heavy clay in a brickyard; this was not forbidden until it became compulsory to send children to school in the 1880s.

* When I was nine years old (in 1840) my work consisted of continually carrying about 40 pounds of clay upon my head from the clay heap to the table where the bricks were made. This I had to do without stopping for thirteen hours a day. Sometimes I had to work all through the night, carrying 1,200 bricks from the makers to the floors where they were placed to harden. During such a night I would walk about fourteen miles. For all this I was paid sixpence. (Edward Hodder, *George Smith of Coalville* 1896)

The cartoonist Cruickshank wanted to draw attention to the low wages paid to the workers (climbing the stairs) which enabled the factory owner to churn out cheap goods. As goods became cheaper so the market for them would be larger so that the profits would continue to grow (bottom left).

which male workers in textile mills achieved the Ten Hour Day. This campaign for the Ten Hour Day was led by Lord Shaftesbury and the opposition to it was led by the economist Nassau Senior – the Poor Law Commissioner. Senior's argument was that if the hours of work are reduced by one hour per day, the profit would be destroyed. This would mean that there would be no money to pay for new machinery. But Britain became richer after the reforms. This may suggest to you that so-called experts are frequently wrong!

Good owners

Many of the reformers were themselves owners of factories or workshops. Robert Owen owned mills in New Lanark and John Fielden owned mills at Todmorden. These and a number of others may have acted out of concern for the workers' lives and conditions. Other factory owners treated their workpeople well because they realised that healthier workpeople were better workers.

Working conditions after 1842

The passage of the Ten Hour Day Act was an important step on the road to factory reform. It meant little or nothing to many workers however since it only applied to workers in the textile industry. Men and women engaged in engineering, construction, iron foundries or mines were not covered by the terms of this Act. And although after 1842 children were forbidden to work in mines until they were ten years old, and in textile mills until they were eight years old, there were plenty of other jobs which very young children were allowed to do. This included heavy, dirty work such as that in clay pits and brickyards, and dirty, dangerous work such as that found in many domestic industries in the Midlands and North. There was a long way to go yet.

In 1836 parliament passed an Act which compelled parents to report the birth of a child to the office of the Registrar-General, who issued a birth certificate. No one born before 1836 had a birth certificate, so that the 1833 Act was difficult to enforce. In 1844 a new Factory Act lowered the age at which children could work in textile mills to eight years. From 1844 onwards children going to work had to produce a birth certificate (if they were born after 1836) or a doctor's certificate if they were born before 1836. Look at the heading to this certificate. Which Queen is referred to in that heading? When did she come to the throne? Why were certificates such as this not mentioned in the 1833 Act?

Documents

a) Yorkshire Luddites

'Great Enoch still shall lead the van, stop him who
    dare, stop him who can,
Press forward every gallant man, with hatchet, pike
    and gun.
Oh the cropper lads for me, who with lusty stroke the
    shear-frames broke, the cropper lads for me.'

b) Nottingham Luddites

By the charter granted by our late sovereign, Lord,
Charles II, the framework knitters are empowered to
break and destroy all frames and engines that fabricate
articles in a fraudulent and deceitful manner, and to
destroy all framework knitters' goods whatsoever that
are so made. An Act passed in 1788 enacted that
persons entering by force into any house, shop or place
to break or destroy frames should be adjudged guilty of
felony. We are fully convinced that such Act was
obtained in the most fraudulent manner; we therefore,
the framework knitters, do hereby declare the aforesaid
Act to be null and void. And we do hereby declare to all
hosiers, lace manufacturers and proprietors of frames
that we will break and destroy all manner of frames
that make the following spurious articles and all frames
whatsoever that do not pay the regular prices heretofore
agreed to by the masters and workmen. And all frames
of whatsoever description the workman of whom are
not paid in the current coin of the realm will invariably
be destroyed. Given under my hand this first day of
January, 1812 at Ned Lud's office, Sherwood Forest.
(Framework Knitters' letter)

c) Revolutionaries?

That at the time the oath was so administered to the
informant, they explained to him that his duty as a
secret committee man would be to attend all meetings
when warned or called upon, to collect money sub-
scribed by the Luddites to defray the expenses of the
delegates and secret committees when required, and to
go when sent to collect information and carry on
correspondence with other committees. The informant
further saith that it is also the business of the secret
committee to bring in new members. The informant
saith that a very great number of Luddites are local
militia men. That the Luddites have in view ultimately
to overturn the system of government by revolutionising
the country. That certain delegates at Ashton-under-
Lyne on the 4th of August last told the informant that
the first measures to be adopted would be to send parties
to the different houses of members of both Houses of
Parliament and destroy them, and then the people in
London belonging to that society would seize upon the
Government.
(Evidence of an informer at Barnsley, reported by
Earl Fitzwilliam, Lord Lieutenant of the West Riding,
1812)

d) When the cloth had been teazled it was cropped by
'shearers' using huge hand-operated shears or scissors.
This produced the smooth surface. Shears could be made
heavier by fixing extra lead weights — seen lying on the
table.

1 *What was 'cropping'? Why did manufacturers
   introduce a steam-driven cropping (or shearing)
   machine? Why were the Yorkshire croppers so
   opposed to this?*

2 *What was the purpose of 'An Act passed in 1788'?
   In what way was this Act contrary to an Act passed
   by Charles II?*

3 *How did the Luddites get the money they needed to buy
   guns and ammunition?*

4 *Why was the fear of revolution greater in 1811–12
   than in, say, 1780?*

5 *Some people thought that the Luddites were
   revolutionaries. Write a short account which one of the
   Luddites might have sent on 'Why I joined the
   movement'.*

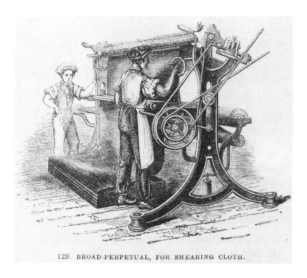

129. BROAD-PERPETUAL, FOR SHEARING CLOTH.

(a) Shearing machines were developed between 1800 and 1810 to replace the hand-shears used by the croppers. The roll of cloth passed over a rotating cylinder on which there was a spiral cutting blade which can be seen at the top of the machine. The croppers in the West Riding woollen industry tried to halt the introduction of this machine; they smashed them whenever they could, using huge hammers, which they nicknamed 'Great Enoch' to do so. Their exploits were commemorated in the jingle (a).

Extracts

Child labour

I worked at Mr Swaine's, at Little Gomersall, near Leeds. I earned half-a-crown (12½p) a week, from six to half past seven. I began when I was six years old. I came to Leicester about three years ago. I came as a spinner. I earn 24 shillings (120p) or 25 shillings (125p) a week, taking full work. Mr Swaine's was a bad factory for cruelty to children in my time. I have marks on me now from ill-treatment that I got there. They would strike us with the billy-roller over the head. I have a bump on my head now, from that. I have begun at five in the morning and worked till half past ten at night. This would be when orders came.
(from the *Report of the Committee on the Factory Bill* 1832)

A progressive owner

As to the conclusions I have come to from the working of my mill for 11 instead of 12 hours each day, as previously, I am quite satisfied that both as much yarn and cloth may be produced at quite as low a cost in 11 as in 12 hours. It is my intention to make a further reduction to 10½ hours, without the slightest fear of suffering loss. I find the hands work with greater energy and spirit; they are more cheerful, and happy.
(A factory owner quoted in *Parliamentary papers* [1845 xxv, 456/7])

Questions on Chapter Eight

1 *What were the advantages of (i) steam power over water power, (ii) the factory system over the domestic system?*

2 *Write a letter from an overseer of the poor in a parish in London to a factory owner in the North, offering some pauper children as factory workers.*

3 *Write a letter which might have been written by one of the children working in a textile mill. (Topics which might be mentioned are noise, hours, machines, other children, accidents, hours, meals and life at home.)*

4 *Trace the stages in factory reform, using 1802, 1819, 1833, 1844, 1847 and 1850 as guiding dates.*

5 *Show how by 1850 the government had begun to interfere in (i) public health, (ii) education, (iii) factory conditions. How was this interference greeted by those who believed in: (i) self-help, (ii) reformers such as Oastler and Shaftesbury?*

6 *Make a collage of headlines which might have appeared above articles on (i) 'Yorkshire Slavery', (ii) the Luddites, (iii) the passing of the 1833 Factory Act.*

Chapter 9

Parliamentary reform - Chartism

Parliament in 1830

Medieval kings first called parliaments together. Wealthy people in the counties and existing boroughs sent two representatives to consult with the king. By 1830 things remained very much as they had always been:

a) the boroughs which elected MPs were the same boroughs that had always sent representatives, and four-fifths of the MPs came from the South and South West of England;

b) most MPs were elected by a corrupt system in which the landowners had too big a say. This might habe been right in 1400, but was wrong once the industrial revolution had started to change the face of Great Britain.

A map showing some of the features of the distribution of constituencies before the Reform Act, 1832.

1 *Why was it right that in medieval times the bulk of MPs should have come from constituencies in East Anglia, the South West and the South of England?*

2 *Name six counties which had more than their fair share of representation in 1830 and six which were underrepresented.* 4

3 *Why was it unfair that both Yorkshire and Rutland had two county MPs?*

4 *Why had medieval kings not called MPs from Bolton or Manchester? Why was it unfair that these places were unrepresented in 1830?*

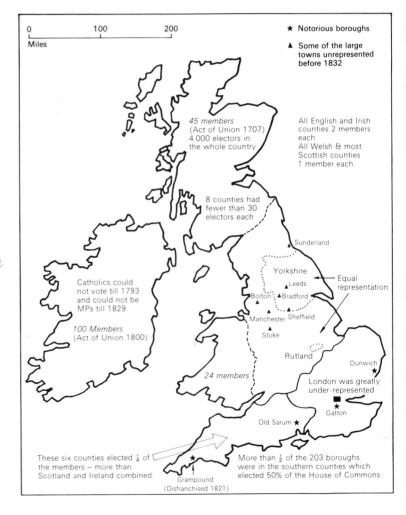

★ Notorious boroughs

▲ Some of the large towns unrepresented before 1832

45 members (Act of Union 1707) 4,000 electors in the whole country

All English and Irish counties 2 members each
All Welsh & most Scottish counties 1 member each

8 counties had fewer than 30 electors each

Sunderland

Yorkshire
Leeds
Bolton ▲ Bradford
Manchester Sheffield
Stoke

Equal representation

Catholics could not vote till 1793 and could not be MPs till 1829

100 Members (Act of Union 1800)

24 members

Rutland

Dunwich ★

London was greatly under-represented

■ ★
Gatton

Old Sarum ★

These six counties elected ¼ of the members – more than Scotland and Ireland combined.

★
Grampound (Disfranchised 1821)

More than ½ of the 203 boroughs were in the southern counties which elected 50% of the House of Commons

0   100   200
Miles

The Peterloo Massacre at St. Peter's Field, Manchester, 16 August 1819. Henry Hunt was the main speaker at the meeting called to bring attention to the need for parliamentary reform. The magistrates sent in the Manchester Yeomanry to disperse the crowd and arrest Hunt. In the process a number of people were killed, more injured and the radicals wrote their own version:

> And the heroic host no more
>   shall boast the glorious feats
>   of Waterloo!
> But this henceforth shall be the
>   toast, the glorious feats of
>   Peterloo!

Industrial change and parliament

One result of the revolution was the growth of new large towns which produced the wealth of Britain. Most of these were not represented in parliament by 1830.

Another result was the growth of a large middle class which, by 1830, was paying as much tax as the landowners. But most of the industrialists and businessmen had no chance to vote in parliamentary elections.

It was men from this middle class who became leaders in the movement for parliamentary reform.

The right to vote

Today everyone over the age of eighteen has the franchise or the right to vote. Until 1832 there was no such simple qualifying rule. In some boroughs every freeman was allowed to vote; in others only resident freemen could vote. In some places the vote was given to men who owned houses with fireplaces able to take a pot containing a stone of potatoes. These were nicknamed 'pot-wallopers'. In other towns the right to vote was given to ratepayers.

One of the demands of the reformers was that there should be one qualifying rule throughout the whole country.

The reform campaign

Reform Associations or Political Unions were set up in most industrial towns. Industrialists gave money needed to pay the expenses of visiting speakers, to hire halls and pay for pamphlets. The most famous union was at Birmingham, led by Thomas Attwood. It was Attwood who demanded that 'the interests of Industry and Trade' be given equal rights with 'the great landed interest'.

The open system of voting. The few people who had the vote had to get through the mob, climb the stairs and announce the name of the man they were going to support. Both candidates bribed the electors and because the election lasted for at least a week voters preferred to wait until near the end before finally casting their vote – and voice. The secret ballot Act (1872) ended this system, which had enabled the rich and powerful to control elections.

The Whigs and reform

In 1830 the Earl Grey became prime minister of a Whig government. Like most members of the landed aristocracy he was afraid that democracy might lead to revolution. But he realised that if he did not do something to satisfy the leaders of the reform movement, they might revolt anyhow as, in 1830, the people of France had revolted against their unreforming King Charles X.

On 1 March 1831 Lord John Russell (son of the Duke of Bedford) brought in the first Reform Bill. This was defeated in the Committee stage of the debate in the House of Commons. On 21 September 1831 Russell introduced a second Bill. This was defeated in the House of Lords. The landowners were not going to give up their power without a struggle.

The Political Unions organised mass meetings throughout the country. In Derby, Nottingham and Bristol there was a great deal of rioting.

The 1832 Act

Russell introduced a third Bill which passed through the Commons and reached the Lords in March 1832. The Lords threatened once again to throw this Bill out. But Grey had forced the King, William IV, to promise that he would create hundreds of new, reforming, members of the Lords if the Bill were not passed. King William and Grey appealed to the Lords and, reluctantly, they agreed to let this Bill pass. The 1832 Act reformed parliament in two ways:

(a) *Constituencies*: 56 towns which had populations of less then 2,000 lost their right to choose MPs; 30 towns with populations of less than 4,000 were allowed to elect only one MP and not, as before, two. There were 142 empty seats in the Commons when these small towns lost one or both their MPs. The 1832 Act gave these seats to the new, industrial areas; 22 large towns were given the right to choose two MPs; 20 smaller towns were given the right to choose one MP; another 6 seats were created in the larger counties, and Scotland and Wales also given extra representation.

(b) *Franchise*: In the boroughs the franchise was given to every man owning or renting property with a rateable value of £10 a year or more; all the old and varied qualifications were abolished. In the counties all the owners of land worth £2 a year retained their right to vote. The right was also given to some tenants (i.e. men who rented land) paying not less than £50 a year and to those holding a long lease on land worth £10 a year.

One result of these changes was that there was an increase in the number of people entitled to vote. In 1830 there were 435,000 voters; after the 1832 Act there were 652,000. You may think that this was not a very great change. Certainly no working class people gained by this Act.

The 1832 Reform Bill receiving Royal assent in the House of Lords.

Chartism

The 1832 Act changed very little. The majority of MPs still came from the agricultural South and South West. The majority of voters were still the landowners, although the richer middle class now had the vote. The working classes had supported the demand for reform. They had attended meetings such as the one at Peterloo. They had gone to the demonstrations organised by the Political Unions. It was the fear of a general revolution that had caused Grey to agree to reform and which had forced William IV and the Lords to let the Bill pass in 1832. Yet the working class had got nothing out of the Act.

In some ways they were even worse off. Their employers now had the vote and some say in the laws which the

A Chartist meeting. Most Chartist meetings were held out of doors since they did not have the money to hire halls. This night-time meeting is going to be addressed by one of the respectably-dressed riders. Most of the Chartists here and nationally were from the working class. Notice the weapons; many people feared that Chartism would lead to a bloody revolution.

reformed parliament passed. And parliament made no attempt to deal with the social problems facing the working classes. Indeed, the Poor Law Amendment Act of 1834 seemed to be a harsh and cruel way of tackling the problems of unemployment, low pay, old age and ill-health (see Chapter 7). It is hardly surprising that some people started a new movement, drawing up petitions or charters to present to parliament, asking for more reform.

One of the first charters was handed in to parliament in 1837. It reads:

'It was the fond hope of the people that a remedy for their grievances would be found in the Reform Act of 1832. They have been bitterly let-down. The Reform Act has meant simply a transfer of power from one wealthy group to another. The people have been left as helpless as before. Therefore we demand universal suffrage (i.e., the right to vote should be given to every man).'

The Six Points
The workers considered that it was essential that their voices

should be heard in parliament if that parliament was to pass laws to improve their working and living conditions. This gave rise to the Six Points which, after 1840 were common to all the petitions, and which appeared in almost all Chartist propaganda:

1 a vote for every man over the age of twenty-one;
2 a secret ballot to replace the open system of voting in which a man's employer might take revenge on him if he did not vote as the employer wanted him to vote;
3 the end of the rule which said that men standing as candidates in elections had to own property worth £2,000;
4 the payment of a wage or salary to MPs so that working men could give up their jobs if they were elected;
5 a further reform of the constituencies so that they were all of roughly the same size;
6 a General Election to be held each year.

NOT SO *VERY* UNREASONABLE!!! EH?"

A cartoon from *Punch*, 1848, showing Lord John Russell, who had introduced the First Reform Act in 1831–32, being presented with the Charter signed by millions of supporters. Russell had said that the 1832 Act was 'the final solution' to the reform of Parliament. 'Finality Jack' as he was called, shared the beliefs of the majority of upper class and middle class people that Chartism was a dangerous menace.

A divided leadership

Parliament ignored the petitions presented in 1837 and in 1839. In the latter year there were outbreaks of violence led by men who believed that parliament would have to be forced to grant their demands. In Newport, South Wales, there was a clash between the army and Chartist supporters who were trying to release some of their leaders imprisoned there. The rejection of a third Charter in 1842 led to more violence. The most important centre was at Preston where workmen ruined many steam engines by pulling out the plugs of the compression chambers. These so-called 'Plug Riots' had little effect other than to strengthen the fear that Chartism was a violent movement.

Some of the movement's leaders welcomed this growing violence. Feargus O'Connor, the owner of a newspaper, the 'Northern Star', wanted an armed uprising. Other leaders believed that Parliament would not give way to violence.

In 1848 the Chartists again tried to put a petition before Parliament. There was a mass meeting on Kennington Common, near the site of the modern Oval Cricket Ground. A procession was formed to accompany the cabs carrying the petition which had, apparently, two million signatures. Rain kept many people away from the demonstration and the march; the police allowed the leaders of the demonstration to go with their Charter across the bridge to Westminster. But they refused to allow the great mass of the demonstrators to cross into London so that there was none of the violence that had been expected.

The Charter was presented and parliament told about its demands and the millions of signatures. Many of them were in the same handwriting. Included among the signatures were such important people as 'Her Majesty', 'Victoria Rex', 'April 1st', 'The Duke of Wellington' and 'Sir Robert Peel'! But there were also many comic signatures such as 'No cheese', 'Pug Nose', 'Flat Nose', and the like. Russell also told the Commons that there were signatures which 'belonged to the name of no human being'. It is little wonder that the Commons and the newspapers made a great deal of fun of this Charter. And nothing fails like a thing that can be laughed at.

The movement died out after this fiasco. Many of its former supporters found an outlet for their energies in the new trade union movement (Chapter 10). By the use of trade unions they hoped to improve living standards by getting higher wages from employers. There was an improvement in Britain's trading position after 1848 – partly the result of Peel's free trade policy (Chapter 11) and partly because the rest of the world wanted to buy an increasing amount of British goods. This led to more employment, better wages and a rising standard of living for the majority of the British people. In this 'best of all possible worlds' there seemed little room for Chartism.

The industrial revolution brought great wealth to many middle-class families. It also brought a great deal of improvement to some working class families. This illustration from a workingman's magazine of 1861 shows a Lancashire workingman and his family enjoying life 'rent free' in their own home, bought with the help of one of the early Building Societies. As people's living standards rose they had a chance to become interested in politics.

1 *Name three items which show that this working class family were better off than the agricultural workers of the late eighteenth century. (p. 66).*

2 *The husband is reading a newspaper. Why was it possible to have nationally-distributed newspapers in the 1860s and not in the 1760s? Why might the reading of the newspaper make the workman more politically minded?*

1867 Reform Act

However the continued growth of the populations of the industrial towns meant that by the 1860s there was need for a further redistribution of seats away from the agricultural areas to the industrial Midlands and North. In 1866 Prime Minister Gladstone introduced a Reform Bill into parliament. He argued that the workers had proved that they were ready for the vote. Many of them now had some education. As a result more of them were able to read the increasing number of newspapers. In almost every town, working men had provided the money to pay for the building of Working Men's Libraries and Institutes. Here they had a chance to continue with their education. Millions of working men paid their money into the new building societies. Many of them borrowed money to buy their own homes. In 1861 Gladstone had set up the Post Office Savings Bank to give the working class a chance to save their money and by 1866, 650,000 working class people had Post Office Savings Books. All this, said Gladstone, proved that some at least of the working men were fitted to vote.

But this Bill was defeated in the House of Commons. Then an even more radical Bill was introduced by the Conservative leader, Disraeli. This was passed in 1867. As a result, all male householders in the towns were given the vote. This increased the number of voters to over two million, the vast majority of them being skilled workers. In time this led to the creation of the demand for a separate political party to represent these new voters. But this is a development which did not take place for another thirty years.

The Hyde Park riots as reported in the *Illustrated London News*, 4 August 1866.

Documents

a) Wellington opposes parliamentary reform, 1830

He had never heard of any measure up to the present moment which could satisfy his mind that the state of representation possessed the full and entire confidence of the country. The representation of the people at present contained a large body of the property of the country, and in which the landed interests had a preponderating influence. He was not prepared to bring forward any measure of the description alluded to by the noble lord. He would at once declare that, as far as he was concerned, as long as he held any station in the government of the country, he would always feel it his duty to resist such measures when proposed by others.
(From Parliamentary Debates [I, cols 5.23])

b) Opposition to Reform, 1867

The Government are proposing to enfranchise one class of men who have been disenfranchised heretofore. I ask the House to consider what good we are to get for the country at large by this extension of the franchise? The effect will be to add a large number of persons to our constituencies, of the class from which, if there is to be anything wrong going on, we may naturally expect to find it. It will increase the expenses of candidates and the management of the elections. You must look for more bribery and corruption than you have hitherto had. The working men of England, finding themselves in a full majority of the whole constituency, will awake to a full sense of their power. They will say, 'We can do better for ourselves. Don't let us any longer be cajoled at elections. Let us set up shop for ourselves. We have machinery, we have our trade unions, we have our leaders all ready. We have the power of combination and when we have a prize to fight for we will bring it to bear with tenfold more force than ever before.'
(Speech by Robert Lowe, 13 March 1866)

c) Cruickshank's view of the danger of Reform.

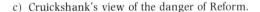

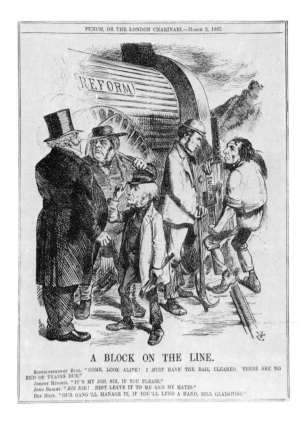

A BLOCK ON THE LINE.

Superintendent Bull. "COME, LOOK ALIVE! I *MUST* HAVE THE RAIL CLEARED. THERE ARE NO END OF TRAINS DUE."
Johnny Russell. "IT'S MY JOB, SIR, IF YOU PLEASE."
John Bright. "*HIS* JOB! BEST LEAVE IT TO ME AND MY MATES."
Ben Dizzy. "OUR GANG'LL MANAGE IT, IF YOU'LL LEND A HAND, BILL GLADSTONE."

d) A block on the line. Punch's view of the question of political reform after the failure of Gladstone's Bill, 1866.

1 *Which class dominated parliament in 1830? Which class claimed that it ought to be represented there? Why were the people of this class entitled to a share in government?*

2 *Do you think that parliament in 1830 had 'the full and entire confidence of the country'? Was it true of the 1866 parliament?*

3 *Which class dominated parliament in 1866? Which class was asking for representation? Why were they entitled to a share in government?*

4 *Compare the arguments used by the middle class in 1830–2 with the arguments they used in 1866.*

5 *Do you think that Lowe's fears were justified?*

6 *Why did Cruickshank think that there was a danger of revolution between 1830 and 1860? Which members of society might have agreed with him? Do you think their fears were justified?*

7 *Briefly summarise the views of the major figures in the Punch cartoon during the period 1866–7. Why did Gladstone fail to deal with the 'block on the line'? What was surprising about the fact that the Conservatives managed to do so?*

Extracts

Division among the Chartists

The whole physical force agitation is harmful and injurious to the movement. Muskets are not what are wanted, but education and schooling of the working people. Stephens and O'Connor are shattering the movement. Violent words do not slay the enemies but the friends of the movement. O'Connor wants to take everything by storm, and to pass the Charter into law within a year. All this hurry and haste, this bluster and menace of armed opposition can only lead to premature outbreaks and to the destruction of Chartism.

(A letter by William Lovett, a carpenter and a moderate among the Chartists)

The presentation of the Charter

Great preparations were accordingly made. The inhabitants along the thoroughfare to Kennington Common kept doors and windows shut. The plans devised by the Duke of Wellington, were on a large and complete scale. The Thames' bridges were the main points of concentration, bodies of foot and horse police, and masses of special constables being posted on either side, a strong force of military was kept ready for instant movement.

(The *Annual Register*, 1848)

A representative parliament?

In the House of Commons there are 658 members, everyone of whom belongs to the middle and upper classes. Labour has not one direct representative — there is not in the House of Commons *one man* whose life has been spent in the workshop in intimate daily experience of the working-man's trials. Working-men, we call on you as a paramount and pressing duty, to return qualified men of your own to parliament.

(From a leaflet written in 1871)

Questions on Chapter Nine

1 *Why did some people believe that the landed gentry should dominate parliament? How far, if at all, was this changed by the 1832 Reform Act?*

2 *What is the qualification for the franchise today? How does the absence of a good system of communications help to explain the varied qualifications that existed in 1793?*

3 *Write a letter which might have been written by someone who had attended a meeting of the Reform Associations.*

4 *Find out the names of three boroughs which lost the right to elect two MPs after 1832, and also three boroughs which gained that right. You will find the complete list in Dawson and Wall, Parliamentary Representation (OUP.)*

5 *Imagine that you were a journalist in 1848. Write your article on the Chartist demonstration and petition. (You might have supported the movement.)*

6 *Which was the more important Reform Act — 1832 or 1867? Why? How important was the Ballot Act, 1872?*

7 *Make a collage of headlines which might have appeared above articles on (i) Wellington and the unreformed Parliament, (ii) riots in favour of Reform, 1831, (iii) the passage of the Reform Act, 1832 (iv) Chartist uprisings in 1839 or 1842.*

Unit Three

The Workshop of the World 1830-70

The 1851 Census returns showed that for the first time there were more people living in towns than lived in the countryside. Britain was well on with its industrial revolution which, after the coming of the railways, had entered a second, speedier and more powerful phase. One result of this 'railway revolution' was the continuing urbanisation of Britain.

By 1851 there was beginning to emerge a new type of workman — a man with skills which employers were willing

PROPOSED CONGRESS OF TRADES COUNCILS

AND OTHER

Federations of Trades Societies.

MANCHESTER, FEBRUARY 21st, 1868.

FELLOW-UNIONISTS,

The Manchester and Salford Trades Council having recently taken into their serious consideration the present aspect of Trades Unions, and the profound ignorance which prevails in the public mind with reference to their operations and principles, together with the probability of an attempt being made by the Legislature, during the present session of Parliament, to introduce a measure detrimental to the interests of such Societies, beg most respectfully to suggest the propriety of holding in Manchester, as the main centre of industry in the provinces, a Congress of the Representatives of Trades Councils and other similar Federations of Trades Societies. By confining the Congress to such bodies it is conceived that a deal of expense will be saved, as Trades will thus be represented collectively; whilst there will be a better opportunity afforded of selecting the most intelligent and efficient exponents of our principles.

It is proposed that the Congress shall assume the character of the annual meetings of the British Association for the Advancement of Science and the Social Science Association, in the transactions of which Societies the artizan class are almost entirely excluded; and that papers, previously carefully prepared, shall be laid before the Congress on the various subjects which at the present time affect Trades Societies, each paper to be followed by discussion upon the points advanced, with a view of the merits and demerits of each question being thoroughly ventilated through the medium of the public press. It is further suggested that the subjects treated upon shall include the following :—

    1.—Trades Unions an absolute necessity.
    2.—Trades Unions and Political Economy.
    3.—The Effect of Trades Unions on Foreign Competition.
    4.—Regulation of the Hours of Labour.
    5.—Limitation of Apprentices.
    6.—Technical Education.
    7.—Arbitration and Courts of Conciliation.
    8.—Co-operation.
    9.—The present Inequality of the Law in regard to Conspiracy, Intimidation, Picketing, Coercion, &c.
    10.—Factory Acts Extension Bill, 1867: the necessity of Compulsory Inspection, and its application to all places where Women and Children are employed.
    11.—The present Royal Commission on Trades Unions: how far worthy of the confidence of the Trades Union interest.
    12.—The necessity of an Annual Congress of Trade Representatives from the various centres of industry.

All Trades Councils and other Federations of Trades are respectfully solicited to intimate their adhesion to this project on or before the 6th of April next, together with a notification of the subject of the paper that each body will undertake to prepare; after which date all information as to place of meeting, &c., will be supplied.

It is also proposed that the Congress be held on the 4th of May next, and that all liabilities in connection therewith shall not extend beyond its sittings.

Communications to be addressed to MR. W. H. WOOD, Typographical Institute, 29, Water Street, Manchester.

By order of the Manchester and Salford Trades Council,

S. C. NICHOLSON, PRESIDENT.
W. H. WOOD, SECRETARY.

The first TUC Congress, called in 1868.

to pay for, a man who rarely suffered the indignity of unemployment. These skilled workmen (Chapter 10) enjoyed a high standard of living. Many of them shared the views of the prosperous middle classes – that men got on by their own efforts and did not need any government to help them. But part of their self-helping efforts led these men to form powerful trade unions. After the Reform Bill of 1867, some of them began to talk about the possibility of forming a political party to represent the working class. Here we have the first sight of one of the strongest attitudes in modern Britain. 'Jack is as good as his master', was the view of some of these confident, well-paid town workers.

But Britain was still dominated by the views of 'the masters' of the middle class. The majority of these middle class men had made their own way into the ranks of the wealthy without any aid from inherited family wealth or government assistance. It is easy to see why they believed in self-help and opposed attempts by governments to interfere with their running of their towns or factories.

The Great Exhibition of 1851 can be seen as part of the middle class wish to show off. It should also be looked at as vivid evidence of the power of Britain, then the envy of the rest of the world. Britain's domination was to be short-lived. By 1871 other countries had learned from Britain's example and had become industrialised. Some of them, notably Germany and the U.S.A., soon outstripped Britain. A major reason for Britain's fall from the leadership of the industrial world was her failure to pay sufficient attention to the question of education (Chapter 13).

Brunel (in top hat, with legs crossed), watching work on his *Great Eastern*.

Chapter 10   The working classes and trade unions

An old class

Almost every society, past and present, has had its working people. Some of these workers possess skills and become craftsmen such as masons, bricklayers, carpenters and millwrights. In medieval times such craftsmen became members of their craft guild. They then worked for a time for a master-craftsman. When they were able to produce a 'masterpiece' of work which satisfied the leaders of the craft guild, they too became master-craftsmen, able to employ apprentices and skilled workers.

The majority of workers, however, were unskilled. They were farmworkers for the most part and their living standards were lower than those of the skilled worker.

A sixteenth century stone crushing plant. Water was carried by a pipe (top right) to turn the wheel. The wheel drove the heavy weights which crushed the stones (centre left).

Early unions

By the end of the seventeenth century the master craftsmen in charge of their guilds had changed their rules. It had now become difficult for skilled workpeople to become masters themselves. This meant that the majority of skilled workmen had to remain *journeymen* (or daily paid labourers) employed by one or other of the masters. It is not surprising that by 1700 these journeymen had formed trade unions to try to force their employers to pay higher wages. Nor is it surprising that the employers should resent this interference with the traditional way of life.

Industrial revolution

The coming of the machines led to the decline of such skilled workers as the handloom-weavers. Machines only required machine-minders and children could be employed to do many of the simple tasks. Many such workers found that their wages were reduced as the result of the industrial revolution. Low wages led to a poor diet and insanitary, overcrowded living conditions. Many shared Cobbett's views on the evils of industrialisation. They forgot the low standard of living that most of their class had to put up with in the so-called 'good old days'.

Sheffield, a painting made in 1850. This was one of the industrial towns which grew rapidly during the nineteenth century. Notice the chimneys of houses and factories, the railway line (centre right of picture) and the way in which people lived near their place of work.

An artist's impression of an initiation ceremony into a trade union in the early nineteenth century. You may think this is an exaggerated view of what happened. In 1831 the Huddersfield Mechanics formed a union. The first things that they bought were curtains (to prevent people peeping into their clubroom), a Bible (on which new members took an oath of loyalty and secrecy) and a pistol – to ensure that the oath was kept. They would not have thought that this artist was exaggerating.

Trade unions and towns

By 1840 the health reformers, such as Chadwick, had forced the unwilling government to examine conditions in the industrial towns. A Commission was appointed to examine the sanitary conditions of the whole country. In 1842 it issued a Report on The Sanitary Conditions of the Labouring Classes which showed that one of the main reasons for the unhealthy state of industrial towns was that they had grown so very quickly. Their Report stated that the population of Great Britain had increased by about 47 per cent between 1801 and 1831. However there had been a much greater percentage increase in the size of industrial towns. Between 1801 and 1831 the population of Manchester had gone up by 109 per cent, that of Glasgow by 108 per cent, Birmingham by 73 per cent, Leeds 99 per cent and Liverpool 100 per cent.

The massing together of large numbers of workpeople, most of whom shared common grievances about their

working and living conditions, was one factor making for the growth of more, larger trade unions.

Trade unions and the government, 1799–1825

Britain was at war with Revolutionary France after 1793. The government was frightened that the British workers might follow the example of the French and support a Revolution. Various laws were passed to try to make sure that this did not happen. Among these repressive laws were the Combination Acts of 1799 and 1801 which forbade workmen to form trade unions. However this did not prevent some workmen joining in the Luddite movement to try stop employers using new machines. The activities of the machine-smashing wreckers only strengthened the government's fears that there was a danger of a British Revolution.

Nor did the Combination Acts stop other workers from forming Friendly Societies into which they paid a few pence

These four drawings made in the 1860s were entitled: 'A socialist parable.' On the opposite page they show (top) that under powerful monarchs only a few people share in the trough and (bottom) that under constitutional monarchy, dominated by a small, powerful group, only the powerful got to the trough. On this page (top) under the banner of 'free competition' there is such a struggle for survival that only the strong got to the trough, while young, sick, injured or elderly were trampled underfoot and (bottom) that only in a democratic society can each person get a fair share from the trough. One of the aims of the trade union movement was to ensure that working people received a fairer share.

each week and from which they received money whenever they were sick, unemployed or too old to work. This, as we shall see, remained one main feature of British trade unionism.

By 1822 Britain had defeated France and the danger of a British Revolution had faded. The government was prepared to relax some of the more repressive laws which had been passed during wartime. In 1824 the Combination Acts were repealed and men were allowed to join unions and to negotiate with their employers about hours, wages and conditions of work.

Legal but unpopular unions
Following this repeal there was a great deal of union activity. Lancashire cotton spinners, Bolton brush makers, Preston weavers and Sheffield file grinders were only four of the dozens of groups to form unions. The names of these unions showed that their members were men of only one craft. Each separate craft jealously guarded its own rights and privileges and was concerned only with the interests of its own members. You will also see from the names that these early unions were local. Until railways were built (after 1830) there was no cheap and efficient method of communication and it was almost impossible to form a national trade union.

Robert Owen was an unusual sort of factory owner. He believed that the workers deserved more than they were getting from their hard work. He argued that there should be free education for the workers' children. But this did not come for another sixty years or so. He tried to get laws passed to make it illegal to employ children in factories or mines. And this did not come for another twenty years or so. Owen was ahead of his time in most things. He was one of those who tried to form a Grand National Consolidated Trade Union (GNCTU), in which workpeople of all crafts and no craft would join. This, he hoped, would force employers as well as government to improve the living and working conditions of all workpeople.

But governments, magistrates and employers were not going to give in as easily as that. Some employers simply sacked anyone who tried to form or join a branch of the GNCTU. Many forced their employees to sign The Document which appeared in 1830, in which they declared that they did not, and would not belong to a union. (p. 105).

If workpeople did form trade unions some employers persuaded local magistrates to punish them. The most famous examples of this involved some Dorsetshire weavers who became known as the Tolpuddle Martyrs. Their condemnation and sentence of transportation was praised by the Whig middle class government.

A warning against membership of a trade union, issued by the magistrates of Dorchester, who later sentenced the Tolpuddle Martyrs.

CAUTION.

WHEREAS it has been represented to us from several quarters, that mischievous and designing Persons have been for some time past, endeavouring to induce, and have induced, many Labourers in various Parishes in this County, to attend Meetings, and to enter into Illegal Societies or Unions, to which they bind themselves by unlawful oaths, administered secretly by Persons concealed, who artfully deceive the ignorant and unwary,—WE, the undersigned Justices think it our duty to give this PUBLIC NOTICE and CAUTION, that all Persons may know the danger they incur by entering into such Societies.

ANY PERSON who shall become a Member of such a Society, or take any Oath, or assent to any Test or Declaration not authorized by Law—

Any Person who shall administer, or be present at, or consenting to the administering or taking any Unlawful Oath, or who shall cause such Oath to be administered, although not actually present at the time—

Any Person who shall not reveal or discover any Illegal Oath which may have been administered, or any Illegal Act done or to be done—

Any Person who shall induce, or endeavour to persuade any other Person to become a Member of such Societies,

WILL BECOME

Guilty of Felony,
AND BE LIABLE TO BE
Transported for Seven Years.

ANY PERSON who shall be compelled to take such an Oath, unless he shall declare the same within four days, together with the whole of what he shall know touching the same, will be liable to the same Penalty.

Any Person who shall directly or indirectly maintain correspondence or intercourse with such Society, will be deemed Guilty of an Unlawful Combination and Confederacy, and on Conviction before one Justice, on the Oath of one Witness, be liable to a Penalty of TWENTY POUNDS, or to be committed to the Common Gaol or House of Correction, for THREE CALENDAR MONTHS; or if proceeded against by Indictment, may be CONVICTED OF FELONY, and be TRANSPORTED FOR SEVEN YEARS.

Any Person who shall knowingly permit any Meeting of any such Society to be held in any House, Building, or other Place, shall for the first offence be liable to the Penalty of FIVE POUNDS; and for every other offence committed after Conviction, be deemed Guilty of such Unlawful Combination and Confederacy, and on Conviction before one Justice, on the Oath of one Witness, be liable to a Penalty of TWENTY POUNDS, or to Commitment to the Common Gaol or House of Correction, FOR THREE CALENDAR MONTHS; or if proceeded against by Indictment may be

CONVICTED OF FELONY,
And Transported for SEVEN YEARS.

COUNTY OF DORSET,
Dorchester Division

February 22d, 1834.

C. B. WOLLASTON,
JAMES FRAMPTON,
WILLIAM ENGLAND,
THOS. DADE,
JNO. MORTON COLSON,

HENRY FRAMPTON,
RICHD. TUCKER STEWARD,
WILLIAM R. CHURCHILL,
AUGUSTUS FOSTER.

G. CLARK, PRINTER, CORNHILL, DORCHESTER.

Robert Owen had boasted that his GNCTU would be able to force the government into granting more money to the poor, better working conditions to the employees and free education for children. In fact his Union was a very weak one. Too few members paid their weekly dues. Too many of the officials were dishonest and ran away with the funds they collected. Too few craftsmen were willing to get involved in disputes which did not concern them. Most workmen preferred to sign The Document rather than get the sack. And the weakness of Owen's Union was proved when he was unable to make the government repeal the sentence of the Tolpuddle Martyrs.

Model unions

Many workers joined in the Chartist movement in the hope that a more democratic Parliament would pass laws that would help them. The failure of this movement led many of them to turn their attention again to developing a strong trade union movement. Their aim was to gain a share for themselves in the increasing wealth of Britain. The bricklayers, millwrights and engineers formed their individual craft unions. Because of the development of the railway system these became national unions — associations of former, local craft unions. The Amalgamated Society of Carpenters and Joiners was one such union; another was the Amalgamated Society of Engineers, founded in 1851. Members of these unions were among the main gainers from the industrial expansion which followed the building of the railways. Regularly employed and well-paid, (with up to £2 a week) they were able to buy themselves and their families a high standard of living. Through building societies many of them became house-owners. With the help of falling prices which were the result of Britain's Free Trade policy, they became prosperous, well-to-do citizens.

An early trade union card.

These were the men who could pay 5p or more per week as a subscription to their trade union. In return a typical union paid 50p a week unemployment benefit for 12 weeks and 30p for a further 12 weeks; 60p a week sickness benefit for 26 weeks and 30p a week for the rest of the illness; accident benefits and an old age pension.

These skilled workers had no need for a government-provided welfare system; they were helping themselves in a way that Samuel Smiles and the Liberal economists approved (see Chapter 11); they would have supported Shaftesbury's opposition to state charity (p. 64).

Confident workers

Good wages, regular employment, rising living standards and

good trade unions gave the new generation of industrial workers a different outlook on life to that of their fathers and grandfathers. Their living standards were better and their expectations were higher. They demanded a share in the Parliamentary system. Middle class politicians were right to be frightened at the emergence of a working class voter. One day they would demand an even greater share in the growing wealth of the nation.

The unskilled workers

However, there were the masses of workers who had no skills and were lowly paid. They fought each other for a badly paid job at such places as London Docks. No wonder that it was discovered that about 30 per cent of the population lived in distressing poverty even as late as 1900.

Unskilled London dockers wait to be chosen for work.

* In a building that would hold very few in comfort, men were packed to suffocation, like the Black Hole of Calcutta. This struggling mass fought desperately, elbowing each other, punching each other to get work for an hour and for a few pence. And the men fought for those few pence as men fight for life. The foreman walked up and down, picking the slaves with brutal carelessness. (Evidence to the Royal Commission on Trade Unions, 1867–9.)

Documents

a) The Manchester worker's Life, 1833

The population employed in the cotton factories rises at five o'clock in the morning, works in the mills from six till eight o'clock, and returns home for half an hour or forty minutes to breakfast. This meal generally consists of tea or coffee, with a little bread. Oatmeal porridge is sometimes, but of late rarely used, and chiefly by the men; but the stimulus of tea is preferred, and especially by the women. The tea is almost always of a bad and sometimes of a sickening quality, the infusion is weak, and little or no milk is added. The operatives return to the mills and workshops until twelve o'clock, when an hour is allowed for dinner. Amongst those who obtain the lower rates of wages this meal generally consists of boiled potatoes. The mess of potatoes is put into one large dish; melted lard and butter are poured upon them, and a few pieces of fried bacon are sometimes mingled with them, and but seldom, a little meat. Those who obtain better wages, or families whose aggregate income is larger, add a greater proportion of animal food to this meal, at least three times in the week; but the quantity consumed by the labouring population is not great. The family sits round the table, and each rapidly appropriates his portion on a plate, or they all plunge their spoons into the dish. At the end of the hour they are all again employed in the mills until seven o'clock.

The average wages of all persons employed in the mills is from nine to twelve shillings per week (45p–60p per week).

(J. P. Kay, *Social Conditions and Education of the People in England and Europe* 1850)

b) Rising living standards for British workers, 1830–1880

The working classes of the United Kingdom have enjoyed a great improvement in wages in the last fifty years, an improvement roughly estimated at 50 to 100 per cent; the hours of labour have been shortened in the same period 20 per cent; there has been a fall in the prices of the principal articles of general consumption, with the exception of rent and meat, where the increase still left to the labourer a large margin for increased expenditure; the condition of the masses has in fact improved vastly, as is shown by the diminished rate of mortality, the increased consumption per head of tea, sugar and the like articles, the extension of popular education, the diminution of crime and pauperism, and the increase of savings bank deposits, as well as of other forms of saving among the masses.

The conclusion is that what has happened to the working classes is a revolution, having substituted for millions of people who were constantly on the brink of starvation, and who suffered untold privations, new millions of artisans and fairly well-paid labourers.

(R. Giffen, *Essays in Finance* 1887)

1 *How many hours did people work in Manchester in 1832?*

2 *What was their average wage; (i) per week, (ii) per hour? in 1833.*

3 *How does the evidence in Document (a) help to explain (i) the low rents people could afford, (ii) the overcrowding in working class areas and (iii) the high death rate common at that time?*

4 *Make a list of the food eaten by most working class families in Manchester in 1832. How often did some 'better-off' families have meat?*

5 *What was a typical wage in (i) 1833 and (ii) 1887?*

6 *If wages rise and prices fall what happens to standards of living? Draw a graph to illustrate your answer.*

7 *Name two articles bought by working class people in 1887 which indicated that there had been a rise in living standards since 1833.*

8 *Why does the growth of savings bank deposits indicate a rising standard of living? Which section of the working class was, in 1887, still unable to save?*

9 *How far was the improvement in living standards due to (i) government action, (ii) free trade, (iii) trade unions?*

c) Chartist rising, Newport 1839

d) An outing in Shirley Hills by working class women, 1912

Extract
Workers or slaves?
I was first yoked to the coal work at Preston Grange when I was nine years of age; we were then all slaves to the Preston Grange laird.

Even if we had no work on the colliery in my father's time we could seek none other without a written licence and agreement to return. Even then the laird selected our place of work, and if we did not do his bidding we were placed by the necks in iron collars, called juggs, and fastened to the wall or 'made to go the rown'. The latter I recollect well, the men's hands were tied in face of the horse at the gin, and made to run round backwards all day.

(Evidence before the *Royal Commission on conditions in Mines* 1842)

1 *What was the main aim of the Chartists' attack on the Newport goal?*

2 *Why did this attack (i) increase the fears of the ruling class, (ii) fail to achieve its aim?*

3 *Document (c) appeared in 1839. Document (d) appeared in 1912. What evidence is there from these two illustrations that there was an improvement in the living standards of the working class between 1839 and 1912?*

e) **The 'Document'**

We, the undersigned, agree with Messrs . . . that we will work for them on the following terms: We declare that we do not belong to the 'Union', or any other society which has for its object any interference with the rules laid down for the government of mills.

We agree with our masters, that we will not become members of any such society while in our present employ.

We will not subscribe or contribute to any such society, or to any strikers whatsoever. And if we are discovered to act contrary to the above agreement, each of us so offending will forfeit a sum equal to a fortnight's wages.
(Evidence before a Parliamentary Select Committee, 1831–2)

1 *How might working men help other men on strike? Why were the 'masters' in one factory determined to stop this?*

2 *How were men to be punished if they 'subscribe or contribute' to a union or 'any strikers'?*

3 *How would a man be punished if he refused to sign The Document?*

4 *The Combination Acts had been repealed in 1824. How far does this extract show that the repeal had little real effect?*

Questions on Chapter Ten

1 *Write a short paragraph to show the differences between a guild and a trade union.*

2 *Explain why trade unions (i) became more numerous after 1760 and (ii) became larger after the development of the railway network.*

3 *Arrange a debate in which one side argues in favour of the passing of the Combination Acts (1799 and 1800) and the other side argues in favour of allowing men to form trade unions.*

4 *In what ways did trade unions, even in 1867, behave as Friendly Societies? Why were the benefits paid by unions (i) welcome to union members (ii) not available to the mass of industrial workers?*

5 *Write a paragraph on the importance of Robert Owen. (See also Chapter 13.)*

6 *Write three paragraphs on (i) the origin of, (ii) the membership of and (iii) the aims of the Model Unions which grew up after 1850.*

7 *Imagine that you were a Luddite. Write two paragraphs to explain (i) why you joined the movement and (ii) how you helped wreck a new machine.*

8 *Write the headlines which might have appeared above reports of (i) the passing of the Combination Acts and (ii) the sentencing of the Tolpuddle Martyrs.*

9 *Draw or paint your own idea of either (i) child labour or (ii) a meeting of union members between 1799 and 1825.*

Chapter 11   Middle class Britain

Class divisions

In 1867 Dudley Baxter wrote, 'The Distribution of the National Income, (1867)', which showed that there were a few very rich people in Britain (less than 50,000) but a much greater number of very poor people (nearly 8 million).

We have already seen that industrialisation led to the growth of large towns and cities in which many members of the working class became comfortably off. But Victorian towns were dominated in many ways by the increasing number of middle class men and their families. These men earned their living in various ways. There were the industrialists – factory owners, coal mine owners, owners of engineering works, canals, railway systems and brickyards. Then there were the people who employed large gangs of *navvies* in their construction companies and made fortunes from the building of railways, town halls, churches, houses and harbours. There were the increasing number of people engaged in financing the growing industrial power of the country such as bankers and their clerks, stockbrokers and their middle class employees in the City of London, accountants and a host of other clerks in offices up and down the country. There were also the professionally qualified. Among these were architects and surveyors, chemists and mathematicians, doctors and lawyers, and a variety of different sorts of engineer, each with its own Institution.

Upper class people leaving a house party. Notice the various men-servants, one of whom is calling for a carriage. Notice, too, the elegant and expensive clothing worn by the women of this privileged class.

The government itself was employing an increasing number of well-paid people such as Factory and Health Inspectors, Medical Officers for Health, Schools' Inspectors and so on. Nassau Senior was one of the men responsible for the Poor Law Amendment Act of 1834. In 1835 Senior wrote to a friend to tell him about the way in which the 1834 Act was working. In the course of the letter he mentioned the 'fifteen Assistant Commissioners, earning £1,000 a year each.

The political influence of the middle classes

We have already seen that the demand for parliamentary reform came from the middle classes (Chapter 9). We have also seen that once they gained power, the middle classes used it for their own ends. They tried to lower the Poor Rate. They tried to prevent the working class from gaining a share in the political system. Above all, they campaigned for the repeal of the Corn Laws.

Middle class people travelled in comfort (above); people of the lower classes had wooden benches and open-sided carriages (below). But they could afford excursions, a sign of rising living standards.

1 *Why did the people in the third class need umbrellas?*

2 *The third class travellers went 'To Brighton and back for 3/6d'. What does this tell you about the prosperity of some of the working class? What effect did cheap travel have on people's leisure habits?*

3 *Trains carried goods as well as people. Explain why railways were important to (i) fishermen in Grimsby (ii) farmers in Cornwall, (iii) housewives shopping in a large town?*

The Anti-Corn Law League

In Chapter 2 we saw how the landed aristocracy had used their political power in parliament to get the Corn Laws passed. After 1832 the middle class shared political power with the aristocracy and a study of the Anti-Corn Law League tells us a good deal about the middle class of Britain of the 1840s. Its simple demand (for the repeal of the Corn Laws) fitted in with the general middle class belief in freedom – from government interference in the nation's economic and social life. Its use of the parliamentary system helps us to understand the system and to appreciate the growth of middle class influence after 1832. The League used the still new railway system to send out its agents into every constituency where they set up local Anti-Corn Law League Associations. The aim of these Associations was to persuade those who had the right to vote to get themselves on the electoral register and to use their vote to get supporters of the League elected to parliament. The League also used the new Penny Post (started in 1841) to send out literature and propaganda, to its supporters in their local Associations. The middle class used its wealth to pay for all the literature, propaganda, postage, speakers' expenses, parliamentary election expenses,

Richard Cobden speaking to the Council of the Anti-Corn Law League. These confident, rich industrialists, merchants and financiers were creating the new Britain in which they were making their own fortunes. They wanted a share in the government of the country and some say in the laws which were passed.

108

and hiring of halls involved. Finally, the success of the League's campaign (in 1846) was due in part to the growing strength of *Free Trade*. This had been demanded by Adam Smith in 1776 and partly put into practice by Huskisson after 1823. It was carried on by Robert Peel between 1841 and 1845. The demand for Free Trade in corn was merely one more aspect of the demand for Free Trade in general. Cobden argued that if Peel thought it right to take import duties off raw materials and manufactured goods, how could he claim the right to keep an import duty on food? However, the landed interest was still influential. It was opposed to repeal, believing that Free Trade in corn would lead to foreign corn pouring into the country – and ruin for them.

The repeal of the Corn Laws in 1846 was a sign of the growing power of the well-to-do middle classes.

PAPA COBDEN TAKING MASTER ROBERT A FREE TRADE WALK.

PAPA COBDEN.—"Come along, MASTER ROBERT, do step out."
MASTER ROBERT.—"That's all very well, but you know I cannot go so fast as you do."

Papa Cobden taking Master Robert for a Free Trade walk. A *Punch* cartoon of 1845, which recognised the increasing political power of the new middle classes.

1 *Who were Master Robert and Papa Cobden? What positions did they hold in 1842.*
2 *When did Master Robert agree to follow Papa Cobden down the road marked Free Trade?*
3 *What was the effect of Master Robert's decision to follow Free Trade on the Tory Party?*
4 *Who was the most bitter critic of Master Robert's conduct?*

Housing

The new middle classes wanted to show off their new wealth. As John Bright, a cotton manufacturer and one of the leaders of the Anti-Corn Law League said, they 'were looking forward to some point which they had not yet reached' — the ranks of the upper class. One way of 'bragging' or showing off, was to pay for the building of a large town house. Around the older industrial towns and cities the new middle classes built their homes. The very rich built their large detached house in its own grounds. The fairly well-off lived in three or four-storied town houses, such as can be seen in their thousands around Bayswater and Kensington in London. The lower middle class lived in more modest semi-detached houses, thousands of which were built in respectable rows in every English town.

And in these houses the middle class employed an army of domestic servants. A man earning £100 a year could afford to employ one living-in maid; a doctor earning £350 a year could afford three or four living-in servants, as well as a daily help for the hard work.

The well-furnished, comfortable home of a Victorian middle-class family.

A group of servants from a large Victorian house.

* The servants live in a large room in a remote part of the house, generally on the ground floor, where all, male and female, eat together. Each servant has a separate bed-chamber in the highest storey. Only the house keeper and the butler have distinct apartments below. Immediately adjoining that of the house-keeper is a room where coffee is made. On the other side of the building is the washing establishment with a small courtyard attached; it consists of three rooms, the first for washing, the second for ironing, the third, which is considerably loftier and heated by steam, for drying the linen in bad weather. (From G. M. Young, *Early Victorian England* 1934.)

Mrs Beeton

The lady of the house, who had probably moved up the social ladder with her husband, turned for help to the 1,172 pages of Mrs Isabella Beeton's *Book of Household Management* (1861). On the title page of this book Mrs Beeton promised to give, '*information for the mistress, housekeeper, cook, kitchen-maid, butler, footman, coachman, valet, upper and under house-maids, lady's maid, maid-of-all-work, laundry maid, nurse and nurse-maid, monthly, wet and sick nurses, etc etc, also sanitary, medical and legal memoranda; with a history of the origin, properties and uses of all things connected with home life and comfort.*'

The usefulness and appeal of this book can be measured by its sales. It came out as an 1,172-page book, price 7s 6d, in 1861. By 1870 it had sold over two million copies. The fact that in ten years this book sold over two million copies gives us some indication of the size of the servant-keeping middle class.

Self-help

In 1859 Samuel Smiles wrote a best-selling book called *Self Help*. In it he praised the way in which successful upper or middle class men had got on by their own efforts. Smiles praised the way in which the early industrialists had made their ways without help from governments or charitable people. Smiles believed that the country would only become stronger, richer and industrially more powerful if men worked as hard as they could, and made themselves as well-

From Mrs Beeton's *Household Management* 1895 edition.

1 *What time was the first breakfast to be served? Name two servants who would have to be up much earlier than this. What time were evening prayers to be said? What was the length of the working day in this household?*

2 *Why were there two breakfasts and two dinners?*

off as possible. He thought that the country would become poorer, weaker and industrially backward if men were taught that they could depend on someone else for their houses, food or clothing. He condemned the idea that governments ought to spend the taxpayers' money to help those who, it seemed, were unwilling to help themselves. These ideas may seem harsh to the modern reader. But they appealed to the self-made middle classes and strengthened their opposition to government attempts to interfere with the ways in which they ran their factories or built their towns.

Self-help also appealed to the more successful members of the working classes. Some of these had formed their own Cooperative Societies, following the example of 28 weavers from Rochdale. In 1844 these weavers had each put £1 into a fund, hired the ground floor of a warehouse in Toad Lane and opened a retail shop. They bought food and other goods from local manufacturers and warehouses. They then sold them at the normal retail prices charged in other shops and made the same profits as normal shops. However the Rochdale Cooperative did not behave like the normal shop when it came to using the profits. Instead of keeping the profits for themselves, the Rochdale Cooperative's organisers handed back a share of the profits to the shoppers. Those who had spent £20 in the shop in a year got twice as much back as those who had spent only £10. Most customers left their share of the profit (or dividend) in the business as a form of saving. This enabled the business to expand so that it became even more profitable. The example set by the Rochdale Pioneers was followed by working people in other towns.

It was clear that some working people were quite able to help themselves in the way Smiles wanted. There were also the self-helping trade unions which provided the skilled workman with his own welfare society (Chapter 10). Work-men also saved money in banks, post offices, building societies and insurance companies and so earned the praise of Smiles and other believers in self-help.

But the spirit of self-help was also responsible for the great opposition to government attempts at social reform. In 1852 the satirical magazine *Punch* wrote about the Englishman's right to 'do with their own what they like' even if this meant the right to throw rubbish in the streets and to build houses without drains or water supply. It was this 'right' that allowed the middle classes to create the unhealthy towns in which the working class lived and died in great numbers.

The well-fed and well-clothed members of a prosperous middle-class Victorian family.

* The creation of wealth in England in the last ninety years is a main fact in modern history. Some English private fortunes reach, and some exceed, a million dollars a year. A hundred thousand palaces adorn the island.
There is no country in which so absolute a homage is paid to wealth. A coarse logic rules throughout all English souls; if you have merit, can you not show it by your good clothes and coach and horses?
The habit of brag runs through all classes, from the *Times* newspaper through politicians and poets, through Wordsworth, Carlyle, Mill and Sidney Smith, down to the boys of Eton. (Ralph Waldo Emerson, *English Traits* 1856)

NOW FOR IT!
A Set-to between "Pam, the Downing Street Pet," and "The Russian Spider."

Palmerston, the favourite of some of the middle class, became Prime Minister during the Crimean War and the British looked forward to beating the Russians as a result of the change.

1 *Palmerston became Prime Minister during the Crimean War. Who was the enemy in this war?*
2 *Did* Punch *approve of the choice of Palmerston for Prime Minister? How can you tell?*

Middle class reformers

It is only fair to the middle class to point out that they were the people who organised industry so that the country became much richer and, later on, could afford to spend money on social reform. Without their drive, ambition and determination to make good and help themselves, Britain would have remained an under-developed country.

And even while this wealth was being created in the first half of the century it was from the men of the middle class that most of the social reformers came. Oastler, Chadwick and Fielden are some of the middle class reformers. Doctors, clergymen, civil servants, journalists and teachers were among those who made known the views of reformers such as Dr John Simon. Simon later became the Medical Officer for Health at the reformed Board of Health (1858).

Confident middle classes

Lord Palmerston was British Foreign Secretary for most of the period 1830–65. It is reported that he was asked: 'If, my Lord, you had not been born an Englishman, what nationality would you have like to have been?' Palmerston, it is said, did not hesitate: 'If I had not been born an Englishman, then I would have wished to have been born an Englishman.' As in so many so-called jokes there is a great deal of folk wisdom in this. Englishmen were confident that they were the best. They considered that they ran the Workshop of the World. They provided the world with goods. The British navy kept peace around the world, or forced less fortunate foreigners to give way to British demands for peace (at a price). In the 1870s a Music Hall song was to reflect this very strong patriotism:

> We don't want to fight
> But by jingo if we do
> We've got the ships, we've got the men
> We've got the money too.

It is important to remember that Palmerston could not have had a vigorous foreign policy if Britain had not been a great industrial power. It is not only progress and social reform that depend on productivity; a nation's standing in the world also depends on her prosperity.

Documents

a) Edward Carpenter's poem on industrialization,
In a Manufacturing Town, 1883

As I walked, restless and despondent through the
    gloomy city

And saw the eager unresting to and fro — as of ghosts
    in some sulphurous Hades —

And saw the crowds of tall chimneys, going up, and
    the pall of smoke covering the sun, covering the
    earth, lying heavy against the very ground —

And saw the huge refuse-heaps writhing with children
    picking them over.

And the ghastly, half-roofless smoke-blackened
    houses, and the black river flowing below —

As I saw them and as I saw again far away the
    Capitalist quarter with its villa residences and its
    high-walled gardens and its well appointed
    carriages, and its face turned away from the
    wriggling poverty which made it rich —

As I saw and remembered its drawing-room airs and
    affectations and its wheezy pursy Church-going
    and its gas-reeking heavy-furnished rooms and its
    scent bottles and its other abominations —

I shuddered:

For I felt stifled, like one who lies half-conscious —
    knowing not clearly the shape of the evil — in the
    grasp of some heavy nightmare.

Then out of the crowd descending towards me came a
    little ragged boy;

Came — from the background of dirt disengaging
    itself — an innocent, wistful child-face begrimed like
    the rest but strangely pale, and pensive before its
    time.

And in an instant (it was as if a trumpet had been
    blown in that place) I saw it all clearly, the lie I
    saw and the truth, the false dream and the
    awakening.

For the smoke-blackened walls and the tall chimneys
    and the dreary habitations of the poor, and the
    drearier habitations of the rich, crumbled and
    conveyed themselves away as if by magic;

And instead, in the backward vista of that face, I saw
    the joy of free open life under the sun:

The green-delighting earth and rolling sea I saw —

The free sufficing life — sweet comradeship, few needs
    and common pleasures — the needless endless
    burdens all cast aside,

Not as a sentimental vision, but as a fact and a
    necessity existing,

I saw

In the backward vista of that face.

(E. Carpenter, *Towards Democracy* 1883)

b) Victorian 'street urchins'. Children like this were often
employed as street sweepers.

1 *Make a list of some of the reasons why towns such as
this had a high death rate.*

2 *Compare life for the well-to-do with that led by the
bulk of the inhabitants. How does this help to explain
attitudes towards (i) self-help and (ii) sanitary reform?*

3 *Why might some of the workers in this town have
wanted to return to the domestic system?*

4 *Who gained and who lost by industrialisation? Give
reasons for your answers.*

5 *Our towns are not as bad as this today. How far is
this improvement due to (i) government legislation and
(ii) action by local councils?*

6 *Write a letter from the poor child in this poem who
has been transported on a time machine into the
1970s. What might he write about?*

7 *Why do these two boys have a brush? Why did
Victorian streets need crossing sweepers?*

8 *Some streets had several sweepers while other streets
had none. Why? Can you suggest the streets in your
town that would have had sweepers?*

9 *Look at the picture. The boys have no shoes. Can
you suggest why, and what effect might this have on
their health?*

10 *Why did Victorian parents allow their children to do
this work which brought in, on average, about one
shilling (5p) a day?*

Extracts

An argument against government interference

In every class they would find men working because they had wives and families to keep up or because they were striving to be as well off as their neighbours. So it was among the working classes; and in interfering with their right to work, the House was violating one of the dearest rights of these people.

(John Bright, cotton manufacturer and one of the leaders of the Anti-Corn Law League, speaking in the debate on the *Factory Bill* 10 February 1847)

A Victorian recalls his childhood

There were no bathrooms then, and all hot and cold water had to be carried from the kitchen and the scullery. But we had baths each day in spite of that. Our household consisted of a cook, houseparlourmaid and a girl. Their wages were £18, £16 and £6 a year. A widow who lived in a cottage nearby came in to bake and help when required.

(quoted in G. M. Young, *Early Victorian England* 1934)

Questions on Chapter Eleven

1 *At the beginning of the chapter there is a reference to the small number of rich and very large number of poor in 1867. What do you think a modern survey of social class would show?*

2 *List three reasons why the middle class formed and supported the Anti-Corn Law League. How does the repeal of the Corn Laws (1846) illustrate (i) the growing power of the middle class, (ii) the effects of the 1832 Reform Act, and (iii) the declining influence of the landed interest?*

3 *How did the middle class 'show-off' their new wealth?*

4 *Find out more about (i) Isabella Beeton and her famous book, (ii) Samuel Smiles and his equally famous book.*

5 *Why could Britain dominate world affairs between 1850 and 1870?*

6 *Arrange a debate on the subject 'The middle classes were the ones who gained most from the industrial revolution'.*

Chapter 12

Public health and medical science

Public Health

Active local councils

Edwin Chadwick was the secretary of the Poor Law Commission (Chapter 6). He and other reformers had set up groups to study the effects of insanitary conditions. It was these studies which first proved the link between the environment and the death rate (Chapter 6).

Parliament recognised this connection when, reluctantly, it passed the first Public Health Act in 1848. Local councils, also showed that they were aware of the need to try to make their towns cleaner and healthier. In 1844 Manchester passed a by-law forbidding the building of more back-to-back houses. Liverpool appointed its first Medical Officer of Health in 1847 and by 1857 the Liverpool council had built 146 miles of new sewers, increased the town's water supply, opened three public baths, two washhouses and a number of public lavatories.

Parliament helped local councils by passing a series of Acts which allowed, but did not compel, councils to build sewers, to make by-laws about housing and to take over the town's water supply. By 1870, 69 towns owned their own water supply. Birmingham built a new reservoir in the Elan Valley in Wales, 70 miles away from Birmingham. Manchester and Liverpool also paid for the building of large reservoirs.

By-law housing in Burnley. Councils were allowed to make laws to ensure that houses were solidly built, properly drained, provided with running water and flush toilets and, sometimes, a gas supply. To us they may seem 'rows and rows of little brown streets.' To the people who left slum houses to begin a new life in these houses they were a great improvement on anything they had known. Many of these houses are still standing – a sign of the way in which they were built.

But most councils did not act in this way. The majority of them were afraid to spend ratepayers' money. Bristol was one such 'inactive' town and late in the nineteenth century only 5,000 of its 30,000 houses had a water supply. The rest had to depend on wells to provide water 'tainted with the matter from cesspools which oozes through the porous soil and intermingles with the water!' Some towns had sufficient water to allow people to have flush toilets in their homes. But these were only introduced into Manchester in 1898. Until then the council carts went around each day to empty the pail left outside each house.

Parliament passes new laws

In 1868 parliament passed the Torrens Act which allowed councils to use some of their rates to pay for slum clearance. The councils could buy slum houses from their owners and pay for them to be pulled down. Then if they wished, they could build new houses on the cleared ground.

In 1870 parliament passed an Act which set up the Local Government Board. This Board took over the duties of the Board of Health and of supervising the Guardians of the Poor. In its own small way this was a very important step. There was now a government department with the job of looking after the conditions in the nation's towns.

The Disraeli government of 1874–80 was responsible for the Artisans Dwellings Act (1875). This gave councils greater powers to deal with slums than they had under the Torrens Act which had only given councils powers to condemn individual houses. The 1875 Act allowed councils to condemn a whole area. Councils could then buy up a whole district, pull down hundreds of houses and put up decent housing.

Westminster Gardens, Millbank. This was an early London County Council housing scheme (1897–1902). The blocks were large but the designers managed to avoid that ugly look which was usually given to Model Dwellings for the Industrious.

Chamberlain and Birmingham

However this Act, like so many others, was not a forceful one. It permitted or allowed councils to use the powers given by the Act. It did not compel them to do so. Few councils, in fact, used the powers offered to them. One man who did was Joseph Chamberlain who was Mayor of Birmingham from 1873 to 1876. He persuaded the Birmingham Council to use the powers given by Parliament. He boasted that Birmingham was 'parked, paved, gas-and-watered and improved, all as a result of three years' active work.' But even the reforming Chamberlain had to admit, in 1884, that 'we cannot burden the ratepayers any more; we have done all that this generation at any rate will be able to do.' And by 1884 all that had been done was to clear 40 acres of slums, to build a brand new Corporation Street Shopping Centre. But no new houses had been built for the less well-off.

By-law housing

Birmingham and other councils, like Liverpool, used their powers to clear slums and then allowed private builders to put up new houses in their place. These houses were sometimes sold off to people who could afford to buy them. Sometimes the builders became landlords and rented the houses off to the better-off who could afford to pay the weekly rent of about 4 shillings (20p). By 1900 Liverpool had cleared about 6,000 slum houses. In their place private builders put up what became known as 'by-law houses'.

Disraeli and public health

The Public Health Act 1875 was the second of the great Acts passed by the Disraeli government. This compelled every council to appoint a Medical Officer of Health and an Inspector of Nuisances. It also permitted councils to build sewers, street drainage, new reservoirs, public parks, libraries, wash-houses, swimming baths and public lavatories. Here you can notice some progress. Councils were now being compelled to use their powers where once they had only been permitted to do so. In time they would also be compelled to use their powers in every field of public health.

Private enterprise and public housing

Even a leading reformer, Lord Shaftesbury, did not think that the government or local councils should provide decent housing at a rent the less well-off could afford (p. 64). He thought that subsidised housing should only be available for extreme cases. In the nineteenth century most people thought that it was right for the government to concern itself only with the environment. Reluctantly, people agreed to pay higher rates so that streets could be properly paved and cleaned, refuse taken away and water supplies laid on to new building. But housing, they thought, ought to be provided by private builders. People should either buy or rent houses from builders or landlords.

This suited the well-off middle class (Chapter 11). It also suited the better-off members of the working class (Chapter 10). They bought their houses through their building societies or paid the rent of between 20 and 30p a week for a three or four-roomed home.

But the poorly paid, who earned as little as 50p a week in 1870 and less than £1 a week in 1900 could not afford to buy a house. Nor could they afford the high rent charged for a new home. They had to crowd together in terraced buildings (or tenements) with one family to a room. These buildings quickly became slums.

George Peabody and other reformers

George Peabody was a wealthy American who came to live in England in 1837. In 1860 he set up the Peabody Trust to which he gave £500,000. The Trust was to build blocks of Peabody Dwellings, the first of which was opened in London's Spitalfields in 1864. The Trust built a total of 50,000 flats for rent.

Octavia Hill was a granddaughter of Dr Southwood Smith, a notable reformer of the 1830s and 1840s. In 1864 she bought three cottages in Marylebone and spent her own money on improving them. She then re-let the improved

(Opposite) Peabody Buildings, Westminster, 1869. The trust put up a number of such Buildings where working class families were provided with room, light, air, water, sanitation as well as facilities for washing and drying clothes. However there was and is a barrack-like look about these Buildings while the rents were too high for the poorer section of the working class.

cottages at a rent which was high enough to repay the money she had spent on buying and improving the cottages. Her success in Marylebone encouraged her to persuade her rich friends to lend her money to buy up other slum property.

Model towns

Octavia Hill's work was of some value. However, even she had to admit that in thirty years she and other private benefactors had succeeded in rehousing only 26,000 people and all of them in London. Private benevolence did not really come to grips with the real housing problems of the ever-larger industrial towns.

In the 1860s the Yorkshire textile manufacturer, Titus Salt, built a new town, 'Saltaire', for his workpeople. The town contained everything that the employees could want. There were parks, baths, public library and social club, but no public-house. W. H. Lever, the soap manufacturer (later Lord Leverhulme) built another 'dry' town at Port Sunlight and George Cadbury, the chocolate manufacturer, followed Lever's example and built Bournville (1879).

But the Model Towns had little to offer to the people living in the overcrowded slums of industrial Britain. They were small towns, built by wealthy employers for their, relatively, small number of work-people. It was possible to imagine that the owners of coal mines or steel works might have followed these examples and built similar Model Towns for their employees. But the majority of people worked for small family firms which did not have the money to plan on this scale.

Saltaire, Yorkshire. You can see, in the centre, the textile mill built by Titus Salt on the banks of the Leeds and Liverpool Canal. The factory was opened in 1853 and the Model Town completed in 1871. The factory employed 3,000 people who lived in Saltaire where they enjoyed many amenities – parks, museums, libraries and so on – which were not available to workers in most industrial towns.

Welwyn Garden City. On 8 March 1908 Lucy Masterman, wife of an eminent politician, visited Hampstead Garden suburb and wrote:

In the afternoon we went by train to Hampstead and saw the garden suburb, dear little clean houses in gardens with splendid sweeps of country all round under snow. It made one nearly cry to think Camberwell and West Ham and Peckham might all have been like that if people would only have taken thought and looked after them.

Garden cities and town planning

In 1898 Ebenezer Howard wrote, *'Tomorrow: a peaceful path to social reform'*, in which he called on the government to follow the examples of Lever, Cadbury and Salt by planning the building of new towns. In 1902 he published a book under the title *'Garden Cities of Tomorrow'*. He showed that a planned garden city could have the advantages of both town and country and avoid the disadvantages of both.

The first of the garden cities was founded at Letchworth in 1903. There was another at Hampstead. Howard's ideas were taken up by some politicians and civil servants. One result of this was the passing of the first *Town Planning Act* (1909) which gave the local councils the right to insist that new housing estates had to be properly laid out. This held out the hope that the industrial towns and cities would, in the future, become places fit for humans to live in.

Medical Science

Operations and anaesthetics

Up until the 1840s hospitals were dirty and dangerous places. As the famous Sir Joseph Simpson said:

'The man laid on an operating table in one of our surgical hospitals is exposed to more chances of death than was the English soldier on the field of Waterloo.'

One of the dangers was that the patient would die from shock during an operation. Only the very simplest of operations such as an amputation of an arm or leg was possible. But even these were events of great horror. The patient had to be strapped to the table or held down by the surgeon's assistants. It is not surprising that the surgeon was regarded by the public with the horror felt for the public hangman.

In 1799 Sir Humphrey Davy had discovered that 'laughing gas' (nitrous oxide) removed pain. He had suggested that it should be used during hospital operations.

Dr John Snow's chloroform inhaler. Before he invented this, chloroform was poured onto a handkerchief which was held over the patient's mouth and nose.

In 1838 his assistant, Michael Faraday, showed that ether had the same effects as nitrous oxide. But nothing came of the work of these two eminent scientists. The only people who used nitrous oxide were travelling showmen who entertained the crowds at fairs by showing the strange effects of inhaling the 'laughing gas'.

In 1846 an American surgeon, John Warren, used ether on a patient who had to have a growth removed from the throat. The operation was a great success. There was none of the tortured screaming that was normal in such operations. Within two months surgeons in University College Hospital, London, were using ether.

James Simpson was professor of midwifery at Edinburgh University. He tried ether, but found it unsatisfactory. He experimented with many other substances before he found chloroform. Simpson used chloroform with great success in 1847 but his use of the new *anaesthetic* became popular only after Queen Victoria used it for the birth of her seventh child, Prince Leopold.

Pasteur and germs

Queen Victoria was given chloroform by Dr John Snow, the first professional anaesthetist and inventor of the first inhaler. Snow was in the forefront of other discoveries. In 1854 he investigated an outbreak of cholera in Broad Street, London, where 500 people died within ten days. Snow proved that those who died had all drunk from one particular pump, whereas people in the street who lived had not drunk from that pump. We know, today, that the pump had been contaminated by a germ called 'vibrio' which causes cholera. Snow did not know this.

The man who proved that disease was caused by germs was a Frenchman, Louis Pasteur. His first discovery showed that germs caused wines, beer and other liquids to go bad. In 1865 he invented a method of heating the liquids so as to kill the germs. This process, known as 'pasteurisation' is now commonly used, especially as a method of making milk a safe drink.

Jenner, Pasteur and vaccination

In 1796 Edward Jenner was a doctor in Gloucestershire. He had to treat a number of patients suffering from smallpox. He noticed that people who had once suffered from cowpox never suffered from the more harmful smallpox. Jenner took some matter from the sores of a girl with cowpox, put it into the arm of a boy, James Phipps, who then had a sore arm and an attack of cowpox. Jenner then gave the boy a small dose of smallpox poison. The poison did not 'take' and Jenner

Louis Pasteur at work in his laboratory.

realised that he had found a cure for smallpox. His process of vaccination was widely adopted — although Jenner was unable to explain how it worked.

In 1879 Pasteur experimented with a cholera vaccine on chickens. He showed that if the animals were given a weak dose of cholera their bodies learned how to kill the germs. When later the same chickens were given strong (otherwise fatal) doses of cholera they were able to defeat the disease, whereas chickens which had not been vaccinated died from similar doses of strong poison.

Pasteur was able to explain Jenner's success. He was also able to go on to prepare vaccines against rabies, anthrax and swine fever. Soon afterwards vaccines were discovered against typhoid, plague, yellow fever and typhus. The modern practice of *inoculation* had begun.

Lister in a ward at the King's College Hospital, London.

Operations and antiseptics

As we have seen many people died from shock during the brutal operations before anaesthetics were developed. Many others, who managed to live through the operation, died because their open wounds became infected. Doctors were unable to understand this until Pasteur showed that germs caused disease. Joseph Lister was professor of surgery at Glasgow University. He studied Pasteur's work and learned that germs were everywhere — on skin, clothes furniture, floor and in the air. Lister realised that it was these germs which infected the open wounds of his patients. In 1864 he used carbolic acid as an antiseptic. He wiped everything that might come into contact with the patient during an operation — surgeon's hands and clothes, instruments, thread used for sewing, sponges. He also used lint soaked in carbolic acid as a dressing over the wound. The result of Lister's work was a sharp drop in the number of his patients who died from infections of their wounds.

Mrs Wardroper who was appointed by Florence Nightingale, with student nurses at the Florence Nightingale School. A high standard was required not only of nursing skill but of dedication. The Nightingale School had a rapid effect on the standard of nursing all over the country.

In 1870 Lister used a hand-operated carbolic spray to kill the germs in the air of the operating theatre. He also began to perform operations which had once been thought impossible — opening joints and wiring together broken pieces of bone. His patients did not die from infected wounds, while they also benefited from the anaesthetics discovered by Simpson. By 1893 other surgeons had adopted Lister's methods and were performing operations on the brain, lungs and other organs. The way was open for the development of that modern surgery of which we are rightly so proud.

Documents

a) Housing Conditions for the Poor, 1883

First, the information given does not refer to selected cases. Secondly, there has been absolutely no exaggeration. This must be to every Christian heart a loud and bitter cry, appealing for the help which it is the supreme mission of the Church to supply.

You have to penetrate courts reeking with poisonous and malodorous bases arising from the accumulations of sewage and refuse scattered in all directions; courts, many of them which the sun never penetrates, which are never visited by a breath of fresh air. You have to ascend rotten staircases. You have to grope your way along dark and filthy passages swarming with vermin. Then you may gain admittance to the dens in which these thousands of beings, who belong as much as you to the race for whom Christ died, herd together. Eight feet square – that is about the average size of very many of these rooms. Walls and ceilings are black with the accretions of filth which have gathered upon them in the boards overhead; it is running down the walls; it is everywhere. A window is half stuffed with rags or covered by boards to keep out wind and rain; you look out upon the roofs and ledges of lower tenements, and discover that the sickly air which finds its way into the room has to pass over the putrefying carcasses of dead cats or birds. As to furniture – you may perchance discover a broken chair, the tottering relics of an old bedstead or the mere fragment of a table; but more commonly you will find rude substitutes for these things in the shape of rough boards resting upon bricks, an old hamper or box turned upside down, or more frequently still, nothing but rubbish and rags.

(Rev Andrew Mearns, *The Bitter Cry of Outcast London* 1883)

1 *Why could the author of this extract claim that his description was one which could be applied to many areas?*

2 *Who, according to the author, should be appalled?*

3 *Why was there a danger of disease as a result of conditions outside the houses?*

4 *What was the average size of a room? Compare this with the size of a room in your own home.*

5 *Why was there a danger of disease as a result of conditions inside the home?*

6 *Why were people forced to live in these conditions?*

7 *These slums would have to be cleared and new houses built. Why would this require: (i) legislation; (ii) a more active local authority; (iii) increased taxation?*

b) Private enterprise, 1875

As soon as I entered into possession, each family had an opportunity of doing better; those who would not pay were ejected. The rooms they vacated were cleansed; the tenants who showed signs of improvement moved into them and thus, in turn, an opportunity was obtained for having each room distempered and papered. The drains were put in order, a large slate cistern was fixed, the washhouse was cleared of its lumber, and thrown open on stated days to each tenant in turn. The roof, the plaster, the woodwork was repaired; the staircase walls were distempered; new grates were fixed; the layers of paper and rag (black with age) were torn from the windows, and glass was put in; out of 192 panes only eight were found unbroken. The yard and footpath were paved.

The rooms, as a rule, were re-let at the same prices at which they had been let before; but tenants with large families were counselled to take two rooms, and for these much less was charged than if let singly; this plan I continue to pursue. Incoming tenants are not allowed to take an insufficient quantity of room. The elder girls are employed three times a week in scrubbing the passages in the houses, for the cleaning of which the landlady is responsible. For this work they are paid, and by it they learn habits of cleanliness.

The pecuniary result has been very satisfactory. Five per cent has been paid on all the capital invested. A fund for the repayment of capital is accumulating. A liberal allowance has been made for repairs.

(Octavia Hill, *Homes of the London Poor* 1875)

1 *How did Miss Hill 'improve' the tenements which she took over?*

2 *What evidence is there that she (i) tried to prevent overcrowding and (ii) forced some people to leave the tenements?*

3 *Find out more about the work of (i) Octavia Hill and (ii) George Peabody.*

4 *Why was Miss Hill's scheme of no value to the poorly paid or unemployed?*

5 *Write a letter from one of those who were helped by Miss Hill (they might mention cleanliness, sickness rates, water supplies, rents and so on).*

6 *Draw or paint your own: 'Before and after Miss Hill's improvement scheme'.*

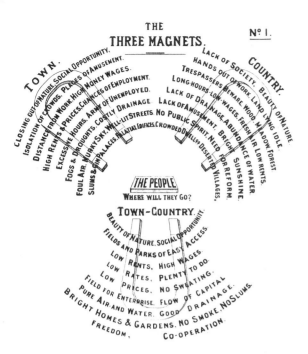

THE
THREE MAGNETS.   Nº 1.

TOWN. ... CLOSING OUT OF NATURE. SOCIAL OPPORTUNITY. ISOLATION OF CROWDS. PLACES OF AMUSEMENT. DISTANCE FROM WORK. HIGH MONEY WAGES. HIGH RENTS & PRICES. CHANCES OF EMPLOYMENT. EXCESSIVE HOURS. ARMY OF UNEMPLOYED. FOGS & DROUGHTS. COSTLY DRAINAGE. FOUL AIR. MURKY SKY. WELL-LIT STREETS. SLUMS & GIN PALACES. PALATIAL EDIFICES. CROWDED DWELLINGS.

COUNTRY. ... LACK OF SOCIETY. BEAUTY OF NATURE. HANDS OUT OF WORK. LAND LYING IDLE. TRESPASSERS BEWARE. WOOD MEADOW FOREST. LONG HOURS. LOW WAGES. FRESH AIR LOW RENTS. LACK OF DRAINAGE. ABUNDANCE OF WATER. LACK OF AMUSEMENT. BRIGHT SUNSHINE. NO PUBLIC SPIRIT. NEED FOR REFORM. CROWDED DWELLINGS. DESERTED VILLAGES.

THE PEOPLE
WHERE WILL THEY GO?

TOWN-COUNTRY.
BEAUTY OF NATURE. SOCIAL OPPORTUNITY. FIELDS AND PARKS OF EASY ACCESS. LOW RENTS, HIGH WAGES. LOW RATES, PLENTY TO DO. LOW PRICES. NO SWEATING. FIELD FOR ENTERPRISE. FLOW OF CAPITAL. PURE AIR AND WATER. GOOD DRAINAGE. BRIGHT HOMES & GARDENS. NO SMOKE. NO SLUMS. FREEDOM. CO-OPERATION.

) The Three Magnets as drawn by Ebenezer Howard in his book *Garden Cities of Tomorrow* (1902). Notice the advantages of living in the town (top left) and country (top right) and how life in a garden city combined the advantages of both while avoiding their disadvantages.

1 *Make a list of (i) the advantages and (ii) the disadvantages which Howard gives of living in the town? Can you add any of your own?*

2 *Do the same for the countryside.*

3 *In the garden city or town-country Howard assumes that rents and rates will be low. Why would this lead to an increase in government assistance to the garden city? Why would this lead to an increase in taxation?*

4 *Make a list of the reasons why the death-rate would be lower in the garden city than it had been in the Victorian industrial town.*

5 *Find out (i) the names of other garden cities and (ii) the date when the first Town Planning Act was passed.*

Write a letter from someone living in an industrial town who had gone with Mrs Masterman (page 121) on her visit to Hampstead in 1908 (the writer might have compared her town with the garden city and have commented on lack of noise and dirt, freshness, appearance of streets and people and so on).

Questions on Chapter Twelve

1 *Show that some local councils were more active than others in making their districts healthier. Explain why some were unwilling to become involved in solving the problems of sanitation, water supply and housing.*

2 *Explain the differences between the Torrens Act (1868) and the Artisans Dwellings Act (1875).*

3 *Explain why the poor were still badly housed in spite of legislation and the work of the private benefactors such as Peabody and Octavia Hill.*

4 *Show that the work of Peabody and Octavia Hill was of some benefit to some working class people.*

5 *What was the importance of the work of Ebenezer Howard? How far was his work of value to working class people (i) during his lifetime (ii) in the long term?*

6 *What were the main risks of a surgical operation at the start of the nineteenth century? How far did the work of James Simpson help to reduce these risks? Show how two other doctors helped to make surgery more likely to succeed.*

7 *Compare the work of Jenner and Pasteur. How far was Pasteur's work of value to British doctors and surgeons?*

8 *Write a paragraph on the work of Simpson, Snow and Lister.*

Chapter 13 · Children and their schools

The sad figure of the governess, lowly paid and treated with contempt.

The boys of a rich family leaving home to go to a boarding school at the end of the eighteenth century. The older boys have been taught not to cry; the younger boy, going away for the first time, has the sympathy of his sisters.

Upper class boarding schools

The sons of the landed gentry – the old upper class – had always received their education either at home with a private tutor, or at one of the nine great schools: Charter-house, Eton, Harrow, Rugby, Shrewsbury, Westminster, Winchester, St Paul's and Merchant Taylor's. Many of them went on to Oxford or Cambridge, looking on a University as a sort of finishing school where they would meet the people whom they would meet later on in their political and social lives.

The girls of these rich families were taught at home – either by a governess or by their mothers. It was not thought proper to 'educate' girls in the way their brothers were. Sewing, embroidery, riding and perhaps a little French, dancing and music were what the well-brought up lady was thought to require.

Middle class boarding schools

In pre-industrial Britain the small number of middle class children had been taught at one or other of the local grammar schools, most of which had been founded in the Tudor period. But during the nineteenth century there was, as we have seen in Chapter 11, a rapid increase in the numbers of these middle classes. Some of them became as wealthy as members of the older aristocracy. The parents of these richer middle class families wanted their sons to be taught like the sons of the older aristocracy. But there was not enough room for

them at the nine 'great schools'. So during the nineteenth century the rich middle class paid for the building of a large number of boarding schools to which they sent their sons.

Grammar schools

Many of the middle class continued to send their sons to the local grammar school. We have already seen (Chapters 1 and 5), that Britain in 1760 was a relatively underpopulated country with most of its people living in small towns or villages. This helps to explain why its schools were small. We should not make the mistake of thinking that eighteenth and nineteenth century schools looked like our modern schools.

The grammar school at Market Harborough, Leicestershire. It was founded in 1607 by Robert Smyth, a rich merchant. In his will he left £20 per year for the education of poor children, and requested that the school should be built on posts in the town's market place.

Private schools

There was also a wide variety of private schools. Some were as bad as Dotheboys Hall, described by Dickens in *Nicholas Nickleby*; others were small Dame Schools in which some gentlelady took in a dozen or so children for a few pence a week — usually teaching them very little, but helping their parents to think that they were a rung above the lower classes.

A Dame School, painted by Thomas Webster. Many such schools were much less pleasant than this one. Children learned little from the 'dame' who acted more as a child-minder than a teacher.

At Bowes Academy in Yorkshire, twenty-five boys died during Mr Shaw's time at the school. They died of starvation, disease and neglect. Charles Dickens wrote about this school which he renamed Dotheboys Hall, in *Nicholas Nickleby*. Mr Shaw was the real-life model for the cruel Mr Squeers.

The lower classes, 1760–1800

At the beginning of the industrial revolution few members of the working classes could afford to send their children to school. Poorly paid, they had no money for school fees. Living in very poor conditions, their children had to work to add their few coppers to the family income. Various charitable organisations had tried to provide some sort of schooling for the children of the lower classes: the Anglican Church had its Charity or Parish schools, the Methodists had started their Sunday Schools, and were copied by such people as Robert Raikes, a well-to-do master printer in Gloucester.

Raikes' intention was to take the children off the streets on the only day when they were not already employed in one or other of Gloucester's factories. He hoped that learning the Bible and the Catechism would make the children better citizens, so that the middle class gardens would no longer be pillaged and middle class ears no longer be offended by bad language.

Monitorial schools

But the continual rise in the number of children being born proved too much for the Churches and the older methods of providing some sort of schooling. However, Joseph Lancaster, a former Quaker, and Dr Andrew Bell, an Anglican vicar hit on a new idea at about the same time. They founded schools in which a teacher would train older pupils to act as helpers or monitors. These monitors would teach the younger children, and in this way one qualified teacher could cope with 500 or more children at a time. Both Lancaster and Bell depended on more well-to-do people providing them with money to build and maintain their schools. One way of collecting money was by having Charity Sermons in churches.

In a monitorial school

Lancaster's school looked like a large warehouse. Other schools were even grimmer than this. Some were old cottages, others were cellars underneath churches. There were no colleges for the training of teachers. Many of the so-called teachers were people who had failed at some other job. Some of them were bullies. Most of them unable to keep order let alone manage to teach the children very much.

And the people who paid for the building of the schools did not expect the children to be taught very much. It was essential that they learn their Bible, so that they could be taught that it was their duty to obey their employers when they left school. Some were taught to write simple words, although in many schools there was no attempt to teach writing. Simple addition and subtraction was taught — to help people cope with their shopping. The early schools were not like those we have today.

A monitorial school with its one teacher and many monitors.
1 *Why could one teacher not teach all these children himself?*
2 *Why was this called a 'monitorial' school?*
3 *Why did it cost very little to run such schools?*
4 *Why were the monitors unable to teach any history, science, geography, etc.?*
5 *Why was much of the learning in such schools merely 'learning by heart'?*

129

Self-help and the schools

We may think that these schools, teachers and methods were bad, but the politicians and most writers of the time thought that they were excellent schools. We have to remember that the principle of self-help, proposed by Samuel Smiles and supported by most industrialists was a very powerful influence, and it influenced people's ideas about educating the working classes.

Some MPs tried to get the government to give some money towards educating working class children. Such attempts failed in 1807, 1819 and 1825. However in 1833 the government finally agreed to give £20,000 towards helping

Many teachers of the early nineteenth century were men who had failed at other jobs. They seemed to enjoy being cruel to children.

I was then sent to a boys' school, to learn to 'write and cypher', thought at that time to be all the education required for poor people. The first master was a severe one, and the second was somewhat worse. On one occasion I saw him hang up a boy by his thumbs for playing truant!
(William Lovett, *The Life and Struggles of William Lovett*)

the societies which had been formed to run the monitorial schools founded by Lancaster and Bell. This was a small sum of money. And even this money was only to be given to the districts where people had already made efforts to provide schools themselves. If the rich people in, say, Plymouth, collected £500 towards the building of a school, the government would provide some money to help them on their way. If, however, the people of a Manchester slum area could not raise money to start building a school they would get nothing. The government was willing to help only those who would help themselves. And even this limited form of help and poor quality of education was opposed by many.

These people might have put up with schools as places where the poor learned their manners, but they feared that giving them a proper education might lead to revolution.

Payment by results

After the government started to help the societies running the Lancaster and the Bell schools in 1833, other societies were formed by Methodists, Catholics and Jews to provide schools for the children going to their churches. The government grant-system helped to build these schools also. One result of this was a great increase in the amount of money paid out by the government, and an increase in the amount of taxation imposed to get that money.

The first meeting of the 53 newly-elected members of the London School Board. Notice that there were some ladies on the Board. One of them was Dr Elizabeth Garrett Anderson, the first woman doctor in England.

* We must not delay. Upon the speedy provision of elementary education depends our industrial prosperity. It is no use trying to give technical teaching to our artisans without elementary education. If we leave our workfolk any longer un-skilled, notwithstanding their strong sinews and determined energy, they will become over-matched in the competition of the world.
(W. E. Forster, introducing the Education Bill of 1870)

By 1860 the grant was over £800,000. About the same time there was a great increase in the amount spent by the government because of the Crimean War (1853–56). Income tax rose to what was considered to be a very high rate of 7d (2½p) in the pound. The government decided to cut its spending on education as well as on other things. Robert Lowe. the Minister in charge of education, announced a new system for payment of the grant. Instead of each school getting a grant automatically each year, there would be an inspection and an examination of the pupils in each class. Government Inspectors would visit each school once a year and set tests in reading, writing and arithmetic (the three Rs). They would also inspect the registers (a fourth R). The school would receive a grant for a) the number of children on the register and in attendance at the examination and b) for the number of passes gained by the children in the examination.

One result of this new system was a drop in the amount paid out by the government. Many of the children were unable to pass the simple tests because they had been badly taught. This meant that the teachers' wages also fell, because the school had less money to hand out. A third result was that the teachers became more efficient – at least in forcing the children to learn, by memory, all the pieces of reading, writing and arithmetic that were going to be tested in the examinations. In time more children managed to pass the tests but only because the teachers spent all their time at the three Rs and gave no time to music, art, science and other subjects that were not going to be tested. This system of payment by results was not ended until the 1890s by which time a tradition of memory-learning had been established.

The 1870 Education Act

But even this system was unable to raise the standard of education quickly enough. The various religious societies were unable to build enough schools and too many children were not going to school at all. By 1870 it was becoming clear that Germany and the U.S.A. were becoming our industrial rivals (Chapter 15). So the government was compelled to take a larger part in the education of the nation's children.

In 1870 W. E. Forster brought in a new Education Bill. He hoped to have a new system which would help provide a better educated workforce for British industry. The Bill was approved and the 1870 Act laid the foundations for the present system of state education.

The government forced local ratepayers to elect School Boards which could collect a local rate, buy land and build schools in which children would pay a small fee. In time the fee was abolished and education at Board Schools became free. In time also, it became compulsory for parents to send their children to school between the ages of 5 and 11. Forster hoped that the Board Schools would turn out boys and girls who would become the workpeople in the new, technologically-based industries. Other people hoped that these schools would take the half-dressed, illiterate and tough children off the streets and turn them into well-behaved citizens. The Board Schools were to be places where the poor were to be trained in good habits.

Secondary Schools for the Working Classes
We have seen that the middle classes sent their children to the fee-paying schools where the children stayed until they were 14 or 16 or 18. These were 'secondary' schools while the Board Schools were only 'elementary' (or first schools)

A Board School in Lambeth, London. Built to look like a church such schools had small playgrounds, no playing fields, but very solid walls.

and the children left at the age of eleven or, later, twelve. We have already seen that in Victorian Britain there was the growth of a more confident skilled working class. Some of these people began to demand more than elementary education for their children. There were also some elementary teachers and School Boards, who were most anxious to provide their working class children with some sort of technical education. This was sometimes provided in Higher Grade Schools which received their grants from the Science and Art department based at Kensington.

But the elementary schools and the School Boards were not supposed to provide such technical schooling for children. They were, in fact, breaking the law when they collected rates to spend on laboratories, drawing boards and mathematical equipment. One opponent of this muddle was Robert Morant, one of the new middle class Civil Servants, who became Secretary to the Board of Education. In 1898 he persuaded a government official called Cockerton to prosecute the London School Board for spending money on technical and higher schools and classes. The judge decided (in the Cockerton judgment) that the School Boards were acting illegally by providing this sort of secondary education. The government was then forced either to close down all the classes and schools or to pass a new Education Act, which it did in 1902. This Act abolished the old School Boards, made the boroughs into Local Education Authorities for elementary education and made the County Councils into LEAs for secondary schools. LEAs were allowed to build their own County Secondary Schools where they could charge fees — as did the existing (secondary) grammar schools.

However, for the children of the working classes this Act provided very little. Not until 1907 was there an Act which said that County Secondary Schools had to provide free places for children who had been to the elementary schools and had passed the 'scholarship' examination from that school to the secondary school. In 1907 there were only 4,700 such free places, but after 1911 the system expanded and by 1913 there were 60,000 free places at the new secondary (grammar) schools. The working class child had a small chance of getting on. But compare these 60,000 places with the 500,000 children leaving primary schools that year.

For most working class children there was no change. Britain had still not begun to catch up with Germany and the U.S.A. And because of the failure of its educational system, its industrial supremacy was successfully challenged by these two rivals.

(Opposite) These three pictures are of children from the same class at Snowfields School, London in 1894, 1924 and 1952. You can see the changing standards of these children of three generations. A Headmaster wrote:

* The boy of 1900 as compared with the boy of 1880. Much more docile; insubordination now almost unknown. Cheerful and eager now, then often sullen and morose. All this, the result of discipline and control at school, reacts beneficially at home. Personal cleanliness — greatly improved; verminous cases among boys rare, but among girls almost universal, due to their long hair. As to dirt, it is necessary to distinguish between recent dirt got at play and the ancient kind that gives the strong smell. The vermin referred to are lice; bugs are rarely seen; but fleas are common, especially on children coming from homes where there is a baby. (From K. Dawson and P. Wall, *Education* 1969)

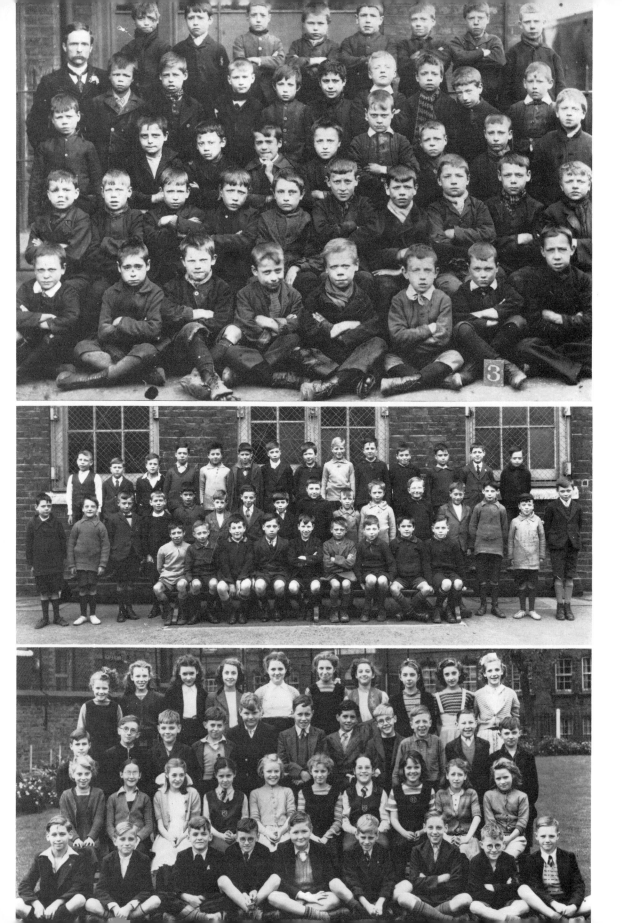

Documents

a) To each class its own school, 1864

The wishes of the parents can best be defined in the first instance by the length of time during which they are willing to keep their children in school. It is found that education can at present be classified as that which is to stop at about 14, that which is to stop at about 16, and that which is to continue till 18 or 19; and we call these the Third, the Second and the First Grade of education respectively.

It is obvious that these distinctions correspond roughly to the graduations of society. Those who can afford to pay more for their children's education will also, as a general rule, continue that education for a longer time.

First-grade

The bulk of those who wish for this grade of education are in two very distinct classes. One class is identical with those whose sons are in the public schools; men with considerable incomes, or professional men, and men in business, whose profits put them on the same level.

The other class of parents, who wish to keep their children at school the same length of time are professional men, especially the clergy, medical, and lawyers, and the poorer gentry. They have nothing to look to but education to keep their sons on a high social level. They are compelled to seek it in boarding schools, and generally in boarding schools of a very expensive kind.

Second-grade

These parents consist of two classes. On the one hand, many of them could well afford to keep the children at school two years, longer, but intend them for employments which ought to begin at 16; as, for instance, the army, civil engineering, and some others. On the other hand, there are very many parents who require their boys to begin at 16 wholly or partially to find their own living.

Third-grade

The third grade of education belongs to a class distinctly lower in the scale, but so numerous as to be quite as important as any; the smaller tenant farmers, the small tradesmen, the superior artisans. The need of this class is described briefly by Canon Moseley to be 'very good reading, very good writing, very good arithmetic'. More than that he does not think they care for; or if they do they merely 'wish to learn whatever their betters learn'. The more their demand is considered the more thoroughly sensible it seems.

(Report of the Schools Inquiry Commission, 1864)

1 *List the various occupations mentioned as suitable for children of (i) the First Grade, (ii) Second Grade), (iii) Third Grade Schools.*

2 *Which classes are not mentioned in this Document? How, if at all, were these classes educated in 1864?*

3 *Why are the parents of children at Second Grade School anxious to have their children educated? Do you think that this is still an important consideration today?*

4 *Why were parents of children in the Third Grade Schools anxious to have their children educated? Is this still true?*

5 *Today, as you know, children of all classes stay on at school until they are sixteen; many of every class stay on even longer than this. Explain why (i) parents can afford to keep their children at school today, (ii) why the government is anxious that children should stay on.*

6 *Why do you think there is no mention in this report of education for girls? Do you think that girls should be as well educated as boys?*

7 *There was an increasing number of schools in all three grades in the Victorian period. Can you say why? What does this increase tell you about the number of middle class families? (See Chapter 11)*

(1)	(2)	(3)	(4)	(5) Passes on Examination				(6) On attendance only	(7)	(8)	(9)
Department	Average attendance	For payment after deduction under Art 4	Presented for examination	R.	W.	A.	Total passes	For payment after deduction Art 4	Infants under 6	For payment after deduction under Art 4	Half Time Art. 47(b)
Boys or mixed under Master	43	43	36	34	30	34	98	98	7	7	—
Girls or mixed under Mistress	35	35	27	22	26	25	73	73	6	6	—
Infants											
Total Day School	78	78	63	56	56	59	171	171	13	13	—

(10)	(11)	(12)	(13) On attendance only	(14)	(15) Total
Department	On average attendance	On examination	Infants under 6	Half time Scholars under Art 47(b)	£ s. d
Boys or mixed	8 12 –	13 1 4	2 56 –		23 18 10
Girls or mixed	7 –	9 148 1	19 –		18 13 8
Infants					
Total Day School	15 12 –	22 16 –	4 4 6 –		42 12 6
Evening					

A School Inspector has examined the children of this small school and the School Managers will be getting a cheque for £42 12s 6d (£42.62½p) as the government's contribution to the running of the school for a year. If more children had passed the examination the teacher might have had a bigger wage. Maybe more effort will be made in the next year.

Extracts

The origin of Sunday Schools

(Robert Raikes was a well-to-do master printer in Gloucester.)

One day, in the year 1780, Mr Raikes chanced to go into the lower part of the town. Nearby, in the street, a swarm of boys were playing 'chuck'. The noise was deafening, the oaths were terrible! Mr Raikes was amazed. 'Something must be done,' said this practical man to himself. But what? Pondering a little he hit upon a new idea — new to him, at any rate: and new to the world at large, as it turned out. The idea was to gather these and suchlike children into schools on *Sundays* — on the day when they made 'hell' in the streets.

(J. J. Wright, *The Sunday School — its origins* 1900)

The argument against literacy

In a Parliamentary debate, 1807, David Giddy said, 'giving education to the labouring classes of the poor, would, in effect, be found to be prejudicial to their morals and happiness; it would lead them to despise their lot in life, instead of making them good servants in agriculture and other laborious employments to which their rank in society had destined them; it would enable them to read seditious pamphlets, vicious books and publications against Christianity; it would render them insolent to their superiors.'

A great waste

We are faced with this fact: that some six million working class children are in our primary schools; that about half a million of these children leave the primary schools every year, and that only a comparatively small number of the half-million can find their way to secondary schools or to evening schools.

The hundreds of thousands of working class children who go from school to the mill and the factory and the workshop must be catered for if we are to furnish ourselves a self-respecting, educated nation.

(J. R. Clynes MP, speaking in the House of Commons 1913)

Questions on Chapter Thirteen

1 *The local librarian will be able to help you to find out whether there was a secondary (grammar) school in your area before 1900. If there was try and find out (in local histories) more about its origins and development.*

2 *Raikes and others (see Sunday School extract) thought that education would help to make children less unruly. Do you think this should be or need be a main aim of education?*

3 *Write a letter from a monitor in which he explains his day's work to his cousins living in a small village.*

4 *Find out more about the work of Lancaster, Bell and Raikes.*

5 *Imagine that you were a teacher in an early Board School. Write to your parents explaining the problems facing you.*

6 *Why was there a growing need for more secondary schools in 1900? How did these schools help some working class children to get a middle class job?*

7 *Write a paragraph on each of the Education Acts passed in (i) 1870 and (ii) 1902.*

Unit Four

The Workshop of the World in decline 1870-1914

Agriculture is Britain's oldest industry and was once the the main occupation of the British people (Chapters 1 and 2). Between 1850 and 1870 this industry experienced a 'golden age' in which farmers and landowners enjoyed continually rising incomes (Chapter 14). Britain, as the Workshop of the World, was able to pay a high price for more and more varied food — and until the steamship had become fully developed, the rest of the world was unable to send Britain the food she needed.

But in 1873 our oldest industry was hit by the beginnings of the 'Great Depression' as American wheat, Australian and Argentinian meat poured into the country at half the prices the British farmer had been used to charging. While it was good for the town worker and the housewife, (Chapter 14), it spelt ruin for the majority of British farmers.

But British farmers were only the first to feel the effects of foreign competition. By 1880, German and American industries had shown themselves to be more efficient, more mechanised and more productive than British industry (Chapter 15). Britain lost her place as the Workshop of the World and started to decline as an industrial power.

The great middle class had once believed in freedom from government regulation and interference. They had supported the moves to Free Trade and up until the 1870s they could have argued that their ideas had helped to make Britain the world's leader. But by the end of the 1880s the lead was lost and many former supporters of Free Trade had become active supporters of the campaign for Fair Trade and, later, for Tariff Reform (Chapter 15).

There was a similar loss of belief in the ability of self-help to produce 'the greatest happiness for the greatest possible number'. By the 1880s it had become clear that the majority of the British people were not able to 'help themselves' to a share in the good life. An increasing number of people began to support the campaign of the various socialist societies (Chapter 16) and demanded an increasingly active role to be played by the government — to provide help for the under-privileged.

The Liberal Party had preached liberty, or freedom from government regulation. However, faced with the evidence of Rowntree and other investigators, the Liberal Party tried to

turn its back on its own history and become a socialist party (Chapter 16). Between 1906 and 1911 the Liberals laid the foundations for the modern welfare state in which the government helps the old, poor, sick and unemployed.

The town workers of the 1880s and 1890s were even less willing than their parents had been to accept their lowly place in society. In larger and more militant trade unions these workmen demanded a fairer share of the nation's wealth; they helped form the Labour Party (Chapter 16) in the hope that this would hasten the pace of change.

We can see many of the roots of our own society beginning to form in the period 1870–1914. The demand grew in this period for equality, education, and state interference. There was a refusal to accept the inequalities that were the result of the self-help, laisser-faire system of early Victorian Britain. One major root we can trace is the beginnings of the Women's Liberation movement (Chapter 18).

The Suez Canal proved to be a vital link with India which took over half Britain's exports in 1869 – Australia and New Zealand as well as smaller colonies in Burma and Malaya. Sailing vessels were unable to use the Canal, which was too narrow to allow them to tack from side to side as sailing ships have to. This gave a great boost to the building of steamships. These were faster, larger and could carry goods more cheaply than could sailing ships. British importers bought meat and other foodstuffs from Australia and New Zealand. While this cheap food was of great benefit to the townspeople, it meant ruin for many British farmers.

Chapter 14   Agriculture and shipping

The golden 'age, 1850–70

Disraeli and other opponents of Peel's repeal of the Corn Laws, (Chapter 11) had forecast that British farmers would be ruined soon after 1846. In fact, British farmers enjoyed greater prosperity between 1850 and 1870 than they had ever known. There was a continual growth in the number of people living in towns, all of whom had to be fed. And this growing urban population had an increasing amount of money to spend, so that they began to eat more, better and more varied food. This food could not be imported from abroad in sufficient quantity until the steamship had been developed. So British farmers were the main source of food supply for this increasingly well-to-do market.

The opponents of the repeal of the Corn Laws believed that British farmers would be ruined by the repeal. This sketch by Richard Doyle in 1849 shows Disraeli speaking to a group of British farmers. Doyle's affluent farmers seemed to have profited from the prosperity of industrial England and were, obviously, not ruined at all – yet.

Better farms

Some British farmers, seeing that they were going to be able to sell more food to the townspeople, tried to make their farms more efficient. They bought some of the new machines invented during this period. Others used new and improved

methods of land drainage to make their land more workable. Some made efforts to understand the work of agricultural scientists, and used the new fertilisers which made their land two or even three times as productive as it had been before.

In 1846 the Royal College of Agriculture had been opened at Cirencester. The College educated a new breed of farmer and farm manager. It also gave demonstrations for visiting farmers, produced pamphlets and articles for farmers' magazines about new methods and new developments. In general, the work of the College and of other similar institutions made British farmers more aware of ways in which they could improve the quantity and quality of their output.

The railway system

The British farmer was also helped by the spread of the railway network after 1850. Until the railways had been built, sheep, cattle, pigs and chickens had to walk to the meat markets in London and other large cities and towns. Welsh cattle for example, were driven from Wales during the spring, fattened on pasture in Sussex and Surrey before being sold for slaughter in London. This was a slow, expensive and wasteful business. After the coming of the railways the animals were brought in trucks, in large numbers, quickly and without having to be pastured on the way. In 1867 1,147,600 sheep were carried by train to the London market alone. It is not surprising that the well-paid townspeople

This is an illustration from a book published in 1866. It shows a threshing machine driven by steam. Seven men plus the machine were able to do in one day the work which had once taken many men many weeks. The machine was expensive and no farmer could afford to pay for one out of his own income. Contractors used to buy these machines and go from farm to farm.

* Even the best new machines are not yet adopted into general use. This incomplete progress may, however, easily be accounted for. The farmer, whose life is secluded has little opportunity of seeing them, and it is remarkable that nearly all our first implement-makers live on the East side of England in these four counties from which the other great improvements have also proceeded. But few even of our best farmers, though they may possess the new implements, carry their use thoroughly out. It seems evident that the new implements require a new system. (Report of the Select Committee of the House of Lords on Improvement of Lands, 1873)

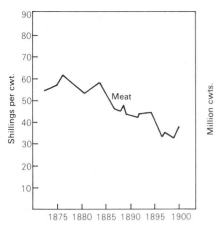

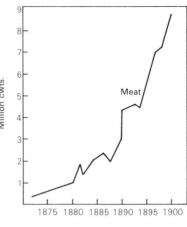

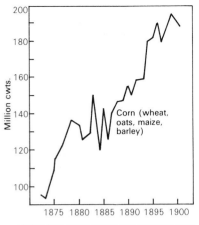

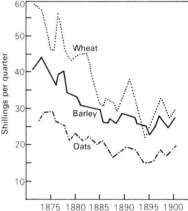

began to eat more meat and so helped provide larger incomes for British farmers. A country parson, looking back over his life, wrote of the 1860s when one of his congregation, a tenant farmer, told him; 'I can save about two thousand pounds a year'.

The depression

But Disraeli was proved right in the long run and British farmers were ruined in the 1870s and 1880s. We know a good deal about this depression because the government set up a number of Royal Commissions to find out what had happened to this once prosperous industry. These Commissioners agreed that the two causes of the rapid decline in the farming industry were:

1 A succession of very rainy summers. None of the crops ripened properly so that harvests were very poor. The wet weather also helped to spread diseases among the animals and many farmers had been forced to slaughter their herds.

But British farmers had faced bad weather before. They had seen other years when harvests had been poor. In the past this had not led to a fall in their income because the prices of the scarce food had risen and the farmers' incomes had not fallen. But in the 1870s and 1880s the bad weather was accompanied by another reason for the decline in the British farming industry.

2 There was a great increase in the amount of food imported from abroad. Wheat from the U.S.A. was sold at half the price that British farmers had been charging. This ruined the British wheat-farming industry. The increase in the amount of cheap imported meat came a little later. But the effect was again to drive down the price of meat and so help to ruin the British farmer.

Graphs of price falls and of rising imports. More food was imported and at much lower prices. British farmers were ruined but British housewives were happy.

1 *Find to the nearest shilling the price of a quarter (28lbs) of wheat in (i) 1870 and (ii) 1895. By how much should the price of a loaf of bread have fallen by 1895?*

2 *'This fall in prices was due to the rise in imports'. What evidence is there for such a claim?*

3 *Why was there a rise in wheat imports before there was a rise in the imports of meat?*

4 *Name four countries which sent food to England in this period. Which ones benefited from the opening of the Suez Canal?*

Wheat being unloaded from an
American ship into a grain
elevator on the Thames, 1880.

The import revolution

Why could farmers in the U.S.A. sell their wheat so cheaply?
They paid very low rent, if any, for their huge farms in the new
lands of the Middle West. Indeed many of them were given
the land by the governments of states anxious to attract
people to their newly established State. It was very hard to
get labour in these underpopulated areas so American
farmers were forced to spend more money on machinery.
This meant that they were able to produce more wheat and
more cheaply than would have been possible on the smaller,
high-rent, British farm where, unfortunately, machinery was
not in common use.

And none of this would have been possible had it not
been for the work of those Englishmen who built the railways.
In Canada and the U.S.A., British railway engines and railway
lines were sold to American railway companies. These were
the means by which the wheat was brought quickly, cheaply,
and in vast quantities, from the prairies to the ports of New
York or Boston. From there it came across the Atlantic by
steamship.

It was more difficult for Australian, New Zealand and
Argentinian farmers to sell their meat in England until, in
the 1880s, an Englishman invented a system of refrigeration
which enabled steamships to bring thousands of tons of

frozen meat over vast distances and, in the case of the first two countries, via the Suez Canal.

The wooden sailing ships

What was the history of these steamships which played such a large part in the agricultural changes? In 1800 all ships were made of wood and driven by sail. The ships varied in size. There were the small ships used on the coastal coaling trade. These ships, of about 100 tons weight, carried coal from Newcastle to London and other ports.

There were larger boats built for carrying timber from the Baltic States. These were usually about 600 tons in weight, a little smaller than the 700-ton ships used by the East India Company to carry goods from China and India.

The best wooden ships were built in the U.S.A. where timber was cheap and plentiful and where ships had to be built to go on long runs along the coast of the U.S.A. Because of their speed the American sailing ships were known as 'clippers' because they could cut down (or clip) the time taken by British sailing ships.

In 1833 the East India Company lost its monopoly of trade with the Far East. Many merchants wanted to get a share of the valuable Indian trade; in particular they wanted to bring back the tea which was growing in popularity in prosperous Britain. So British shipbuilders copied the American style and built 'clippers' for the East India Company and its rivals. These boats were long, narrow and carried a huge amount of sail. They could go three times as fast as previous East India Company ships. To strengthen the hulls and to make them lighter than they would otherwise have been, these ships had an iron frame, covered with a wooden skin.

But there were limits to the size of a wooden ship. Experience showed that when wooden ships were more than about 300 feet long, they tended to buckle under the strains imposed on the ship by the sea. More importantly, the wooden ships were unable to stand up to the constant shaking and vibration caused by the steam-engines which were brought into use after 1830.

Iron sailing ships

We have seen that the new machines in the textile industry were built of iron. It is not surprising that men should have thought of using iron instead of wood for their ships. In 1787 Wilkinson, who had helped Watt develop his steam-engine, built the first iron ship. Iron was stronger than wood so that it was possible to build larger ships. Iron was also lighter than wood. An iron ship weighed only half as much as a wooden

The *Sirius*, an early 703-ton steamer chartered in 1838 to sail from London to New York via Cork with 40 passengers.

ship of equal size and capacity. However, experience showed that iron ships quickly became useless because their hulls (or bottoms) quickly became fouled by the growth of barnacles and other marine animal life. Wooden ships did not foul so quickly. This helps to explain the building of the composite ships – where the frame was made of the stronger and lighter iron while the 'skin' was made of planking.

The steam-engine

The first steamship was the *Charlotte Dundas*, built by William Symington and used from 1802 on the Forth-Clyde Canal. It travelled at 6 miles per hour. A steam-driven ship had some advantages over a sailing ship. It did not depend on the wind, so that it could sail on a regular time-table. It could turn and manoeuvre more easily than could a sailing ship which had to tack (i.e. go in a criss-cross direction to take advantage of the wind) while the steam ship could take a direct line.

In 1806 Robert Fulton built the *Clermont* for use on the River Hudson in the U.S.A. and in 1812 Henry Bell built the *Comet* which not only worked on the River Clyde but became the first sea-going steamship when it ventured out into the Clyde estuary. This encouraged other people to build sea-going steamships — for the coastal trade and for the short crossing from Britain to Ireland and to Europe. By 1830 there were 200 steamships sailing from British ports.

Crossing the Atlantic

These first steamships had inefficient engines which drove the paddles at each side of the ship. These had to be adjusted according to the depth of the ship in the water. This changed according to the amount of cargo and fuel carried in the ship. As the fuel was used up, the paddles had to be adjusted.

The engines used a great deal of fuel. Most of the space below deck was taken up by coal bunkers, so there was little room for cargo. The early steamships concentrated on carrying passengers and the mail.

The first steamships which crossed the Atlantic used a mixture of sail and steam. In 1819 the American ship, *Savannah* crossed from New York to Liverpool in 25 days during which it used its engines for only 85 hours. In 1833 a Canadian ship, *Royal William*, crossed the Atlantic using only steam power. But the engines had to be stopped several times to clear the boilers of the salt drawn in from the sea water.

In 1838 Brunel's *Great Western* crossed from Britain to New York in 15 days. But it could only carry 94 passengers and it would not have been profitable to try to use it on the Transatlantic run. The Canadian shipping company owned by Samuel Cunard was able to operate a steamship service because it won the British government contract for carrying the mail from Britain to America.

Later steamships

Throughout the period 1830–70 the only method of bringing cargoes from Australia and India was the sailing ship. New

The *Campania*, one of the later steamships of the nineteenth century. She was nearly 13,000 tons and 620 feet long. An early Cunard steamship, the *Britannia* of 1840, is shown alongside for comparison.

CUNARD LINE
Royal & United States Mail Steamers.

ESTABLISHED 1840.

NOTICE.

The Steamers of this Line now come alongside the Liverpool Landing Stage, and London Passengers depart from or arrive at the Riverside Station on the Quay adjoining.

FIVE & THIRD-DAY PASSAGES.

Paddle Wheel R.M.S. "Britannia," 1840. Length 207 feet. 1,139 tons.

ATLANTIC FLEET.

Twin Screw R.M.S. "Campania" and "Lucania," 1893. Length 620 feet. 12,950 tons.

CAMPANIA   12,950 tons.   Captain HAINS, Lieut. R.N.R.

and faster 'clippers' were built for the tea run and the Australian wool run. One of the last, the *Cutty Sark* was built in 1869 and you can see it if you visit Greenwich.

However there were a number of developments which made the steamship a better proposition than even the best 'clippers'. During the 1840s the awkward paddles were done away with when the screw (propeller) engine was invented and improved. In 1854 John Elder invented a compound engine – called compound because it had more than one piston and cylinder. This meant that the same fuel as had been used to drive a simple one-pistoned engine could now be used to drive a two-, three- or (later) a four-pistoned engine. This meant that the later steamships could go two, three or four times as far and as fast as the first screw-driven ships. By 1872 coal consumption had been halved and by 1900 steamships were only using a quarter of the coal that had been used in the 1840s. This meant that there was plenty of room for cargo.

In 1897 Sir Charles Parsons invented the steam turbine engine which proved to be even more economical in using fuel and able to drive the ships much more quickly. By this time most steamships were being made not from iron but from steel. This was lighter and stronger than iron, which meant that the engines did not have to use much of their power simply to push the ship itself through the water. Steel ships were able to carry much more cargo – and so were more profitable. Steel was also much cheaper especially after the developments of Bessemer and Gilchrist and Thomas. In 1859 it had cost £40 a ton; in 1880 it was only £5 a ton. It is not surprising that by 1900 the famous 'clippers' had been replaced by the lighter, larger, stronger and more spacious steel ships which could use the Suez Canal on their route to India, Australia and New Zealand and which could cross the Atlantic in six or seven days, sailing a regular timetable.

The *Cutty Sark*. Clippers like this competed with the steamships on the long distance routes to India and Australia until the end of the nineteenth century.

Industrial benefits of steamships

The coal, steel, engineering and shipbuilding industries all gained a great boost from the growth in the number of steamships. Since Britain was the world's largest trading country, it is not surprising that British shipping companies should have owned about 60 per cent of all the world's merchant shipping. Nor was it surprising that they should have bought their ships from British shipyards – on the Clyde, the Tyne and the Tees where coal, steel and engineering industries had already been developed, so providing a good environment for the growth of the shipbuilding industry.

Since British shipyards had the experience of building for

British shipping companies, it was easy for them to build for foreign shipping companies at cheaper prices than could be offered by foreign shipyards. So it was that British yards built about three-quarters of the world's ships in 1900, providing good jobs and high wages for thousands of workers in Scotland and the North East of England. It was only in the 1920s and 1930s that this industry fell into depression as the volume of world trade slumped so that there was a fall in the demand for ships.

The failure of British farmers

Thus it was that the development of the steamship was largely responsible for the decline in British agriculture after 1870. But it seems likely that no matter what British farmers might have done before 1870 they would not have been able to meet the competition from foreign farmers. But, unfortunately, most farmers had made little real effort to improve. Most of them had bought none of the new machinery. In some cases this was because the farmer did not even know about it: in other cases they did not buy it because their farms were too small. If a machine cost £1,000 and you owned 1,000 acres then the real cost of the machine was only £1 per acre; if, however, you were the typical British farmer and had only 50 acres then the cost of the machine was £20 per acre. It is possible that a farmer might make enough profit to afford a machine if he owned a large farm; it was not possible to make enough profit on a small farm.

Free Trade – a good thing?

American wheat and Australian and New Zealand meat were brought to this country on the new steamship at prices with which the British farmer could not compete. Between 1841 and 1860 Britain had become a Free Trade country. There were no import duties on foreign goods. There were no barriers to stop people importing food and other goods.

Because foreign food was cheaper than home-produced food, the British farmer had to make a choice. Some went out of business altogether. Many of these men had rented their farms from owners of vast estates. These, too, suffered through the depression because they had no rent-incomes from their land. This is one reason for the decline of the importance of the landed aristocracy in British politics. Rents fell, on average, by one quarter between 1870 and 1914; in some areas the rents fell by half. In one case, in Steeple in Essex, a farmer paid £760 a year for 638 acres up to 1873. In 1886 the annual rent of this farm was only £1.

The other choice facing the British farmer was to change from wheat or animal farming to something else. Many did

The development of the railway network allowed the nationwide sale of branded goods, such as Pears' Soap and, advertised here, Cadbury's Cocoa. Advertisers used the Queen in their posters and the prosperous townspeople bought ever increasing quantities of their goods – a sign of rising living standards.

1 *Where, according to this advertisement, was Queen Victoria when drinking this cocoa?*
2 *Cadbury's cocoa was made in Birmingham. Why was it easier to sell this throughout the country after the coming of the railways than it had been before?*
3 *Name three other kinds of food that are manufactured by large firms and sold throughout the country. Why are these goods cheaper than they would be if they were made by small, local firms?*
4 *How did the sale of branded goods (such as Cadbury's cocoa) help to (i) show that the standard of living was rising (ii) help to raise that standard of living?*
5 *How did advertisements such as this help the development of the newspaper industry? Why were there few such advertisements before the development of the railway network?*

so and went in for vegetable farming. Others became chicken farmers, producing millions of eggs for sale to the prosperous townspeople. Still others turned to fruit farming and British townspeople were able to buy greater quantities of apples, plums and other soft fruits.

Who gained?

One man's price fall is another man's rising living standard. During the period 1876–86 many farmers were ruined by the flow of cheap imports. But during this same period wages remained fairly steady for most town workers, who saw the cost of food, wool, clothing and other things fall. So they were able to buy the same quantity of goods for less money; they had money left over to buy other things – more and varied food, better clothing and furniture, tickets for the theatre and outings to the seaside.

The benefits of the industrial revolution had at last begun to get down among the ranks of the lower classes. For the next twenty years or so they enjoyed a steep rise in their living standards – and when this rise was checked after 1900 they became more militant, more demanding and less willing to accept a return to the old ways.

Documents

a) The development of the steamship and its effect on food prices

Do you think that the cost of the carriage (of American corn) will increase or diminish? – I think that the strong tendency is to diminish, for this reason, that if you take first the sea transport, all this trade is being now carried on by steamers. The cost of constructing a steamer is now much less than it was 10 years ago . . . In addition to that you have to consider, not only that the cost of the construction of the ships is very much less than it has been, but the cost of working ships has diminished probably 30 or 40 per cent, owing to the improved style of engines that have been put into the ships; less coal is burnt; fewer men are required to work them; improved appliances, such as steam winches for loading and discharging cargo, take the place of hand labour and everyone knows what an immense amount of saving that is; improved appliances are used even for the working of the sails.

Vessels that used to be employed for the American trade were ships constructed to carry a couple of thousand tons, and now it is a very common thing to have vessels employed that carry 4,000 tons, and we all know that a vessel of that size can be worked at very much less than double the cost of a vessel that carries 2,000 tons. So that the whole tendency, as far as sea transport goes, is towards a reduction of the cost of transport.

From your experience as a very large ship-owner, and being thoroughly acquainted with the trade, both in corn and cattle, to this country, do you think that this country has ground for the apprehension that we may be interfered with by the American trade? – It seems to me that the farmers in this country must be interfered with pretty heavily at present, and I feel perfectly certain that will continue and probably grow stronger. Every line of railway that is projected in America, brings an additional corn-growing area into competition with the farmer here; and you see what the cost of conveyance is, it is so trifling. For all practical purposes, Chicago is no further distant from this country than Aberdeen is from London.

(R. R. Leyland to the Richmond Commission,
Her Majesty's Commissioners on Agriculture, 1882)

1 *'all this trade is being* now *carried on by steamers'* How was it 'carried on' before? Why was the steamship (i) quicker and (ii) more reliable in its time of arrival and departure than the sailing ship?

2 *The fall in 'the cost of constructing a steamer' was due largely to the invention of a new and cheap method of making steel. Find out more about the work of Bessemer who invented this new method.*

b) A grocer's shop in Dudley, 1900 – a well-stocked shop anxious to serve the prosperous people of industrial Dudley. There were thousands of similar shops in towns and cities up and down the country.

3 *'the improved style of engine' was largely the work of an Englishman, C. A. Parsons. Find out more about his work on the turbine engine.*

4 *'vessels that carry 4,000 tons' Why were men unable to build larger sailing ships?*

5 *Make a list of the reasons why steam shipping provided a cheaper method of sea transport in the 1890s than it had done in the 1870s.*

6 *Explain the significance of the railway system to (i) the British farmer (ii) the American farmer (iii) the depression in British farming after 1870.*

7 *Why did the grocers' shops have a wider variety of food to offer in 1900 than they would have had in 1870?*

8 *Why were British housewives able to afford to buy more and more varied foods in 1900 than they had been able to afford in 1870?*

Questions on Chapter Fourteen

1 *Give four reasons why British farmers (i) produced more food and (ii) employed less labour on their farms between 1850 and 1870.*

2 *How did the development of railways help (i) Cornish vegetable farmers, (ii) Grimsby fishermen, (iii) the opening of chain stores such as Lipton's, W. H. Smith or International Stores.*

3 *Give four reasons for the decline in the prosperity of the British agricultural industry after 1870. Show how this decline was accompanied by a rise in the standard of living for many townspeople.*

4 *Which farmers prospered after 1870? Why?*

5 *Write a letter from someone who remembered the 'golden age' of British farming but who later experienced the depression.*

6 *Make a collage of headlines which might have appeared above articles dealing with (i) the arrival of the first grain shipment from the U.S.A., (ii) the arrival of the first refrigerated ship from New Zealand, (iii) the drastic fall in farm rents in some parts of the country, (iv) the rise in the townspeople's living standards after 1870.*

Extract

The views of a famous economist
It is doubtful whether the last ten years, which are regarded as years of depression have not on the whole contributed more to solid progress and true happiness than the booms and depressions of the rest of the century.
(Alfred Marshall in *Contemporary Review*, March 1887)

Chapter 15

Industrial decline and tariff reform

A lost lead

In 1881 a British economist, Edward Sullivan, wrote:

'Thirty years ago England had almost a monopoly of the manufacturing industries of the world; she produced more of everything than she needed; other countries produced very little. The rest of the world had to buy from Britain because it could not buy anywhere else.

Well, that was thirty years ago. Now, France and America and Belgium have got machinery – our machinery, our workmen and our capital. Each year they sell an increasing volume of their goods here in Britain. On the other hand, year by year, these countries are closing their markets to our exporters.'

'Thirty years ago' was the year of the Great Exhibition when the confident middle class (Chapter 11) boasted that Britain was the Workshop of the World. Britain's leadership had been a very short one. By 1881 Germany, the U.S.A., France and other countries had overtaken Britain who had had such a long start in the industrial race. How had they managed this?

Steel, a case history

Men had been able to make steel for many centuries. They knew it had many advantages over iron. It was lighter and

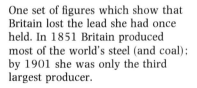

One set of figures which show that Britain lost the lead she had once held. In 1851 Britain produced most of the world's steel (and coal); by 1901 she was only the third largest producer.

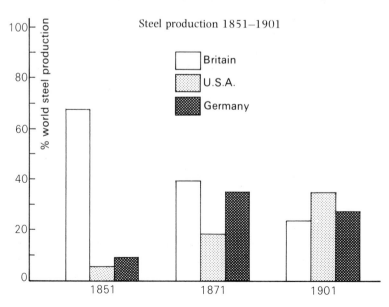

Steel production 1851–1901

Britain
U.S.A.
Germany

% world steel production

therefore more suitable for armour and for cutlery. It was almost free from carbon impurities and was therefore less brittle than iron which has a higher carbon content. This meant that steel did not crack or snap as easily as iron. But they could only produce it in small amounts and by expensive methods. In 1740 Benjamin Huntsman a Doncaster watchmaker had developed a *crucible* method which produced very high quality steel – but only by an expensive and slow process. Iron was cheaper to produce.

In 1856, during the Crimean War, Henry Bessemer was looking for a way to produce more and cheaper wrought iron. He invented a converter. The molten iron was poured into this container and air was blasted through it from holes in the bottom. The oxygen in the air burnt out the carbon in the iron. Bessemer found that he had unexpectedly produced a new form of *mild steel*. Unfortunately the Bessemer process could not be used with iron ore which contained much phosphorus – and British ores had a high phosphorus content. This led to the importing of non-phosphorus ores from Sweden and Spain and a shift of the iron and steel industry from the iron fields to the areas around the ports in South Wales and the North East.

In 1866 William Siemens invented the *open hearth furnace*. He put limestone into the molten pig iron; this combined with the carbon to form a slag. Siemens melted the

Steel-making was revolutionised by the inventions of Henry Bessemer, Siemens and Gilchrist Thomas. In this illustration you can see a Bessemer plant in use. On the left is a furnace in blast; air is being blown through the molten pig iron. This burns out the carbon. You can see the flaming gases roaring from its mouth. When the 'blow' has been completed, the converter holding the iron is tipped out (as on the right) and the molten steel poured into a large ladle. This is then swung around to fill the semicircle of moulds.

One of the causes of rising unemployment was the fall in Britain's share of world trade. Germany (shown in this cartoon) and the U.S.A. had developed their own industries and were taking trade away from Britain.

* Our manufacturers are more and more excluded from the markets of the civilised world, not by fair competition, but by oppressive tariffs. At home they are met by the unrestricted competition of every article which can be made more cheaply in any country by dint of longer hours of work, lower wages, and a meaner style of living on the part of the workers. They enjoy the one advantage of cheap food, it is true; but that is purchased, as they are finding to their cost, by the ruin of those dependent upon agriculture, and the consequent paralysis of the home trade in the rural districts.
(W. Farrer Ecroyd, *Fair Trade* 1881)

CAUGHT NAPPING!

iron by using hot gases which were aimed at the surface of the molten metal. This process was slower than Bessemer's. But it was much cheaper and was easier to control. The steelmaker could tap the furnace to get the steel out when he saw that the carbon content was just right. However, as with the converter so too with the open hearth; neither could use the British ores because of the high phosphorus content.

The answer to this problem came from two cousins; Sidney Gilchrist Thomas and P. C. Gilchrist, a chemist working in the Blaenavon ironworks in Wales. In 1878 they lined a furnace with dolomite limestone. This extracted the phosphorus from the molten iron and the result was high quality, phosphorus-free steel.

Unfortunately British steel makers had by now invested heavily in either the Bessemer converter or the Siemens open hearth furnace. They were not prepared to scrap these methods, which depended on a supply of imported ore, in favour of the new method which could use British ore. The Germans were much quicker — they used the ores from their Lorraine fields. So, too, were the Americans where a Scottish immigrant, Andrew Carnegie, made his fortune out of the new Gilchrist-Thomas method. It is not surprising that by 1900 both countries had overtaken Britain in steel making.

The home market
Another reason for the success of other countries was that they built much bigger, more efficient machines than the British. With larger furnaces and machines the foreigners were able to produce goods of a better quality and at a lower price than

the British could manage on their smaller, old-fashioned machines. One reason why the foreigners were prepared to build bigger plants and buy larger machines was the larger size of their markets. Britain had a population of about 45 million; manufacturers could hope to sell goods to that number of people. The American manufacturer had a larger population in his own country plus the nearby populations of Canada and countries in South America. He could hope to sell to this much larger number of people. Similarly with Germany. Her own population was growing and, more importantly, Germany could expect to sell, fairly easily, to the people in neighbouring countries in Europe.

It was not surprising then that the more efficient foreigner produced better and cheaper goods than did the British. Nor was it surprising that these goods sold in markets which once upon a time had taken only British goods.

Tariffs

Sullivan's statement that 'year by year, these countries are closing their markets to our exporters', gives another clue to the success of foreign manufacturers. Foreign governments in the U.S.A., Europe, the old colonies of Australia, Canada and New Zealand, all tried to help their own manufacturers by putting taxes on imported goods. These taxes pushed up the price of the imported article and so made the home-made article even more of a good buy. Since Britain was the largest exporter, these taxes (or *tariffs*) hit the British manufacturer. They led to a fall in the amount of goods sold abroad. British governments, on the other hand, stuck to their policy of Free Trade. They allowed foreign goods to come into Britain without having to pay any tariffs at all. This had already ruined the British farming industry (Chapter 14); after 1880 it became clear that this Free Trade policy was harming British industry.

Education and industry

A third major reason for Britain's decline was touched on in Chapter 13. There we saw that one reason for the passing of the 1870 Education Act was the government's fear that British workpeople were not getting enough education. But Britain's children did not go willingly to school. Nor when they got there did they learn enough to help them become technically qualified. There was far too little attention paid to education in Victorian Britain. The upper class knew little, if any, science. The middle classes who ran industry knew as little, while the lower classes had none of the skills that the foreign workmen learned in a variety of technical schools. Brawn may have been enough when industry relied mainly

A drawing from the *Illustrated London News* of 1876 by which time the London School Board had made attendance compulsory. This drawing shows an Attendance Inspector, aided by the police, rounding up boys who were playing truant. The poverty of the children is clear from their clothing. British industry had to depend on boys like this – poor, unwilling to go to school and probably unable to learn much when they did go.

on muscle. The new, chemical, electrical, petro-chemical and electrical engineering industries needed both highly qualified inventors and designers as well as well-educated technologists and technicians. Britain was not producing enough of either type.

Self-satisfied industrialists

By 1880 the people in charge of the country's factories and mines were the grandchildren or great-grandchildren of the people who had taken Britain through the early stages of the industrial revolution. It was the efforts of these earlier pioneers which had given Britain its lead. But their descendants did not have the same spirit of adventure nor the same drive. They had plenty of money: their mines or factories were ticking over and producing enough for them to live well. They saw no reason to push for greater exports, to learn about the new industries or to buy the new, expensive machinery. Their failure to keep ahead – as their ancestors had done – was a major reason for Britain's decline.

Lost markets

And what were the results of this failure by British industrialists and the success of the foreigner? One was the loss of markets which Britain had once dominated. Another was the failure to capture sufficient of the market in the newly-industrialising countries of Europe. Thirdly, there was the growth of imports from foreign countries, even of cotton goods which had spearheaded Britain's earlier industrial progress. By 1880 Britain was importing more cotton goods from Germany than she was exporting to that country. British firms were unable to produce the high-quality goods produced in Germany's mills. Other British firms were unable to compete with the Germans in chemicals, earthenware, dyes, musical instruments, scientific apparatus and specialised machinery. It was this German success which persuaded Joseph Chamberlain to take up the case for Tariff Reform. Speaking in Glasgow on 8 October 1903 he noted that since 1872 the export trades of the leading countries had changed as follows:

> Britain – up by £22 million (i.e. 7½% while population went up by 30%)
> Germany – up by £56 million
> U.S.A. – up by £110 million

In relation to her population the British export trade was 'practically stagnant for thirty years' declared Chamberlain.

Unemployment

As Britain ceased to be the workshop of the world, and as foreign goods drove British goods out of both foreign and

The pawnshop. In the 1870s there was a decline in the British iron and steel industries. Unemployed people as well as lowly-paid workers had to pawn their few possessions to get money for food and rent. One of the signs of improvement in living standards over the last forty years has been the disappearance of many pawnshops.

home markets, there was a rise in the number of skilled men who were unemployed. These men had once been supporters of the principle of self-help which provided them with a seemingly endless rise in living standards.

In the 1880s this rise in standards came to an end for many. And for many more there was the fear that maybe they too would suffer the horror of a long period of unemployment if their employer failed to sell his goods. You will see in Chapter 16 how these workmen had once looked down on the unskilled workers and at their attempts to form a Labour Party. They had never felt the need for state-help; they had always believed in self-help. After the 1880s many of them had to suffer the sort of poverty which the unskilled had always suffered. The skilled workers then became anxious to join the Labour Party and to get state-help.

Fair Trade vs Free Trade

British workmen were not the only ones who began to lose their faith in freedom and self-help. British manufacturers had once had great faith in the virtues of Free Trade. But by 1881 some of these same manufacturers were less certain of its merits. In 1881 Farrer Eckroyd wrote *Fair Trade* to express the claims of British manufacturers. In this book he demanded that Britain ought to impose a general tariff of 10 per cent on all imports. This could be used, by the government as a bargaining point with foreign governments which imposed their own tariffs. The British government could offer to lower the tariff on the goods of countries which promised to do the same for British goods entering their countries.

But in 1881 the majority of politicians and manufacturers

still thought that Free Trade was the true faith and had to be maintained in spite of the difficulties it produced and against the claims of its critics.

Tariff Reform

By 1903 there had been another twenty years of evidence that Free Trade was not going to help Britain recover her former position as the workshop of the world. There was also evidence that Britain was no longer able to dominate the world's affairs as she had done in Palmerston's time. Germany, in particular, had become a possible rival not only in trade but in foreign affairs as well. This was one of the reasons which led Joseph Chamberlain to start his Tariff Reform campaign at the end of 1903.

Having pointed out that British manufacturers were failing to hold their own with foreign manufacturers, Chamberlain said that a system of British tariffs would 'gain work for the enormous number of those who are now unemployed'. Chamberlain had once been a Radical Liberal and had resigned from Gladstone's government in 1886 because the 'Grand Old Man' would not follow socialist policies intended to help the less well-off. By 1900 Chamberlain had become Colonial Secretary in the Conservative government. He was mainly responsible for the attempts to make that Empire, in Africa and Asia, into a growing market for British goods. If British manufacturers were being pushed out of one lot of markets, then the British government would help them find new ones in an expanding Empire.

Politics and Tariff Reform

It might have been easy for the British government to impose tariffs on foreign imports, although this would have been opposed by the die-hard Liberals. But Britain wanted more than this. In the attempt to knit the Empire together, Chamberlain tried to persuade Australia, Canada and New Zealand to alter their tariffs so that lower tariffs were put on British goods than on foreign goods. This was known as Imperial Preference. The Colonies would not agree to this unless Britain agreed to put tariffs on food imports from countries outside the Empire but not on food coming from the Colonies. This would have given their farmers an advantage over American and other farmers. But this was too radical a proposal even for most Conservatives who otherwise might have supported Chamberlain's proposals. The Conservative Party split into those who supported and those who opposed Tariff Reform. Chamberlain had resigned from the government to give himself time to tour the country to explain his ideas to mass meetings. But wherever he went he was

Britannia and her boys, an engraving by G. Durand. While Britain was losing her former share of world trade she was busy acquiring an Empire. Some people hoped to find new markets in these new colonies. One writer commented:

* It is not too much to say that the modern foreign policy of Great Britain is primarily a struggle for profitable markets of investment. To a larger extent every year Great Britain is becoming a nation living upon income from abroad, and the classes who enjoy this income have an ever-increasing incentive to extend the field of their private investments, and to safeguard and improve their existing investments. This is, perhaps, the most important fact in modern politics. Aggressive Imperialism, which costs the taxpayer so dear, which is of so little value to the manufacturer and trader, which is fraught with such grave incalculable peril to the citizen, is a source of great gain to the investor.

followed, during the next week or so, by a leading Liberal, Henry Asquith, who showed that a tariff on food imports would put up the price of food within the country. Bakers would either charge more for a loaf of bread or they would make a smaller loaf for the same price as they had once charged for a larger loaf. The Liberals argued for 'a cheap breakfast table', a 'Free Trade loaf', and ignored the beneficial effects which a tariff system might have brought to the unemployed. In the 1906 Election the divided Conservatives were heavily defeated, the Liberals winning 400 seats while the Conservatives won only 157.

But the most significant feature of the 1906 Election was spotted by Balfour, the unhappy leader of the small Conservative Opposition. He looked at the 53 Labour MPs who had been elected in 1906 and remarked

'We have here something much bigger than a Liberal victory'.

In politics as well as in industry and trade a new era was dawning.

Joseph Chamberlain speaking at Bingley Hall, Birmingham, 1904 during his Tariff Reform campaign. The Liberals had said that one effect of a tariff on imported wheat would be to make the loaf more expensive — or, if the price were to remain the same, to make the loaf smaller. Chamberlain agreed. Here he is holding up a 'Free Trade Loaf' and a 'Tariff Reform Loaf' which was slightly smaller. He is asking the audience whether they can actually tell the difference, which was very small.

Chamberlain's Tariff Reform campaign split the Conservative Party and helped the Liberals to win a great victory in the General Election of January 1906. In this cartoon, labelled *Gaining Ground*, the artist was making fun of Chamberlain who had declared on the eve of the election that support for his ideas was 'gaining ground'.

Documents

a) Needy children on a Salvation Army outing.
   About one third of working men earned less than £1 a week at the time. About one in eight men were unemployed and received no social security payments. For their families there was a choice of taking charity such as this or of going to the workhouse.

b) **John Bright on Free Trade, 1884**
   I observe that your Tory candidate and his friends are seeking support as Fair Traders in opposition to Free Traders. They complain that we are allowed to buy freely all the products of foreign countries, and that, owing to some foreign tariffs, we cannot sell our own products as freely as we wish to do.

   Let your workmen reflect on the change which Free Trade has wrought. The price of tea is now less than the duty paid upon it in former days. Sugar is not more than one third of its cost.
   (Letter written by John Bright, 1884)

c) **Joseph Chamberlain and Tariff Reform, 1903**
   The original object of Mr Cobden and his colleagues nearly sixty years ago was to secure a free exchange of products between the nations of the world at their natural price, but for many years the example of the open door set by the United Kingdom has not been followed by other countries, and hostile tariffs have everywhere interfered with the natural course of trade.

   These tariffs designed to exclude British manufactures, have enabled foreign producers to undersell the British manufacturer in neutral markets and even seriously to attack his home trade.

   The Tariff Reformers believe that by re-arming themselves with the weapon of a moderate tariff, we may still defend our home market against unfair competition, and may secure a modification of foreign tariffs which would open the way to a fairer exchange of products than we have hitherto been able to obtain.

   But they attach even greater importance to the possibility of securing arrangements with our Colonies towards a great development of trade within the Empire. They believe that these objects can be promoted by a slight transfer of existing taxes which will raise the revenue required for defence, while adding greatly to the amount of employment for our ever-growing populace.

   The questions thus raised, although they interest every class, are more vitally important to working men than to any other, since they alone depend upon the daily employment for their daily subsistence.
   (Article written by Joseph Chamberlain at the end of his Tariff Reform Campaign, November 1903)

A. J. Balfour's uncertainty, 1904

I'm not for Free Trade, and I'm not for Protection,
I approve of them both, and to both have objection.
In going through life I continually find
It's a terrible business to make up one's mind.
So in spite of all comments, reproach and predictions,
I firmly adhere to Unsettled Convictions.
(Sir Wilfred Lawson's parody of Balfour's views, 1903)

1 Why was Bright in favour of Free Trade? Why was he
supported by many working class men? How did their
support of Bright affect the success of Chamberlain's
campaign?

2 Who was Cobden's nearest colleague in the campaign
for Free Trade 'nearly sixty years ago'? How did Free
Trade fit in with the principle of self-help?

3 How did tariffs interfere 'with the natural course of
trade'? Which countries might have wanted to alter
that course and which countries favoured the freedom
advocated by Free Traders?

4 See if you can find five aims behind the Tariff Reform
Campaign outlined by Chamberlain. How do they fit
in with the argument that Chamberlain was a social
reformer?

5 Why was Balfour uncertain of the policy to adopt?
What effect did this have on the fortunes of the
Conservative Party?

6 Arrange a debate between Fair Traders and Free
Traders.

7 What was the link between the children in Document
(a) and the growth of foreign competition?

8 How would these children benefit from (i) a system of
British tariffs, (ii) Imperial Preference.

9 How would they suffer from Imperial Preference?

10 Why did many working class families vote for the
Conservatives in 1900 and not do so in 1906?

Questions on Chapter Fifteen

1 Make a list of the advantages enjoyed by Germany and
the U.S.A. when they became leading industrial nations
in the 1870s. What was significant about (i) the
successful unification of Germany – completed in
1870–1 and (ii) the victory of the North over the
South in the American Civil War, 1861–5?

2 What is a tariff? How do tariffs on American cars
imported into Britain, (i) increase the price of the
car, (ii) help the British car industry? Why did
Britain have no tariffs on imports in the late nineteenth
century?

3 British exports were still increasing at the end of the
century. What was Chamberlain complaining about?

4 Make a list of the reasons why Chamberlain supported a
policy of Tariff Reform.

5 What were the advantages of Imperial Preference to
(i) Britain, (ii) Colonial farmers? Why was this
Preferential system opposed by (i) Colonial
industrialists, (ii) the Liberal Party, (iii) many
working class people?

6 Find out more about the work of Bessemer, Siemens,
Gilchrist and Thomas. How did their work effect the
well-being of the British steel industry?

7 Make a collage of headlines which might have appeared
above articles dealing with (i) the increase in imports
from Germany and the U.S.A., (ii) Britain's loss of
markets in Colonial countries, (iii) Chamberlain's
campaign for Tariff Reform, (iv) the Liberal Party's
defence of the policy of Free Trade.

Extract

An appeal for tariffs at home, expansion abroad
In the first place we all desire to keep and increase our
national strength and the wealth of Great Britain. In
the second place, our aim should be the creation of an
Empire such as the world has never seen.
(Joseph Chamberlain speaking in Glasgow, 6 October
1903)

Chapter 16

Trade unions – the rise of the Labour Party

A divided society

By 1870 a small number of people had a very high standard of living. Some skilled workers had a much higher standard than their parents had ever known (Chapter 10). But most workers were unskilled and, like London's dockers, earned as little as 1p per hour. Their standard of living was very low.

We know a good deal about these poor people. Many people wrote about them and tried to help them including William Booth, the founder of the Salvation Army. During the 1890s Charles Booth, a rich shipowner, sent out dozens of people to visit the homes of the poor in London and found that about one-third of the London working class lived in terrible poverty. In 1900 Seebohm Rowntree, the chocolate manufacturer from York, sent out people to visit every house in that city. In his book, *Poverty, a study of Town Life*, Rowntree showed that over 40 per cent of wage-earners, about one-third of the population of York, lived in poverty.

And in 1900 neither of the two main political parties did much to help these people. The feeling remained that the state should not be asked to help the poor with their housing or other social problems.

Socialism

In 1870 most politicians believed in the idea of self-help. But by 1900 there were a growing number, even of the ruling class, who no longer believed that self-help was enough. Free Trade was part of the self-help idea. By 1890 a number of people believed that this Free Trade was one reason for Britain's decline (Chapter 15) and there was a demand for Tariff Reform. The work of Booth and Rowntree showed that self-help and non-interference did not produce a good life for the British working class. Alongside the demand for Tariff Reform there grew up the demand for a socialist government.

An American, Henry George, wrote *Progress and Poverty* in which he called for increased taxation and a government 'war on poverty'. A clergyman, Andrew Mearns, wrote *The Bitter Cry of Outcast London* in which he described the wretched housing conditions in which many people lived (p. 124). He called for government action to provide decent and cheap housing. William Booth, Charles Booth and Rowntree all added to the demand for government action.

Socialist societies

And it was not only the authors of learned books who were asking for this. In 1881 Henry Hyndman founded the Social Democratic Federation (SDF) in which he hoped to unite the activities of all radicals and those workers who wanted a change in the political and social system. William Morris had once belonged to the SDF but in 1884 this gifted poet and artist founded his own Socialist League.

Also founded in 1884 was the Fabian Society which produced a number of pamphlets and books which described conditions in Britain and suggested how these could be improved. Most of the Fabians were well-educated. Among their leaders were H. G. Wells, the scientist-author, George Bernard Shaw, the Anglo-Irish playwright and the two Webbs, Sidney and Beatrice, who were rich enough not to have to work for a living. The majority of Fabians were Liberals. They hoped that their books would force the Liberals to become more socialist-minded.

The London Dockers' Strike, 1889

The socialist societies and authors wanted governments to pass laws which would make life better for the poor. The

A painting of an upper-class wedding, 1908. Notice the clothing, hats and the new method of transport – the motor-car.

The children of a middle class family listening to their father.

The children of a poor family with their parents.

* Now, John, what are the evils of which we complain? Lowness of wages, length of working hours, uncertainty of employment, insecurity of the future, low standards of public health and morality and the existence of false ideals of life.
I will give you a few examples of the things I mean. It is estimated that in this country with its population of 36 millions there are generally about 700,000 men out of work. There are about 800,000 paupers. About 8 millions exist always on the borders of destitution. About 20 millions are poor. About 30,000 people own five-sixths of the land and capital of the kingdom, but of 36 millions of people only $1\frac{1}{2}$ millions get above £3 per week. The average income per head of the working classes is about £17 a year, or less than 5p a day.
(Robert Blatchford, *Merrie England* 1895)

(Opposite) The Manifesto of the dockers showing how many unions were involved in the London Dockers Strike and the objects for which each was striking.

unskilled workers had no trade unions until the 1880s. Few people thought that they were capable of doing much to get things changed.

However in the 1880s, urged on by members of the SDF and the Fabians, some unskilled workers did act. Annie Besant, a journalist and a Fabian, formed a union among the girls in the match-making factory owned by Bryant and May. She led them into a strike and helped them get a wage increase from their employers. Will Thorne, a member of the SDF, led his fellow-stokers in the London Gas Works to form a union. The owners of the Gas Company gave in to the men's

SOUTH SIDE
CENTRAL STRIKE COMMITTEE,

SAYES COURT, DEPTFORD.

SEPTEMBER 10, 1889.

GENERAL MANIFESTO.

Owing to the fact that the demands of the Corn Porters, Deal Porters, Granary Men, General Steam Navigation Men, Permanent Men and General Labourers on the South Side have been misrepresented, the above Committee have decided to issue this Manifesto, stating the demands of the various sections now on Strike, and pledge themselves to support each section in obtaining their demands.

DEAL PORTERS of the Surrey Commercial Docks have already placed their demands before the Directors.

LUMPERS (Outside) demand the following Rates, viz:—1. 10d. per standard for Deals. 2. 11d. per stand. for all Goods rating from 2 x 4 to 2½ x 7, or for rough boards. 3. 1s. per std. for plain boards. Working day from 7 a.m. to 5 p.m., and that no man leave the "Red Lion" corner before 6.45 a.m. Overtime at the rate of 6d. per hour extra from 5 p.m. including meal times.

STEVEDORES (Inside) demand 8d. per hour from 7 a.m. to 5 p.m. 1s. per hour overtime. Overtime to commence from 5 p.m. to 7 a.m. Pay to commence from leaving "Red Lion" corner. Meal times to be paid for. Holidays & Meal times double pay, and that the Rules of the United Stevedores Protection League be acceded to in every particular. *conceded*

OVERSIDE CORN PORTERS (S.C.D.) demand 15s. 3d. per 100 qrs. for Oats. Heavy labour 17s. 4d. per 100 qrs. manual, or with use of Steam 16s. 1d. All overtime after 6 p.m. to be paid at the rate of ½d. per qr. extra.

QUAY CORN PORTERS (S. C. D.) demand the return of Standard prices previous to March 1889, which had been in operation for 17 years.

TRIMMERS AND GENERAL LABOURERS demand ⑥d per hour from 7 a.m. to 6 p.m. and 8d. per hour Overtime; Meal times as usual; and not to be taken on for less than 4 hours.

WEIGHERS & WAREHOUSEMEN demand to be reinstated in their former positions without distinction.

BERMONDSEY AND ROTHERHITHE WALL CORN PORTERS demand: 1. Permanent Men 30s. per week. 2. Casual Men 5s. 10d. per day and 8d. per hour Overtime; Overtime to commence at 6 p.m. Meal times as usual.

GENERAL STEAM NAVIGATION MEN demand:—1. Wharf Men, 6d. per hour from 6 a.m. to 6 p.m. and 8d. per hour Overtime. 2. In the Stream, 7d. per hour ordinary time, 9d. per hour Overtime. 3. In the Dock, 8d. per hour ordinary time, 1s. per hour Overtime.

MAUDSLEY'S ENGINEER'S MEN. Those receiving 21s. per week now demand 24s., and those receiving 24s. per week demand 26s.

ASHBY'S, LTD., CEMENT WORKS demand 6d. per ton landing Coals and Chalk. General Labourers 10% rise of wages all round, this making up for a reduction made 3 years ago.

GENERAL LABOURERS, TELEGRAPH CONSTRUCTION demand 4s. per day from 8 a.m. to 5 p.m., time and a quarter for first 2 hours Overtime, and if later, time and a half for all Overtime. No work to be done in Meal Hours.

Signed on behalf of the Central Committee, Wade Arms,

BEN. TILLETT,
JOHN BURNS,
TOM MANN,
H. H. CHAMPION,
JAS. TOOMEY.

Signed on behalf of the South side Committee,

JAS. SULLI...
CHAS. H...
HUGH J...

The Angel, Socialism, represented as the salvation of downtrodden Labour.

demand for a reduction in the working day without any loss of pay.

But the most famous action by the unskilled took place on London Docks where the unskilled workers (led by Ben Tillett), formed themselves into a union and went on strike in support of their demand for an increase in pay from 2p to 2½p an hour.

Few people thought that these men could unite. But Tillett and his friends from the SDF, Tom Mann and John Burns worked hard. They persuaded the more skilled workers to come out in support of the unskilled men. This brought the docks to a halt. Burns organised a series of marches through London to show the better-off how poorly-paid, badly-dressed and ill-fed were the families of the unskilled workers. A Committee of working people organised collections of money and handed out food and clothing to the families of the strikers. Dockers in Australia sent £30,000 to help their fellow-dockers in London.

The Lord Mayor of London set up a Conciliation Committee on which the men, their employers as well as leaders from Church and public life, worked out an agreement which gave the men what they had asked for.

Effects of the strike

But even a wage of 2½p an hour was not going to help the unskilled dockers to buy their own homes or to afford the rent for a decent one. They still did not have enough to save for their old age or take out insurance policies against unemployment or sickness. The socialist societies argued that only when there was a socialist government would the poor get cheap housing, old age pensions, unemployment benefit, free medical care and so on.

The London Dockers had shown that they could act, in unity, in the industrial field. Why should they not act to form a political party and so force social reforms through Parliament? They had found their own strike-leaders. Could they find their own political leaders? There had been a demand for a working class party soon after the passing of the 1867 Reform Act. During the 1890s this demand grew stronger and more persistent.

Keir Hardie and the Labour Party

There were a number of working men in parliament in the 1890s. Most of them were elected for mining constituencies where the Liberals knew that one of their richer candidates might not have done so well. In these areas the local Liberal Association chose a working man as their candidate. When elected, these Lib-Labs sat with the Liberals.

In 1888 a Scottish miner, Keir Hardie, asked the Liberals in mid-Lanarkshire to allow him to be their candidate in a by-election. They refused. Hardie stood in that election and came bottom of the poll. He then boldly announced that he was forming the Scottish Labour Party.

Hardie visited a number of English constituencies during the next few years, persuading working men to form their own local Labour Party. He was very successful in Yorkshire, Lancashire and the working class districts of London. In the General Election of 1892 Hardie was elected MP for West Ham and John Burns, MP for Battersea. The arrival at the Commons of the Scottish leader of the first working-men's party was well-publicised.

In 1893 Hardie called a meeting of the representatives of the various local Labour groups at Bradford. Here they formed themselves into the *Independent Labour Party*. However, at the 1895 Election all their candidates, including Hardie and Burns, were defeated.

This did not lessen the enthusiasm of Hardie's supporters. During 1896 over 70 new branches of the ILP were formed, mainly in Yorkshire and Lancashire. Working men had begun to see the value of political action.

Keir Hardie. A hostile reporter wrote:

* Mr Keir Hardie drove up to the House in a toil-stained working suit with a cloth cap on his head and accompanied by a noisy brass band followed by a noisy and disreputable throng from the dockside slums which included many undesirable foreign elements who should be driven from our shores before they infect our good and sensible working men with their bloodthirsty beliefs. (The *'Morning Post'*, August 1892)

The Unions and the ILP

Many of Hardie's supporters were trade unionists. Some became delegates to the annual conferences of the *TUC*. Here they asked the leaders of other unions to join them to form a strong working class party. Year after year they were turned down by the leaders of the unions for skilled workers. They had the most powerful voice, the most votes and the support of their own Lib-Lab MPs.

But the writing of the socialists and the fear of unemployment (Chapter 15) slowly persuaded the skilled workers to change their minds. In 1899 the TUC agreed that a Conference could take place where representatives of the various socialist societies, the ILP and of any unions which wished to go along, might work to form a new Workers' Party.

This Conference took place in the Memorial Hall, Farringdon Street London on 28 February 1900. There were representatives from a number of unions representing about 500,000 men, as well as delegates from three socialist societies representing only about 23,000 members. They decided to name their new Party the Labour Representation Committee, with an Executive of twelve; seven from the trade unions, and two each from the ILP and SDF and one from the Fabian Society.

Bloody Sunday, 1887. Fighting in Trafalgar Square, London. There were similar clashes in industrial areas throughout the country as the police were called upon to put down demonstrations by the unemployed.

John Burns speaking at Derby in support of Richard Bell (seated left). Bell had been an ILP MP in 1900 and was an official of the Amalgamated Society of Railway Servants.

Skilled workers and the LRC

After the success of the Dockers' Strike there were other large unions formed for unskilled workers. There was a danger that the smaller unions for skilled men would be swamped by these larger unions. So the leaders of the older unions changed their rules to allow unskilled men to join.

The older unions had generally been happy to negotiate with their employers, preferring not to strike. But the depression of the 1890s (Chapter 15) and the fear of unemployment drove many of the older unions into following the more militant policies of the newer unions. This increasing militancy was a feature of life in the 1880s and 1890s. There were fights with the police, attacks on property and huge demonstrations. These frightened the middle class, who were also suffering from the effects of the depression.

Taff Vale, 1 9 0 0– 0 2

In August 1900 workers on the Taff Railway Company went on strike when the Company tried to transfer a man from one district to another against his wishes. Their union, the Amalgamated Society of Railway Servant (now the NUR) supported their action and the strike was an official one. The general manager of the Company, Mr Beasley, claimed damages from the union for this act. In July 1901 the House of Lords decided that the Union had to pay the Company £23,000 and pay legal costs of £19,000. This encouraged other employers to fight their unions through the Law Courts and in 1902–3 the Yorkshire Mining Association claimed £150,000 damages from the miners' union.

This was an attempt to lessen the power of the unions. If they could be made less willing to strike for fear of the damages they might incur, employers would hold the whiphand during negotiations. It was this Taff Vale decision which drove the leaders of the skilled unions into the ranks of the Labour Representation Committee – which they had not joined in 1900 and whose formation they had for years opposed.

In February 1901 only one third of the trade unions had joined the LRC. By February 1904 over two thirds had done so. This had a great effect on the infant Party because the older unions for skilled men had better organisation, more able leaders and more money than the unions for the unskilled. One effect of this larger membership was success at the elections. Between 1900 and 1906 the LRC won three seats. In 1903 the Liberal Chief Whip, Herbert Gladstone, arranged an electoral pact with Ramsay MacDonald, the secretary of the LRC. They agreed that at the next General Election they would withdraw their candidates in certain

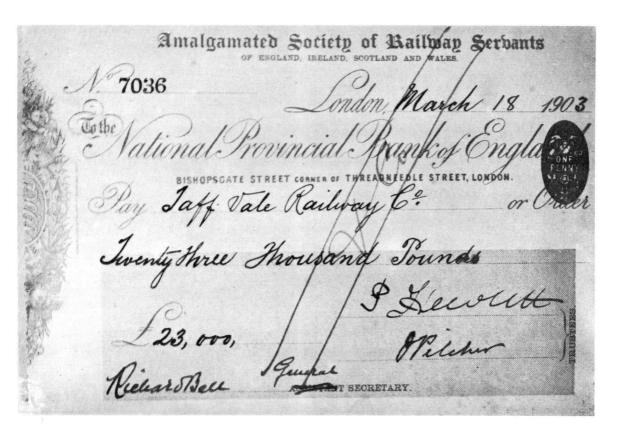

Amalgamated Society of Railway Servants
OF ENGLAND, IRELAND, SCOTLAND AND WALES.

N°. 7036

London, March 18 1903

To the National Provincial Bank of England

BISHOPSGATE STREET CORNER OF THREADNEEDLE STREET, LONDON.

Pay Taff Vale Railway C°. or Order

Twenty three Thousand Pounds

£23,000,

Richard Bell

General
ASSISTANT SECRETARY.

TRUSTEES.

constituencies to allow a straight fight with the Conservative candidate. In the General Election of 1906 the LRC put up fifty candidates and won twenty-nine seats. In addition there were twenty-three Lib-Labs, mainly from mining constituencies. These joined the newly-elected 29 and the enlarged group dropped the title LRC and called itself the Labour Party. A new era had dawned and the days of self-help were coming to an end.

The cheque made out to the Taff Vale Railway Company as settlement of that Company's claims against the ASRS.

Documents

PUNCH, OR THE LONDON CHARIVARI.—May 16, 1906.

A BIT OF A BREEZE.

C.-B. (*Organ Grinder, to* Independent Labour Party). "AIN'T YOU A-GOIN' TO JOIN IN WITH YOUR FRIEND, MISS?" I. L. P. "NOT ME! SHE AIN'T MY CLASS!"

a) Keir Hardie and the ILP refuse to join the MPs who dance to the tune played by the organ-grinding Liberal leader.

b) **Slum Dwellers, 1890**

The foul and fetid breath of our slums is almost as poisonous as that of Africa. A population eaten up by every sort of social and physical malady, these are the denizens of Darkest England which may be said to have a population of three million men, women and children; the Submerged Tenth.

(William Booth, *In Darkest England and the Way Out* 1890)

c) **Conditions in Bermondsey**

The food of the poor too, here, is irregularly supplied. There are few who prepare a dinner, except on Sunday. The children unless they have free meals given to them, subsist on bread and butter or bread and jam.

One case I had this bitterly cold week without a bit of bed clothing, five or six little ones, the husband a labourer; not much work. I had lent two blankets out, so was unable to lend her one.

(Charles Booth, *Life and Labour and the People of London* 1891)

d) **Living in York, 1902**

The wage for a labourer in York is from 18 shillings to 21 shillings, the minimum expenditure necessary to maintain in a state of physical efficiency a family of two adults and three children is 21s 8d, or, if there are four children, 26 shillings.

The wages paid for unskilled labour in York are insufficient to provide food, shelter and clothing adequate to maintain in a state of bare physical efficiency, even if the diet is less generous than that allowed in the Workhouse.

And let us clearly understand what 'bare physical efficiency' means. A family living upon the scale allowed for in this estimate must never spend a penny on railway or omnibus; never go into the country unless they walk; never purchase a halfpenny news-paper or buy a ticket for a popular concert; never write letters to absent children, for they cannot afford the postage. They cannot save, join a sick club or Trade Union; they cannot pay the subscriptions. The children have no pocket money for dolls, marbles, or sweets. The father must not smoke or drink. The mother must never buy any pretty clothes for herself or for her children. 'Nothing must be bought but that which is absolutely necessary for the maintenance of physical health, and what is bought must be of the plainest and most economical description.' Finally, the wage-earner must never be absent from his work for a single day.

If any of these conditions are broken, the extra expenditure is met and can only be met, by limiting the diet; or in other words by sacrificing physical efficiency.

(Seebohm Rowntree, *Poverty, a Study in Town Life* 1902)

1 *What was the name of the leader of the Liberal Party in 1906?*

2 *Who was the leader of the Independent Labour Party in 1906?*

3 *Which group of working class voters were represented by the Lib-Labs? Explain why, until 1906, they did not join the ILP.*

4 *Explain why the Lib-Labs came to join the ILP in the new Labour Party.*

5 *Why did the York labouring class live in inadequate housing?*

6 *Why was there a heavy death rate among the families of unskilled workers?*

7 *Write a letter from a child in a poor family living in York or in a poor area of London describing 'a day in my life'.*

8 *Draw or paint, as part of a frieze, 'The submerged Tenth', 'The Bermondsey Poor', 'The York labourer's Family'.*

9 *Why did the mothers and children in these families try to find work? How did their conditions affect the education of the children?*

10 *Look at the final two sentences of Document (d). Why was the labourer likely to 'be absent from work'?*

Extract

The Socialist dream

At the moment there are two classes of society. One possesses the wealth and owns the means of producing more wealth. The other produces the wealth but only for the use of the owners. What remedy do we propose? All the means of production must be treated as if they were the common property of all the people. Every man will receive the full value of his work. Everyone will have enough free time to follow his own intellectual or other pursuits.

(William Morris, *How I became a Socialist* 1896)

Questions on Chapter Sixteen

1 *Find out more about the work of Robert Blatchford, the editor of the 'Clarion'; Ben Tillett, one of the leaders of the Dockers' Strike; William Morris and Keir Hardie.*

2 *1900 has been called 'a turning point in social history'. Name five people, events or organisations which helped to make 1900 a turning point.*

3 *Most of the early Fabians were either Liberals or friends of leading Liberals. What did they hope to do? Why did they finally decide to help to form the Labour Representation Committee?*

4 *Write a letter from one of the men who went on strike in the London Docks in 1889. (He might write about wages, working conditions, unemployment, his family's living standards, housing, Burns, Tillett, processions or the Conciliation Committee.*

5 *Explain why most skilled workers were (i) unwilling to support the LRC in 1900, (ii) eager to join after 1901.*

6 *Use the following dates as guides in writing a short account of the early development of the Labour Party: 1888; 1893; 1900; 1901; 1906.*

7 *Make a collage of headlines which might have appeared above articles dealing with (i) the Dockers' Strike, (ii) Hardie's election at West Ham, (iii) the Memorial Hall meeting, (iv) the Taff Vale decision, (v) the miners' MPs decision to join the Labour MPs in the House of Commons.*

Chapter 17   New Liberalism in a restless society

New Liberalism

The work of Booth, Rowntree and other investigators between 1886 and 1902 proved that a large part of the working class lived in great poverty.

The existence of so much poverty and suffering in the middle of much wealth led many people to demand greater government activity in social and economic affairs. The call for such action had first come from the Liberals themselves. In 1885 Joseph Chamberlain, then a Radical Liberal, issued an 'unofficial programme' outlining the social reforms which a future Liberal government should carry out. But in 1885 the Liberal Party was led by Gladstone who condemned Chamberlain's ideas. He argued for the old policy: 'The spirit of self-help must be preserved in the minds of every member of the working class'

Chamberlain disagreed with his ageing leader. In 1886 Chamberlain left the Liberal Party. After he left there was no Radical leader to try to bring the Liberal Party to the Socialist road.

The rich had very large, comfortable houses. In this picture the artist shows that such comfort did not always bring happiness.

(Opposite) An East End home around 1900 when over one-third of the British people had no house but only a room or two. Many large families lived in single rooms where they were born, lived and died. There was no sign for these people of that good life promised by those who preached self-help.

Socialism developing

This movement towards socialism was helped on its way by the work of the great investigators (Chapter 16) and by the Boer War (1899–1902). There was a rush of volunteers to join the Army in 1899. Over half of them were too unfit to serve. These were the products of a century of progress and self-help. These were the people on whom depended Britain's industrial future. Most important of all these were the people who would have to fight for King and Country if ever one of the newer industrial nations, such as Germany, challenged Britain's imperial power.

One argument in Britain against government interference had been the fear that higher taxes and new welfare schemes would cripple the country. In other countries, including Germany, governments had already laid the foundations for their own welfare states. Germany had a good welfare state and, at the same time, was overtaking Britain in the industrial race.

Liberal achievements, 1906–14

In 1906 Sir Henry Campbell-Bannerman formed a Liberal government with Lloyd George at the Board of Trade and Asquith as Chancellor of the Exchequer. When Campbell-Bannerman resigned owing to ill-health in 1908, Asquith

Chamberlain (riding the horse labelled 'Socialism') and the Tory Radical, Churchill, battling to win the 'Votes' of the working class in 1885. The leaders of the parties, Gladstone and Salisbury, are horrified at the antics of their younger colleagues.

* It is therefore perfectly futile and ridiculous to tell us that these things are to be excluded from the Liberal programme. We have to account for and to grapple with the mass of misery and destitution in our midst. I shall be told tomorrow that this is Socialism. Of course it is Socialism. The greater part of municipal work is Socialism, and every kindly act of legislation by which the community has sought to discharge its responsibilities and its obligations to the poor is Socialism, but it is none the worse for that.

(Joseph Chamberlain, during the election campaign, August 1885)

THE POLITICAL POLO MATCH.

became Prime Minister and Lloyd George became Chancellor. His place at the Board of Trade was taken by Winston Churchill. These were the men responsible for the social reforms of the next five years.

1 Workmen's Compensation, 1906
Under this Act employers were forced to pay compensation to any workman who might have been injured while at work.

2 School Meals Act, 1906
In 1906 the government passed the School Meals Act to help the children of the very poor. It was the teachers who had pointed out that hungry, sick and diseased children were unable to benefit from education. Under this Act, local authorities were allowed to collect a rate to pay for a School Meals Service. During the debate on this measure a number of MPs argued that the government was being wickedly extravagant in offering to give one meal a day to the very poor children. The Gladstonian opposition to social reform had not yet died out.

The Liberal government also compelled local councils to open child welfare clinics where mothers could take their children and where doctors and nurses could check on the children's health and progress. In this way, it was hoped, some at least of the common diseases and sicknesses could be overcome.

3 Old Age Pensions Act, 1908
The old formed a large section of those living in poverty as defined by Booth and Rowntree. Under this Act, people aged

Inside a tailor's sweat shop where women worked long hours for very little money.

70 or over were to receive 25p a week, payable at the Post Office, provided that they had less than £21 a year from any other sources. The first payments were made on 6 January 1909.

The *Woman Worker*, one of the radical magazines of the time, showed how one pensioner had spent her first 25p. (In the list you should notice that 1p = about 2½d, or old pennies.)

In the 1890s there were thousands of children like these – badly clothed, ill-fed and poorly-housed. They were the product of a century of industrial progress and self-help.

Rent	2s 3d	2lb loin of mutton	1s 0d
Pint of paraffin	1½d	half bag of flour	1d
14lb of coal	2½d	pint of porter	1¾d
		(for Sunday's dinner)	
2oz tea	1d	pepper, salt, vinegar	1½d
2lb of potatoes	1d	one loaf	2½d
			4s 5¾d

The old lady said that she intended to have a first-class dinner on Sunday, with perhaps 1d worth of cheese. Later in the week, she would purchase 'a ha'porth of beans' together with 'a pennorth of onions', and after that, she calculated, she would have enough over to afford '1d for a herring on Friday, and then it will be time to draw my pension again'.

But even this small handout was condemned by the richer taxpayer.

4 Trade Boards Act, 1909

People working in trades and occupations not covered by existing Factory Acts had often been forced to work long hours for low pay in appalling conditions. In future there would be government regulations controlling the pay, conditions and hours of work of these people. A Board of government officials was set up to supervise each of the trades involved.

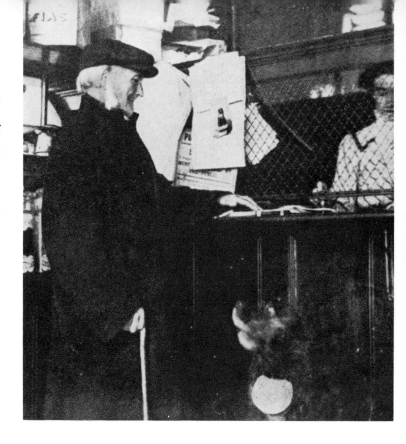

One of the first old age pensioners getting his money from a Post Office in London in January 1909.

* Friday was the beginning of a new era for the aged poor of this country, as on that date the first payment of Old Age pensions was made. In Norwich there were old people waiting for the doors to open at 8 o'clock, and by 9 o'clock the stream of callers was in full flow. As was to be expected the business done at the GPO was overwhelmingly larger than anywhere else. The first pensioner, an old man, made his call at 9.15. Close on his heels came an old lady. They produced their coupon books without a word, answered one or two routine questions, made their signatures, pocketed their money and walked out. (The Norwich 'Mercury', 9 January 1909)

5 Labour Exchanges, 1909

Closely linked with the later National Insurance Act (Part Two) was the setting up in 1909 of a nationwide chain of *Labour Exchanges*. Lloyd George and William Beveridge, who helped him draw up the scheme, wanted the Exchanges as places to which the unemployed would go to prove that they were genuinely looking for work. They also hoped that employers would get in touch with the Exchange when they needed workers. This would mean that the unemployed need not tramp for miles in search of a job.

6 National Insurance Act, 1911 (Part One)

Part One of this Act set up a National Health Insurance Scheme. All manual workers earning less than £160 a year were forced to become insured under this state scheme. The workman paid 4d into a fund, his employer paid 3d and the state added 2d. The insured workman was then entitled to receive free medical attention from a doctor who would be paid out of the fund. He would also receive 10 shillings a week (50p), for up to 26 weeks when off work owing to ill-health – after which he could claim a disablement pension. He would also be able to go to a special hospital if he had tuberculosis, then a particularly common disease, while his

Waiting outside one of the new Labour Exchanges, 1910.

A Conservative view of Lloyd George, the Chancellor who wanted to push up the taxes to pay for social reform.

wife was entitled to claim a maternity benefit of 30 shillings (150p) when she was going to have a baby.

7 National Insurance Act, 1911 (Part Two)

Unemployment was a major cause of poverty, since it meant the loss of family income if the only wage-earner were thrown out of work. Part Two of the 1911 National Insurance Act applied only to men in the following trades: building, construction of works, ship-building, mechanical engineering, iron-founding, construction of vehicles and sawmilling. This insurance scheme was nothing like the comprehensive schemes which we have today. The Unemployment Fund was built up out of the contributions of employers, workmen and government, and the payment was made out of that Fund to the unemployed and insured workman. (p. 181).

The Budget, 1909

These reforms had to be paid for, and in the 1909 Budget, Lloyd George proposed to collect an extra £16 million in taxation to pay for these reforms and for the building of new battleships. He proposed an increase in *income tax* from 5p in the pound to just under 7p for people who had incomes above £3,000 a year with an additional 6 pence (or about 2p) in the pound, to be paid by those with incomes above £5,000 a year. He also increased *death duties* and proposed a new form of land tax (which had to be dropped because it was found too difficult to enforce).

The budget and its increased taxation and the social reforms that these taxes would pay for, aroused the anger of the richer classes, and in particular of the House of Lords. They threw out the budget when it came to their House. This had never been done before. A political crisis occurred which led to a General Election in January 1910. The choice lay between 'Peers or People'.

Lloyd George led the attack on the members of the Lords. The rich taxpayers saw Lloyd George as the robber-tyrant who wanted to take away their money. The Gladstonian belief in self-help was not going to die without a struggle.

The Parliament Act, 1911

The result of this General Election left the Liberals with 272 seats and the Tories with 271. The third largest party in the Commons were the Irish Nationalists led by John Redmond.

Asquith, Lloyd George and Winston Churchill invited the Irish MPs to support them in their struggle with the Lords over the budget. In return the Irish demanded that the Liberals give *Home Rule* to Ireland. The Liberals agreed. But the Irish pointed out that a Home Rule Bill might pass the

A sign that trade unionists were more militant than they had been; Ben Tillett speaking to a crowd of workers on Tower Hill, London during the first-ever national transport strike, 1912.

Commons and then be thrown out in the Lords as the budget had been. So in addition to a Home Rule Bill, they also demanded a Bill which would limit the power of the House of Lords. This the Liberals willingly gave them in the Parliament Act, 1911. Under the terms of this Act the House of Lords could not amend or reject any Bill which had passed through the Commons if that Bill was concerned with taxation (eg a Budget). The Lords could amend or reject all other Bills, but if a Bill was passed by the Commons in three successive sessions, (having been rejected twice by the Lords) then the Bill would be signed by the Monarch and so become an Act of Parliament without being sent back to the Lords for the third time.

A restless society

We have already seen that the larger trade unions were more militant after 1910 than they had been before (Chapter 16). We will also see that about this time middle class women were becoming violently militant in their demands for 'Votes for Women' (Chapter 18). The Lords had created a political crisis over the 1909 Budget and now it was the turn of the Conservative Party and the Protestants of Ulster. In 1912 the Liberals brought in their promised Home Rule for Ireland Bill. Because of the Parliament Act, this Bill, if it went through the Commons in three successive sessions, would have to

A scene at the Albert Hall in December 1908 when Lloyd George was making a speech on Woman's Suffrage. Miss Ogston, a militant supporter of Mrs Pankhurst, heckled the Chancellor. When the stewards came to throw her out she lashed out with a whip she had brought with her. She had chained herself to her seat and was dragged out only after a violent struggle in which 'respectable' gentlemen assaulted 'respectable' women. A restless society, indeed.

Sir Edward Carson was a Protestant lawyer from Southern Ireland. He organised the Ulster Protestants in their opposition to Home Rule and helped to arm a Protestant army which was ready to fight against the government if Home Rule was passed.

become law in August 1914. The Conservatives led by Bonar Law and the Ulster Protestants, led by Sir Edward Carson, were not willing to accept this. They prepared to make Civil War on the Liberal government. Protestant officers in the British Army decided that they would not march into battle against their 'kith and kin' in Ulster. The Liberals were faced with a double danger of having to fight in Ulster without the backing of their own army.

There was little comfort for the Liberals in all this as they faced the prospect of a civil war in Ulster, a militant *suffragette movement*, hostile workers in militant trade unions, and continued splits in their own ranks over the issue of social reform. The onset of the war in 1914 healed the breach between Ulster and the Liberals, at least for a time, but as we shall see it widened the splits in the Liberal Party which had been the party of self-help and had tried to become the party of social reform.

Documents

a) Against Old Age Pensions, 1908

Sir,

The strength of this kingdom, in all its past struggles, has been its great reserve of wealth and the sturdy independent character of its people. The measure will destroy both. It will extort the wealth from its possessors by unjust taxation and will sap the character of the people by teaching them to rely, not on their own exertions, but on the State.

(C. H. T. Crosthwaite, letter to the 'Times' 3 July 1908)

b) Divided Liberalism, 1911

Sir,

Mr Lloyd George while he poses as a Liberal is at heart a Socialist.

It was precisely against the danger of such a bureaucracy as is now growing under Mr Lloyd George that the voice of the guide of the Liberal Party 50 years ago was raised in solemn warning. If John Stuart Mill was alive today and could see the things that are being wrought in the name of Liberalism he would assuredly think that the force of irony could go no further.

('A Liberal of the Old School', in a letter to the 'Times', December 1911)

c) Radical Liberalism 1906

Liberalism supplies at one the highest impulse and the practicable path. By sentiments of generosity and humanity, by the process of moderation Liberalism enlists on the side of progress hundreds of thousands whom a militant Socialist party would drive into violent Tory reaction. It is through the agency of the Liberal Party alone that Society will in the course of time slide forward almost painlessly – for the world is changing very fast – on to a more even and a more equal foundation. This is the mission of the Liberal party. Our cause is the cause of the left out millions. We are all agreed that the State must concern itself with the care of the sick, of the aged, and, above all, of the children. I do not want to limit the vigour of competition, but to mitigate the consequences of failure.

(Winston Churchill, from a speech in 1906)

THE DAWN OF HOPE.

Mr. LLOYD GEORGE'S National Health Insurance Bill provides for the insurance of the Worker in case of Sickness.

Support the Liberal Government
in their policy of
SOCIAL REFORM.

d) The dawn of hope. Lloyd George's Insurance Bill, 1911

3 *Do you agree that increased state aid – to the old, young, unemployed etc, 'will sap the character of the nation'? How has the government helped you to enjoy a better life than was led by the majority of people in 1900?*

4 *Why did 'A Liberal of the Old School' call Lloyd George a Socialist? Would Winston Churchill have accepted this as a description of his closest colleague?*

5 *Why did Churchill believe that Liberalism was the best way to prevent the spread of Socialism? Would the Old Liberal have agreed? What does this tell you about the nature of the Liberal Party between 1906 and 1914?*

6 *Write a letter which an Old Age Pensioner might have written after receiving the first payment in January 1909.*

7 *Make a collage of headlines which might have appeared in newspapers carrying stories based on the three documents.*

8 *Look at Document (d). What did Lloyd George promise the people who were (i) sick or (ii) unemployed? Make a list of the ways in which the modern National Health Service differs from Lloyd George's National Health Insurance Scheme. Why did the 1911 Act lead to an increase in taxation?*

1 *Income tax had to be raised to pay for the social reforms including the payment of the Old Age Pensions. Which class argued that this was 'unfair taxation'? How did they show their anger in 1909 and 1910? Who would have welcomed the Old Age Pensions?*

2 *In Lark Rise the novelist Flora Thompson says that 'people cried in gratitude' on receiving their first Pension payment of 25p. What does this tell you about their standard of living?*

Extract

Tackling unemployment

The compulsorily insured trades were building, construction of works, shipbuilding, mechanical engineering, ironfounding, construction of vehicles and sawmilling. Every workman in those trades had to have an 'unemployment book'. To this book the employer had for each week of employment to affix a 5d (2p) insurance stamp, and was entitled to deduct half the value that is $2\frac{1}{2}d$ (1p) from the workman's wages. The benefit was 7 shillings (35p) a week up to a maximum of fifteen weeks in a year. The workman obtained his unemployment book from an Exchange. He claimed and received benefit there; he proved his unemployment and his capacity to work by signing an unemployed register there in working hours daily. The contributions were paid into, and the benefits taken from, an unemployment fund which was meant to be self-supporting. If the fund became exhausted, it could obtain a loan from the Treasury.

(W. H. Beveridge, *Unemployment*, 1909)

Questions on Chapter Seventeen

1 *How did Gladstone differ from (i) Chamberlain on Free Trade, (ii) Lloyd George on social reform?*

2 *Name five people, events or societies which helped to persuade the Liberals to undertake social reform after 1906.*

3 *Write a letter from a seamstress who has read about the Trade Boards Act, 1909.*

4 *Name four social reforms which led to an increase in taxation. Which political party (i) opposed this increase, (ii) supported it, (iii) wanted even larger increases?*

5 *The 1911 Insurance Act has been called 'a small step forward'. Make a list of the ways in which Part I (on Health) did not help the insured worker and his family. Make a similar list of the ways in which Part II (on Unemployment) did not help the insured worker and his family.*

6 *Give three reasons for the passing of the Parliament Act 1911, showing how three different political parties had their own interests in limiting the power of the Lords.*

7 *Make a collage of headlines which might have appeared above articles dealing with (i) the School Meals Act, (ii) the Old Age Pensions Act.*

Chapter 18

Women's search for freedom

Men's opinion of women, 1850

Today we are used to women doing many different jobs; even schoolgirls are allowed to vote. Victorian men had a very low opinion of women, thinking that they were inferior to men and that their only job was to be a wife and a mother.

Middle class Victorian women

Most Victorian mothers, like their mothers and grandmothers before them, had large families. In the early nineteenth century, most children had died before reaching the age of five. Things improved as the century progressed and it was quite common for the Victorian family to have seven or eight children surviving the dangers of early childhood. In middle class homes bringing up a large family was made easier by the employment of a large number of servants. By 1900 there were over one million domestic servants working and living in the homes of the well-to-do. To help the lady of the Victorian house, Mrs Beeton had written her *Book of Household Management*.

Working class Victorian women

For many women in the working class life was much harder. Their husbands were often lowly paid and frequently unemployed. Many working class mothers were forced to try to earn a little money, doing whatever jobs they could get.

There had been a number of Factory Acts since the 1830s

A middle class family at home in Norwood, London 1900. The dominant position of the husband and father is a reflection of the opinion on the Victorian novelist, Thackeray, who wrote (on women):

* An exquisite slave; a humble, flattering tea-making, pianoforte-playing being, who laughs at our jokes, however old they may be; coaxes us and fondly lies to us throughout life.

and it was forbidden to employ women in coal mines or to work them for more than ten hours a day in textile mills. There was nothing to stop employers in brickyards, engineering works, iron foundries or steelworks from employing women for long hours at hard, dangerous, dirty and poorly-paid jobs. In the large cities there was an ever increasing demand for women to work in sweat shops to make the clothes for the richer middle class women.

The wives of the more prosperous and skilled workers thought that they had made a step forward when they no longer had to go to work. Their well-paid husbands earned enough and there was no need for the mother to go to work. She was free, or emancipated, from the slavery of the factory bench or the sweat shop.

Emancipation

Some books suggest that the demand for Votes for Women was the only, or at least the main, demand by women looking for emancipation (or freedom). In fact, women wanted freedom to have the same sort of education as their brothers had. They wanted freedom to get the same sorts of jobs and the same wages as the men got. They wanted to be really free, not only to vote. In 1882 Parliament passed an Act which allowed married women to own property. Before that date any property she may have had by inheritance or gift or by her own earnings, became the property of her husband. Women were, it seems, incapable of looking after property.

Rebels against male society

Young girls from all classes were supposed to prepare themselves for marriage. This was seen as the natural role for all women. But 25 per cent of Victorian women simply could

13 March 1970. Susan Wallace, who was eighteen on 10 February 1970 made history as Britain's first schoolgirl voter in a by-election at Bridgwater in Somerset. She may be taken as the living proof of the stupidity of the Victorians who agreed with an eminent scientist, Huxley, who said in 1850:

* In every excellent characteristic, whether mental or physical, the average women is inferior to the average man. Even in physical beauty the man is superior.

Women at work in a pen-grinding factory. There was no chance for the working class girl to develop 'idle hands'.

A *Punch* cartoon of 1863, 'The Haunted Lady or the Ghost in the Looking-glass'. The owner of the shop (left) is saying to the rich lady, 'We would not have disappointed your Ladyship at any sacrifice, and the robe is beautifully finished'. Sweated labour among dressmakers was common. *Punch* sarcastically noted:

* There are no slaves in England, of dear no, certainly not. It is true we make our milliners work fifteen hours a day and twenty-four upon emergencies, but then of course you know their labour is quite voluntary.

PUNCH, OR THE LONDON CHARIVARI.—JULY 4, 1863.

THE HAUNTED LADY, OR "THE GHOST" IN THE LOOKING-GLASS.

not get married, because there were more women than men. A number of men emigrated each year. Others died in one or other of the many Colonial Wars. Still others simply did not want to get married. What was to happen to the women who could not get married? Some middle class spinsters took jobs as governesses at less than 1p an hour. Others learned to sew, knit, paint, play the piano and lead an idle life.

There were a few women who decided to break this tradition that middle class women either got married or led a useless sort of existence.

Punch's view of an art class, showing middle class girls learning a 'useful' pastime. In 1913 a leading suffragette recalled:

* I myself was one of that numerous gang of upper class leisured class spinsters, unemployed, unpropertied, unendowed, uneducated, without equipment or training for public service. Posts are barred to them in nearly all professions, in even those few they are allowed to enter. Posts of Government are exclusively for men. They are for the most part dependents from childhood to the grave.
(Lady C. Lytton, *Prison and Prisoners* 1913)

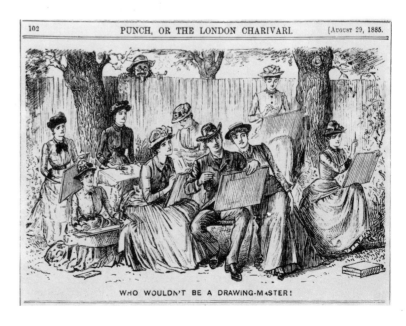

102   PUNCH, OR THE LONDON CHARIVARI.   [August 29, 1885.

WHO WOULDN'T BE A DRAWING-MASTER!

Education

In 1850 Miss Buss founded the North London Collegiate School. In 1858 Miss Beale founded Cheltenham Ladies College. In schools such as these, the girls were taught by women who believed that they should have the same sort of education as their middle class brothers had. Here the girls were prepared for Civil Service examinations, for entrance into business, the Universities or one of the learned professions.

It was only the progressive-minded father who was willing to pay for his daughters to go to one of these fee-paying secondary schools. Most parents were reluctant to 'waste' their money in this way.

The gymnasium of the North London Collegiate School for Girls. Many parents were reluctant to spend money on their daughters' education. One well-educated man remembered:

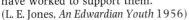

* We were a family of six, two girls and four boys. My father had no hesitation in spending a wholly disproportionate amount upon myself. My next brother went to St Andrews and eventually to Cambridge, but with no margin to buy, from time to time, a little jam to spread upon his bread and butter. But next to nothing was ever spent upon his girls. They were neither educated to support themselves, nor given opportunities of meeting young men who might have worked to support them.
(L. E. Jones, *An Edwardian Youth* 1956)

The first woman doctor

In the 1850s Florence Nightingale had been called in by her friend Sidney Herbert to help organise hospitals in the Crimea. On her triumphant return to Britain after the Crimean War, the 'Lady with the Lamp' used her influence and money to set up the Nightingale School for Nurses (1860). This established nursing as a respectable profession into which well-educated and 'genteel' ladies could enter. (p. 123).

But British medical schools refused to allow women to become medical students trying to qualify as doctors. The first Englishwoman to become a doctor was Elizabeth Blackwell, but she had gone to the U.S.A. for her education. In 1859 she lectured in England and inspired Elizabeth Garrett (who became Garrett-Anderson after her marriage) to try to become a doctor. Miss Garrett was allowed to attend lectures at the Middlesex Hospital, and it seemed that she might be the first woman to qualify in England. However, the male students protested and Miss Garrett was forced to leave. She finally qualified in Paris.

When she returned to Britain she founded the Elizabeth Garrett-Anderson Hospital where all the staff were women and where women students could train to become doctors. In 1876 the government passed a law which allowed medical schools to admit women as students. By the 1890s a number of women had qualified as doctors, although most male doctors, and patients of both sexes, were suspicious of them.

University education

The secondary schools founded by Miss Buss, Miss Beale and other reformers provided the basic education needed by girls who wanted to become medical students or nurses. Miss Emily Davies carried the education struggle several stages further. She was a great friend of Dr Garrett-Anderson and of Mrs Fawcett who was to become a leader in the demand for 'Votes for Women'. Miss Davies persuaded the Universities to allow girls to take the same school examinations as boys were already taking. In 1865 Cambridge allowed girls to take what we now call 'O' level. Other Universities followed this example soon afterwards.

Miss Davies also tried to persuade the Universities to let girls enter as ordinary students. London refused. So Miss Davies opened her own Hitchin College with six students who were taught by male lecturers from nearby Cambridge University. This College was soon moved to Girton at Cambridge, the first of the women's colleges at our universities. Newham College, Cambridge, was founded shortly afterwards and in the 1870s London finally agreed to allow women to enter as students.

A demonstration against the admission of women to the University of Cambridge, 1897. The middle-class males then at the University shared their parents' opinions that 'there is no place for you maids'. In 1860 male students at the Middlesex Hospital, London had also opposed the admission of Miss Garrett as a medical student.

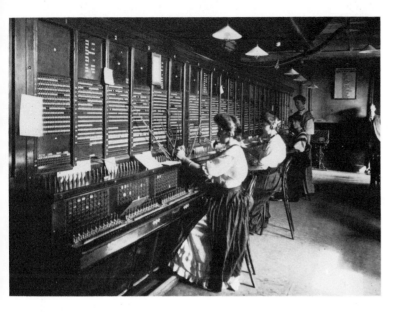

A telephone switchboard, 1900. Job opportunities for middle class girls were provided by technological developments such as the telephone and the typewriter.

Educated middle class girls

These schools and university colleges, and the professions of nursing and medicine were open only to the daughters of rich middle class families who could afford to pay the fees. And not all the educated girls could become doctors, even if all of them had wanted to do so. What were they to do after leaving school, or, for some of them, university? The freedom of the less rich middle class educated girl was increased towards the end of the nineteenth century by a number of technological developments. The telephone called for the employment of switchboard operators, supervisors and the like. The typewriter allowed the employment of women in business and government offices. Here they replaced the older male clerks who had written everything by hand in bulky ledgers. The newer firms (such as that started by Lord Leverhulme) with national outlets for their products, set up large administrative offices. Women were employed in a variety of jobs in these commercial centres. The opening of the large departmental stores, such as Selfridge's in London, or Bentall's in Kingston, allowed many women to take jobs as buyers, supervisors or saleswomen.

Votes for women

And so by the end of the nineteenth century middle class women had begun to take important steps along the road to freedom and equality. But they were still regarded as second-class citizens by most men. One obvious sign of this lower status was that women were not allowed to vote in parliamentary elections. They could vote in elections for local councils and for school boards. They could sit as members of school boards

Emily Davison threw herself beneath the feet of the King's horses at the Epsom Derby in 1913. This was her violent method of drawing attention to women's demands for equality. The *Times* reported:

* The woman rushed from the rails onto the course as the horses swept round Tattenham Corner. She did not interfere with the racing but she nearly killed the jockey as well as herself and she brought down a valuable horse. A deed of this kind, we need hardly say, is hardly likely to increase the popularity of the cause.
(5 June 1913)

and as Guardians of the Poor. But they were not allowed to vote in parliamentary elections. In this they suffered along with over half the men in the country because the voting qualification was that one had to be an adult male householder. Men over twenty-one, who lived at home with parents and men living in cheap, rented lodgings or in blocks of flats, did not qualify for the vote.

In the 1860s a number of local committees had been formed throughout the country to organise demands for 'Votes for Women'. In 1897, Millicent Fawcett linked these committees together to form the National Union of Women's Suffrage Societies (NUWSS). She hoped to persuade male politicians to give women a vote on the same terms as men. By 1903 some women had become dissatisfied with peaceful persuasion. Mrs Emmeline Pankhurst formed the Women's Social and Political Union (WSPU). This organisation decided to take more violent action in pursuit of their claim for the vote. In this they were in tune with the violent period in which they lived (Chapter 17). One of their tactics was to interrupt public meetings by heckling the speakers. The result was that they were usually thrown out of the meeting with great force.

Cat and Mouse

Accounts left by Mrs Pankhurst and her colleagues of the way in which they began their campaign and of men's violent reaction to their heckling gives us some idea of the impact of the *suffragettes* campaign. Women hecklers were whipped, arrested and sent to prison. Here they were joined by

A suffragette wrote about her own suffering while being forcibly fed:

* They push a tube up the nostril which goes wriggling down into the stomach, then there's a funnel on the end of the tube they pour the water − pour the food in, you see. And all the time they were pushing this bally tube down, I kept up coughing, coughing and coughing incessantly. In almost no time intense pains, not little bits of ones, but intense pain came all round my chest and it was almost impossible to breathe. I didn't know what was the matter, but I was glad. I should think that if you should ask what was the best time, I should think that was the best time when I realised that it didn't look as if they would be able to keep me in for months as they had some people. Well, I didn't know what was the matter, but I understood it was double pneumonia and pleurisy, due to food getting into the lung . . . But when I got out I sent a postcard to my parents on which I wrote 'Out, double pneumonia and pleurisy but quite all right'.
(Lilian Lenton quoted in Mrs E. Pankhurst, *My Own Story* 1914)

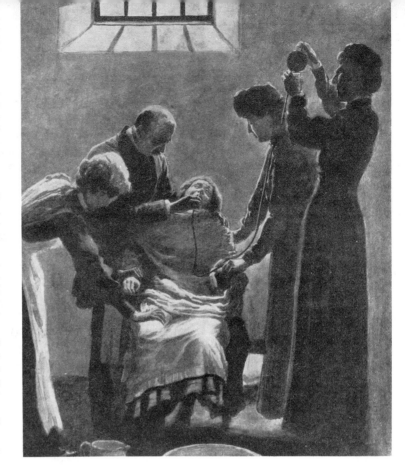

other suffragettes who had been found guilty of chaining themselves to railings in Downing Street or at Buckingham Palace, or women who had smashed every window in the new department stores in Oxford Street.

In prison some women tried to draw attention to their campaign by going on hunger strike. The prison authorities, with the approval of the Liberal government, decided to feed these demonstrators forcibly so that no one would die in prison. This led to a public outcry and to the passing of the 'Cat and Mouse' Act. Under the terms of this Act a hunger striker could be released only to be rearrested whenever the authorities felt it was convenient.

War 1914
The militant campaign by women, like the threat of civil war in Ulster, was called off in August 1914 when Britain declared war on Germany. Mrs Pankhurst changed her cry to 'the right to serve' and by 1918 over a million women had worked in munitions factories, on farms, or had served in the Armed Forces.

Documents

a) Why did women want the vote?

The demand of the women for the vote is fundamentally different from the demand of the man for the extension of the franchise to himself. His protest is against a discrimination between those who own much and those who own little. His manhood is not insulted by the discrimination; he is only injured as an individual or as a member of a class. But the woman's claim springs from deeper sources. It is not political, but elemental. She claims the vote, not as an instrument merely, though it is that too, but as a flag – the flag of her freedom from the sex-subjection of the past. The vote to her is what the removal of the bandages from the feet is to the Chinese woman. It is not only a release from physical or political restraints; it is a symbol of spiritual emancipation.

(A. G. Gardiner, *Pillars of Society* 1913)

b) The Liberals versus the Suffragettes, 1913

The activities of the militant Suffragettes had now (1913) reached the stage at which nothing was safe from their attacks. Churches were burnt, public buildings and private residences were destroyed, bombs were exploded, the police and individuals were assaulted, meetings broken up, and every imaginable device resorted to in order to inconvenience or annoy His Majesty's lieges. When any offenders were caught and convicted they were sent to prison; but as they generally resorted to a hunger strike and as there was a feeling against allowing the law to take its course, which would have resulted in death, they were released and immediately repeated their former offences. A Bill was introduced, called the Prisoners' Temporary Release Bill, soon nicknamed the 'Cat and Mouse Bill', the purport of which was to permit the release of offenders on licence, with a provision that in the event of a subsequent offence being committed the licence should be cancelled and the offenders re-arrested.

(Viscount Ullswater, *A Speaker's Commentaries* 1925)

1 Name two societies seeking 'Votes for Women'. Why did they hope for more from the Liberals than from the Conservatives? How does this expectation help to explain the violence after 1906?

2 What were the qualifications for the franchise (or right to vote) (i) after the Reform Act 1832 and (ii) after the Reform Act 1867? Find out what percentage of adult males received the vote for the first time in 1918.

3 When can people use their right to vote? Do you think that this right is (i) important (ii) more important than the right to get the same wages as men for doing the same job? What does the author of Document (a) mean by describing women's campaign for the right to vote as 'a symbol of emancipation'?

4 Name two leaders of the militant suffragettes. Name two politicians against whom they campaigned after 1906. Do you think that the women achieved anything by this violent campaign?

5 Why did the government decide that women prisoners on hunger strike would have to be forcibly fed? Why did this lead the government to pass the 'Cat and Mouse' Act?

6 Make a collage of headlines which might have appeared above articles dealing with (i) the arrest of Mrs Pankhurst, (ii) the announcement of the decision on forcible feeding, (iii) the interruption of Sir Henry Campbell-Bannerman's speech. (Opposite.)

THE RIGHT DISHONOURABLE DOUBLE-FACE ASQUITH.

VOTES FOR WOMEN

Women's Social and Political Union. 4, Clement's Inn, London, W.C.

Citizen Asq–th: "Down with privilege of birth—up with Democratic rule!" | *Monseigneur Asq–th:* "The rights of government belong to the aristocrats by birth—men. No liberty or equality for women!"

c) Double faced Asquith versus women's suffrage

1 Explain why Asquith was involved in a struggle with the House of Lords after 1919. Which political parties thought that this struggle was a sign of political progress? Which party thought that Asquith was too radical?

2 Why did the artist show the woman in a convict's uniform? Why, according to the government, were the women in gaol? Why, according to the women, were they there?

3 Why did the women think that Asquith was 'double-faced'?

4 Who was the founder of the WSPU? Why did this Union adopt more violent methods than those used by other campaigners for women's suffrage?

Extract

A suffragette demonstration

We did not begin to fight, however, until we had given the new (Liberal) Government every chance to give us the pledge we wanted. On December 21 (1905) a great meeting was held in Royal Albert Hall, London, where Sir Henry surrounded by his cabinet, made his first utterance as Prime Minister. Previous to the meeting we wrote to Sir Henry and asked him, in the name of the Women's Social and Political Union, whether the Liberal Government would give women the vote. We added that our representatives would be present at the meeting, and we hoped that the Prime Minister would publicly answer the question. Otherwise we would be obliged publicly to protest against his silence.

Of course Sir Henry Campbell-Bannerman returned no reply, nor did his speech contain any allusion to women's suffrage. So, at the conclusion, Annie Kenney, whom we had smuggled into the hall in disguise, whipped out her little white calico banner, and called out in her clear, sweet voice: 'Will the Liberal Government give women the vote?'

At the same time Theresa Billington let drop from a seat directly above the platform a huge banner with the words: 'Will the Liberal Government give justice to working-women?' Just for a moment there was a gasping silence, the people waiting to see what the Cabinet Ministers would do. They did nothing. Then, in the midst of uproar and conflicting shouts, the women were seized and flung out of the hall.

(Mrs E. Pankhurst, *My Own Story* 1914)

Questions on Chapter Eighteen

1 *Find out more about the career of Florence Nightingale between 1850 and 1860. Was her work (for nursing) of importance only to middle class girls in Victorian Britain?*

2 *Find out more about the work of Miss Buss and Miss Beale. Do you consider that their work for women's education was more or less important than Mrs Pankhurst's work for women's suffrage?*

3 *Find out more about the careers of (i) Dr Elizabeth Blackwell, (ii) Elizabeth Garrett Anderson. Show how both of them contributed to women's struggle to become qualified doctors.*

4 *Arrange a debate between someone who supports Thackeray's view of women and someone who supports Mrs Pankhurst's views.*

5 *Write a letter from a suffragette imprisoned in 1912.*

6 *Make a collage of headlines which might have appeared above articles dealing with (i) Elizabeth Garrett's attempts to become a student at the Middlesex Hospital, (ii) the passing of the Married Women's Property Act, 1882, (iii) the death of Emily Davidson, (iv) the window-smashing campaign of 1 March 1909.*

Unit Five

The Workshop of the World in depression 1914–39

The soldiers on the Western Front suffered from the stupidity of their generals ('Lions led by donkeys') and from the dirt, rain and mud of which an Englishman wrote:

* The mud makes it all but impassable. Sunk in it up to the knees, I have the momentary terror of never being able to pull myself out. Such horror gives frenzied energy, and I tear my legs free and go on.

For their suffering they were promised 'Homes fit for heroes'

It has been said by many historians that the nineteenth century came to an end with the First World War (1914–18). In this war – the most destructive that the world had seen – about 700,000 British soldiers, sailors or airmen were killed and nearly 2,000,000 were seriously wounded. Many of the wounded were never fit to work again. The war also destroyed that sense of security that was a mark of Victorian and Edwardian Britain, and that confidence that the world was going to go on getting to be a better place than it had been in the past. The mood at the time was expressed by the Foreign Secretary, Sir Edward Grey, when he said 'The lamps are going out all over Europe, we shall not see them lit again in our lifetime'.

The first non-stop Transatlantic flight was made by two former RAF flyers, John Alcock and Arthur Whitten-Brown. They left Newfoundland on 21 June 1919 in a Vickers-Vimy bomber. Their flight lasted 15 hours and 57 minutes before they crash-landed in a bog in Co. Galway, Ireland. Their flight was one symbol of the new age which had its dawn sometime during the First World War.

One effect of this war was that Britain's industrial decline was accelerated (Chapter 20). The war was one of the causes for the onset of the depressed years of mass unemployment. But the war also increased working class people's awareness of their dignity, power, and right to a share in the good life. They had begun to develop this awareness in the late nineteenth century (Chapter 18) but the war helped to develop it. This more confident working class resented middle class attempts to cut back on their living standards. Eventually this led to the General Strike (Chapter 20).

But the period 1919–39 was not one of total depression and gloom. It was also a period in which many new industries developed. Millions of well-paid workmen whose families enjoyed a long period of great prosperity were employed by these industries (Chapter 21). The government had got used to spending vast sums of money during the war. After the war it continued to spend more money than the Liberals had ever dreamt of spending, and so the Welfare State developed (Chapter 22).

Among the new science-based industries which developed in this period (1919–39) were electrical engineering, chemicals, oils, plastics and among the most important, the motor car (Chapter 21). This was one of the new methods of communication which, along with radio, the aeroplane and the vastly expanded national press, helped to make the British people more knowledgeable and better educated than their parents and grandparents had been.

Chapter 19

Social and economic effects of the First World War

On 28 June 1914 the Austrian Archduke Franz Ferdinand, heir to the thrones of Austria-Hungary, was shot dead by a Serbian revolutionary. The Austro-Hungarian governments wanted to punish Serbia for this murder. Russia agreed to come to the defence of her Slavonic neighbour. This led Germany to come to the aid of her Austrian ally and declare war on Russia, and on France, Russia's ally. Britain was not involved in this European entanglement until Germany invaded Belgium on 3 August 1914. Britain demanded that German troops withdraw from Belgium. When they had not done so by midnight, Britain declared war on Germany.

A typical First World War recruiting poster. One veteran remembered:

* The great emotion was excitement. We had the largest, and the most powerful navy in the world; we had only a small army, about 100,000 men, but they were perfect soldiers. So the average person in Britain felt confident and in fact they said 'We're going to teach this old Kaiser Bill a lesson and pull him down a peg or two'. All the young people wanted to be in on it before it finished, and when they called for volunteers the recruiting officers were beseiged because they thought it would be over by Christmas.

Decline in exports

During the war British exporters were unable to send goods to foreign customers. Some then learned to make the goods for themselves and the Lancashire textile industry found it difficult to recapture lost markets after the war. Other customers had learned to use a substitute – and the increasing use of oil, electricity and gas meant that British coal would not be in such heavy demand after the war. More customers had gone to other suppliers. In this way Japan and the U.S.A. had captured many former British markets. So British exports slumped (Chapter 20). At the same time Britain still had to

An artist's impression of a 'dog-fight' between enemy aircraft. The top speed of these canvas-and-wood machines was about 60 mph. The pilots had few navigational aids – compasses could not withstand the shuddering movement.

import – food, raw materials and some manufactured goods – both during and after the war. Wartime demands for raw materials – copper, wool, timber and so on – sent their prices rocketing, which encouraged the producers to develop new sources of supply. But when the war ended prices dropped very sharply. (Between 1918 and 1925, for example, the price of wool fell by about half.) This meant that people like the Australian farmer, Rhodesian copper miner and Malayan rubber planter, had a sharp drop in their incomes. They could therefore afford to buy fewer goods from Britain.

War and progress

As a result of the war, however, there was progress in some directions. During the war governments poured money into armaments and research. Until 1905 the motor car had been a plaything for the very rich, who enjoyed travelling in the 'horseless carriage' that was hand-built at great expense. During the War, however, governments demanded lorries, buses, cars and tractors. Producers expanded their businesses. When the war ended they could turn out many more and much cheaper motor cars and engines.

Similar expansion took place in the aircraft industry. Bleriot had crossed the Channel in 1909, but few people had paid much attention to this new form of transport. During the war, however, many thousands of men became involved in designing, building, flying and maintaining the aeroplanes which poured out of the many factories set up to build the new war machine. After the war many of these aviation pioneers kept up their interest in flying (Chapter 23).

The chemical and petroleum industries also expanded during the war as did the food-processing industry. Indeed it has been said that without the development of the food-canning industry, the trench warfare of 1914–18 could never have been fought. How would the commanders have fed their millions of infantry without corned beef, and tins of plum and apple jam? When the war ended these were industries which poured out their products for use in peace-time, and gave employment to an increasing number of men and women (Chapter 21).

Government and Wartime industry

We have already seen that the government had begun to play a part in the nation's economic and social life before 1914 (Chapter 17). But during this War this interference took place in many more fields and at a greater pace.

By 1918 the government was running the nation's railway system. After the war it forced the hundred and

Women at work in a government-run munitions factory. Lloyd George wrote about these women:

* On 18 July 1915, they headed a great Women's War Pageant, in which thousands of women demonstrators marched for miles along London streets through rain and mud, escorting a deputation that waited on me, as Minister of Munitions, to express their welcome of the National Register, and to offer their services to help the country. While voicing the demand of the women to be permitted to take part in war work, Mrs Pankhurst also put in a plea for wage conditions which would safeguard their standard of living and prevent them from being sweated or exploited by manufacturers. In reply I gave a guarantee that they should have a fair minimum wage for time work and should receive for piece work the same rates as were paid for men. These conditions, sedulously enforced by the Ministry throughout the duration of the War, had a permanent effect upon the status of women workers in this country.
(D. Lloyd George, *War Memoirs* 1934)

forty pre-war railway companies to amalgamate into four gigantic companies.

The coal industry had been the property of about 3,000 owners in 1914. By 1918 the government had taken over this industry. The miners who had demanded the nationalisation of their industry in 1913 believed that they had achieved their object by 1918. However, they were to be disappointed. The government handed the industry back to the many owners in 1921.

The government also compelled steel and munitions companies to produce armaments at prices fixed by the government. It also forced shipbuilding companies to build the vessels required to fight the War.

After 1916 the government forced every man over the age of eighteen to join the forces (under the Conscription Act) or to work in one of the essential industries.

Food rationing

In 1918 the government controlled the nation's food supply and had set up a rationing system to ensure that everyone had a fair share of the scarce food. The usual rations each week were: 8 ounces of sugar; 5 ounces of butter and margarine; 4 ounces of jam; 2 ounces of tea; 8 ounces of bacon. Everyone had the same ration, everyone was subject to the Conscription Act. This helped to break down the class barriers which had been such a feature of pre-war Britain.

Lord Rhondda was a coal mine owner and a friend of his fellow-Welshman, Lloyd George. He was appointed to introduce a rationing system which was intended to provide 'fair shares for all'. Everyone was to receive the same amount of food. Here he is shown opening a communal kitchen in 1918.

Mobilisation of resources

Supporters of the old Liberal policy of 'laisser faire', and self-help, which had made Britain great in the nineteenth century, did not think the government should control major industries, or dictate to other industrialists. They opposed the conscription of the nation's men and women and the rationing of food.

Most people however, accepted that the stress of war forced the government to mobilise all the nation's resources in order to defeat the national enemy – Germany. But what when that war was over? Should the government throw away all its controls, disband its army of civil servants and hand back the nation's affairs again to self-helpers? Many people demanded that the nation's resources should be mobilised even in peacetime to make a 'war' on poverty, slum housing, sickness and other social evils. It is worth noting that the Ministries of Transport and Health were set up in 1918. This was a sign of the increasing role that the State was going to play in the nation's life, even in peacetime.

Taxation

When Lloyd George became Chancellor in 1908, income tax was $2\frac{1}{2}$p in the pound. The Liberal reforms after 1908 forced the government to increase this to 6p. You will remember

Lloyd George walking towards the hall at Versailles where the Peace Conference was being held in 1919. He had smashed the power of the House of Lords in 1911, had led the country to victory over the Germans but had also smashed the Liberal Party.

that this had caused the House of Lords to revolt (Chapter 17). However, during the War income tax was raised to over 30p as the government tried to get money to pay for the muni- it required to win that war.

No-one rebelled at this gigantic increase. By 1918 people had got used to paying this new, high proportion of their salaries, wages and profits to the government. The government had then used this money to wage war against Germany. But what about when the War ended? The government had got used to collecting and spending huge sums of money which taxpayers had got used to paying. After 1918 governments continued to collect and spend huge sums. Now they spent it, not on munitions but on an enlarged unemployment benefit system, new and better pension schemes, more and better welfare provisions for mothers and children (Chapter 22).

Political changes
The Liberal Party breaks up, 1914—18
The Liberals under Prime Minister Asquith were divided in July 1914 as to whether Britain had any part to play in the European War which had already broken out. It was the invasion of Belgium that convinced some of the waverers that Britain had to support Russia and France in their war

against Germany and Austria. However, some Liberals refused to support even this war, and resigned from the Liberal Party in August 1914. Asquith and the older Liberals hoped that the war could be fought and won with the minimum of government interference: 'Life as usual' was the slogan. But, as we have seen, the government was compelled to take over large sections of industry. This was too much for some other Liberals and they too resigned. Prime Minister Asquith was forced, in May 1915, to invite the Conservative Opposition to join him in a Coalition government in the hope that this would help the war effort. Lloyd George became Minister of Munitions and proved highly successful in getting industry to produce the materials required. In June 1916 Lord Kitchener (whose familiar face appeared on a recruiting poster saying 'Your country needs you') was drowned on a journey to Russia, and Lloyd George took his place as Secretary of State for War.

Lloyd George had been the Conservatives' main enemy in pre-war Britain (Chapter 17). But in 1916 he proved to be the leader of those who wanted to wage an all-out war. This meant conscription (compulsory recruitment into the services) and food rationing. Asquith was quite unwilling to take these un-Liberal steps. The Conservatives agreed to support Lloyd George and in December 1916 they forced Asquith to resign to make way for Lloyd George as Prime Minister.

About half the Liberals supported Asquith and resented his overthrow by Lloyd George. Their opposition continued until the Election of 1918 often called the Coupon Election, which followed the ending of the war in November.

The annihilation of the Asquithian Liberals in this election and the success of the Lloyd George Coalition gave the country a parliament composed – said Stanley Baldwin, a future Prime Minister – of 'hard-faced men who look as if they have done very well out of the war'.

Celebrating the end of the War in London, 11 November 1918.

Political changes
The Labour Party becomes stronger, 1914–18

The Labour Party had been split in 1914. Some of its members opposed British entry into the war. Keir Hardie was howled down at a meeting in Trafalgar Square in August 1914, when he asked the British people not to take part in 'the capitalists' war'. Ramsay MacDonald, another pacifist, lost his seat in 1918 Election. Other Labour members refused to obey the Conscription Act, 1916, and went to gaol as conscientious objectors.

But by 1918 many former Liberals had joined the small

Keir Hardie addressing an anti-war demonstration in Trafalgar Square, August 1914. The majority of Labour supporters backed the government in its decision to fight – and so help to provide additional work for millions of people. Hardie's pacifism split the Party for a time. However, this very pacifism won the respect and support of the many former Liberals who opposed the decision to go to war.

Labour Party – which seemed to offer them a more moral home than the Liberal Party led by the enthusiastic war leader, Lloyd George. Many young people, voting for the first time in 1918, refused to support the warmongers and voted Labour, so that the Party gained seats and became the second largest party in the House of Commons. Labour was now official Opposition to the Lloyd George Coalition government.

By 1918, many more people had joined trade unions. The Labour Party's funds grew. Many union leaders had been invited by the government to join wartime committees that had been set up at national and local level to help make the war machine work more smoothly. Their experience in consultation and administration gave them a new confidence and a taste for power. Their aim was to use that experience and power for the benefit of the working class after the war. Many people enjoyed a much better standard of living during the war than they had in 1913. They too, supported the Labour Party in the hope that they could maintain that improvement in peacetime.

Votes for Women, a cartoon in *Punch* January 1918.

Women

In 1913 women had been campaigning for the right to vote (Chapter 18). However, as soon as the war broke out they changed their demand. Lloyd George had opposed Mrs Pankhurst and her supporters in 1913. However, he praised their wartime efforts.

Women served in the forces, on the land, in munitions factories and in the enlarged civil services. They learned to supervise other workers and to enjoy a wage packet of their own. They became more confident and more demanding of equality than they had been in 1913. Women were among the main gainers from the First World War.

The right to vote

It is often forgotten that in 1913 only about half the men in the country had the right to vote. In 1918 there was a new Reform Act which extended the vote to all men and some of the women.

The Act of 1918 only gave the vote to women over the age of 30. Apparently a 30 year old woman was only as intelligent and capable as a 21 year old man. In 1928 another Act gave the vote to women aged 21. At last the suffragettes had their victory.

Documents

a) **Conscripts and medical examinations, 1916**

Of every nine men of military age in Great Britain, on the average three were perfect, fit and healthy, two were on a definitely inferior plane of health and strength, whether from some disability or some failure of development, three were incapable of undergoing more than a very moderate degree of physical exertion and could almost (in view of their age) be described with justice as physical wrecks; and the remaining man was a chronic invalid with a precarious hold on life.

(Report on conscription)

b) **Working class diet improves 1914–18**

We have found in the evidence of budgets of working-class expenditure that in June 1918 the working classes, as a whole, were in a position to purchase food of substantially the same nutritive value as in June 1914. Indeed, our figures indicate that the families of unskilled workmen were slightly better fed at the later date. This conclusion is more than confirmed by the reports we have obtained from the Medical Officers of the Education Authorities of the great cities. From London it is officially reported, after inspection of all the children entering school, that 'the percentage of children found in a poorly nourished condition is considerably less than half the percentage in 1913'. The general impression, especially of the poorer children is favourable, and the view that parents are now better able to give their children the necessary food is borne out by the information we have received as to the number of meals provided to 'necessitous children' by the local education authorities. The last available figures for England and Wales, those for 1917, compared with the estimated number of 1914, show a decline by about four-fifths in the country as a whole.

(Report on working class diet)

c) **A middle class woman on the War**

On one point, I should imagine every one will agree, that class distinctions have positively toppled down since the war; or rather, social barriers have been removed, not entirely by the upper classes becoming less exclusive, but much more by a general uplifting in the standard of living of the workers. Luxuries once enjoyed by the few are now regarded as ordinary expenditure by young people whose immediate antecedents were unaccustomed to any such amenities, and in the case of the same people their standard has gradually altered in the same way. Take, for example, the telephone, wireless, electric light, motorcars, 'pictures'. It might be said that these are all recent inventions brought into common use by the developments of science; but, unless the standard of living had been considerably raised, these would still have been considered great luxuries to be only used by the wealthier classes, and it is largely due

to the high wages paid for munitions during the war and to industrial workers in 1919–20 that luxuries have gradually come to be regarded as commonplace expenditure by the poorer classes.

(F. W. Hirst, *The Consequences of the War to Great Britain* 1934)

1 *What percentage of conscripts were (i) fit, (ii) of inferior health, (iii) physical wrecks, (iv) chronic invalids in 1917? Make block graphs to illustrate your answers.*

2 *Can you suggest why so many people were unfit in 1916?*

3 *Suggest some reasons why fewer people failed medical tests during the Second World War 1939–45.*

4 *What evidence is there that the middle class believed that the working class were enjoying a better life in post-war Britain than they had done in 1913? Look up the figures for income tax again. Why were the middle classes not enjoying as high a standard in 1920 as they had enjoyed in 1913?*

5 *Why were there fewer children 'poorly nourished' in 1917 than 1913?*

6 *Arrange a debate on 'War is an evil'.*

The Cleator Mill Strike Committee, 29 April 1915. During the First World War women workers were made aware for the first time of the power of their organized labour. The result was strikes such as the one organized by the women shown above.

Extracts

The 'coupon' election

To the country Mr Lloyd George and Mr Bonar Law and their Liberal and Unionist colleagues appealed as a *Coalition*. Liberals, on the other hand, entered the election with forces divided. A large number associated themselves with Mr Lloyd George. Others protested against the Prime Minister taking advantage of the national enthusiasm for an electoral purpose. Supporters of the Government received from their allied leaders a letter endorsing their candidature – a 'coupon' it was derisively called. Mr Asquith stood as a Liberal, 'without prefix or suffix'. Only a few of the Liberals 'without prefix or suffix' survived the contest. Mr Asquith and his lieutenants fell.

(A. Mackintosh, *From Gladstone to Lloyd George* 1919)

Lord Birkenhead's opinion of women's suffrage

Le me describe to your Lordships, how gradually, yet how inevitably, we descended the slippery slope. First of all it was not proposed that women should be included. Then a member of the House of Commons, and an important one, said that whoever was included or was not included, it was quite impossible to exclude from the franchise the brave men who had supported our cause in the field. That argument in the spirit of the moment was accepted with facile enthusiasm, and accordingly the soldiers were admitted, subject to the qualification of age and without reference to any other very rigorous examination. Then another member of the House arose and said: 'If you are extending the franchise to our brave soldiers in recognition of their valour on the field how about our brave munition workers?' That argument, too, was difficult to resist when once you had yielded to the first. Then an insidious and subtle member of the House said, 'How about our brave women munition workers?' And having once on principle yielded to the first argument, it was absolutely impossible to resist the second.

(Lord Birkenhead, formerly F. E. Smith, speaking in the House of Lords, 1928)

Questions on Chapter Nineteen

1 *In 1909 the House of Lords had thrown out the Budget. What was the level of income tax that Lloyd George proposed in that budget (Chapter 17)? What was the level of income tax in 1918? Why was there no revolt against this much higher level?*

2 *Write a paragraph on each of (i) the fall of Asquith, (ii) the Coupon Election, 1918.*

3 *Why was the Labour Party (i) split in 1914, (ii) more powerful in 1918?*

4 *'We demand the right to serve', said Mrs Pankhurst. Give three examples of ways in which women served during the war. How, do you think, did this experience affect the women involved?*

5 *'We expect something better after the War' said the Chairman of the TUC in 1917. How do you explain this rise in working class expectations? What might they do if their expectations were not realised?*

6 *Make a collage of headlines which might have appeared above articles dealing with (i) the declaration of war in 1914, (ii) voluntary recruitment for the forces, (iii) the Conscription Act, (iv) food rationing, (v) the fall of Asquith, (vi) the Coupon Election, (vii) the 1918 Reform Act.*

Chapter 20

Old industries – the General Strike and the Depression

During the 1920s and 1930s the level of unemployment was always depressingly high. There were rarely fewer than $1\frac{1}{2}$ million men out of work and often the figure was much higher than this – and we have to remember that during this period there were very few married women at work so that many families had no wage-earner in the house. We should also remember that there were very few immigrants coming into the country – so that the political extremists, such as Mosley's Fascists, had to look for other people to blame for Britain's depressed state. They chose to attack the Jews. The modern fascists, the National Front, try to put the blame for modern unemployment on the coloured immigrant. They are wrong, and so was Mosley. There were basic economic reasons for the high level of unemployment from which Britain suffered in the inter-war period.

Foreign competition

We have already seen that by the end of the nineteenth century Germany and the U.S.A. had become major competitors of once-dominant Britain (Chapter 15). We have also seen that the First World War encouraged the development of industries in many overseas countries. India and Hong Kong developed their own textile industries. Japan and the U.S.A. enlarged their industrial capacity and there was a declining demand for British goods (Chapter 19).

Joseph Chamberlain had seen many foreign goods entering the British market to compete with British produced goods. He had advocated a system of tariffs to exclude these goods. But Britain rejected his policy in 1906 and continued to be the world's only Free Trade country until 1932.

And while there were more countries producing coal, textiles and steel, there were more substitutes for these products. Rayon and artificial silk provided cheap and attractive alternatives for textiles. Oil and electricity provided more efficient forms of fuel than coal.

Prices

British prices were often much higher than prices charged by the foreign competitors. There were many reasons for this – the foreigners often used more efficient machinery and could produce goods more cheaply than could the more old-fashioned British firms. Polish and German coalmines were much more mechanised than were British mines.

In 1925 this situation was made worse when the Chancellor of the Exchequer, Winston Churchill, revalued the British pound, so that it was to be worth $4.86 as it had been in 1913. In fact, this rate of exchange overvalued the pound by about 10 per cent and the following example helps to illustrate the effects of this:

Price of British car *Price in U.S.A.*
£200   at $4.42 to £ (10% less) = $884
        at $4.86 to £ (10% more) = $972

It was harder to sell the British car in the U.S.A. at $972 than at $884.

Tariffs

Every country except Britain erected a wall of tariffs against imported goods — to help their own infant industries to develop, and to cut down on the volume of imports so that their own balance of payments might be healthy. These tariffs made the job of selling British goods more difficult.

The Wall Street Crash, 1929

Post-war American business boomed, and on the Wall Street *Stock Exchange* many people shared the growing profits. Others wanted to join in. They borrowed money from their banks to buy stocks and shares. This drove up the prices of the shares — and brought profits to those who had bought at a low price and sold at the higher price. It all came to an end when, in the autumn of 1929, the American banks asked for their money back. This forced people to sell their shares — but there were not enough buyers (since the banks refused

Outside the New York Stock Exchange, Wall Street, after the Great Crash of October 1929.

to lend money). This forced the prices down and ruined many people. (Someone who had borrowed to buy shares at, say, $100 each might have found in late 1929 that they could not sell the share for $1).

Hundreds of banks lost all their money – since their borowers could not repay their debts. These banks closed down and ruined many people who had deposited their savings in such 'safe banks'. Companies as well as individuals were ruined. This led to a depression in the formerly booming U.S.A. There was a fall in American demand for British goods. There was also a fall in American demand, for example, for Brazilian coffee. There was therefore a fall in Brazilian demand for British goods since Brazilians had less money to spend.

People sometimes suggest that the depression began with this Crash. But in March 1921 about 15 per cent of British workmen were unemployed and although there was some recovery in the 1920s, there were still about that percentage out of work in 1929 when the Crash took place. So it did not cause a depression. What it did was to deepen the existing depression so that 23 per cent of British workmen were out of work by August 1932, when about three million men were unemployed and they and their families (totalling about six or seven million people) lived on the dole.

Unemployment figures for 1928–36. Unemployment increased as world trade declined. With recovery in trade, unemployment also fell. During this period, the prices of raw materials fell by 56 per cent and of food by 48 per cent.

1 What was the level of unemployment in (i) April 1930, (ii) April 1931? When did the level of unemployment start to go down?

2 Which were the main industries in (i) Jarrow, (ii) Merthyr and (iii) Maryport? Why was there a very high level of unemployment in these towns?

3 Why was there a low level of unemployment in (i) Oxford and (ii) Coventry?

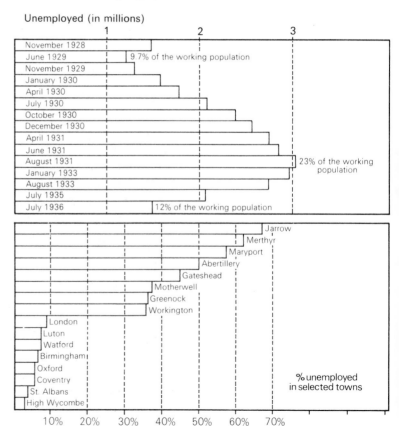

The 1931 British financial crisis

The Bank of England had been delighted with Mr Churchill's decision to go back to the 1913 rate of exchange. This was one step along the road which the Bank and the financiers of the City of London took to put Britain back again in the position she had occupied in the nineteenth century. During that century British merchants and industrialists dominated the world. They sold their goods everywhere, earning vast amounts of gold from foreign countries. Some of this they brought home and shared with their shareholders. Some of it, however, they loaned back to the foreign countries that were anxious to industrialise.

By the 1920s Britain was no longer earning these huge surpluses. She was barely earning enough (from selling goods) to pay for her imports. So the Bank of England and the City borrowed from foreign banks and then lent the money out to other overseas countries.

The advantage of this can be seen from this table:

Borrow from France, to whom the City pays 2% interest
Lend to India, whom the City charges   8% interest
                    Profit made by the City 6%

However, there was one major disadvantage. When an Indian industrialist borrowed from Britain he promised to repay the money over 20 years or more. This was a long term borrowing. But, when the British borrowed from foreign countries they promised to pay the money back whenever it was asked for. This was a short term debt.

Now after the Wall Street Crash foreign bankers became frightened of lending their gold. In particular they became worried about letting Britain have the money after 1929, when a Labour Government took over. Would Ramsay MacDonald and his Labour colleagues bring in some sort of communist legislation? Could Britain be trusted with foreigners' money?

In July 1931 these fears were brought to a head by the news that the Labour Government wanted to spend more than it intended to collect in taxation. On 25 August 1931 the Labour Government fell.

The General Strike

How could British manufacturers and industrialists make their goods more attractive to foreign buyers? They wanted to cut wages, but the post-war working class were less willing to accept such attacks on their living standards. The Trade Union Congress had created a General Council in 1920 which was responsible for organising union opposition to attempts to cut workers' wages. When the mine owners wanted to cut

Miners' Union leaders in 1926. The General Secretary, A. J. Cook (centre), was the man who thought up the slogan 'not a minute on the day, not a penny off the pay'. Herbert Smith, the Union President, was a very tough Yorkshireman.

miners' wages in 1925, the miners received the support of the General Council of the TUC which threatened to bring millions of workers out on strike if these cuts were ever to take place.

In 1925 the government intervened in this quarrel between miners and the owners by providing a subsidy to the industry so that wages could be maintained while discussions about the industry's future went on. The miners regarded this as a victory. The government set up the Samuel Commission which reported in March 1926 and recommended a cut in wages and an extra hour's work. The government subsidy was to end on 1 May 1926. Many trade unionists had been misled by their success in 1925, when they had forced the government to give a subsidy to the industry.

Meetings of owners and miners at the end of March ended in disagreement. Meetings between the General Council and the government in April did not break the deadlock and the General Council decided that it would call a General Strike of its members to support the miners if there was no settlement.

On Sunday 2 May, the talks between the government and the General Council broke down and on Monday 3 May the General Strike began. However, the government had made its preparations after its climb-down in 1925. Milk and other supplies were organised. Soldiers and sailors were brought in to run electricity generators and maintain the power supply. Volunteers from the middle classes ran a skeleton transport system.

The end of the Strike

The members of the General Council were caught in a trap. What did they hope to achieve? Was the TUC going to force the government to change its policy? If so, who in fact governed the country? Many members of the General Council were themselves politicians – such as Jimmy Thomas, leader of the National Union of Railwaymen and a future Labour Cabinet Minister. Most of the Council were strict believers in law and order, discipline and legality. After all, they depended on these things to help them govern their own unions. As the Strike went on through a week of anxious waiting, many members realised that they would have to climb down. The TUC met Herbert Samuel and together they drew up a memorandum of terms by which the Strike could be settled. There was to be a renewal of the subsidy and no cuts in miners' wages. But this memorandum was not a government document. The miners' leaders refused to accept it, but they were overruled by the majority of Council members, and the Strike was called off on 12 May.

The miners continued their strike until November. They were then forced to accept the owners' conditions – large wage cuts were made part of the price that had to be paid for the revaluation of the pound.

Keynes and the Depression

Owners, government, manufacturers and industrialists all believed that the solution to Britain's problems lay in cutting wages, getting Britain back to the gold standard and to the 'good old days' of Edwardian England.

Few people agreed with the opinions of a leading economist, J. M. Keynes. He wanted the government to spend

Unemployed men in a library reading room. Some went to look through the 'Situations Vacant' columns of the newspapers, in the hope that they might find a job. Others, who had given up hope, went to get in out of the cold. A London journalist interviewed some unemployed men in Merthyr in 1936:

＊I went first to the centre of relief, the public assistance offices. Three relieving officers deal with 1,000 cases a week. The insured population of this borough is not quite 21,000 and 60.6 per cent of it is unemployed. People told me with great sadness, of things they had seen in Merthyr. One spoke of a man lying asleep on the only bed in the only room he had; at his head stood a coffin in which the dead body of his child. He had nowhere else to put it before burial.
(Dudley Parker, The *Evening Standard*, 17 November 1936)

The cartoonist, Low, showing the Chancellor of the Exchequer, Neville Chamberlain, about to 'balance the budget'. In the dark suit, J. M. Keynes leads a group of economists who want the government to 'unbalance' the budget by spending more – on public works – than it collected in taxation. The government did not listen to these experts and so did little to create employment.

1 *The government (i) lowered the level of income tax and other taxes and (ii) cut its spending to keep a balance between its taxes and its spending. Why did this lead to more unemployment among firms in the housing and road building industries?*

2 *Keynes wanted the Chancellor to 'unbalance' the budget. Did he want (i) lower taxes and the same spending or (ii) the same taxes and higher spending? If the government spent more money than it collected in taxes how might it have spent the extra money? Why might this have led to an increase in employment?*

more money as a means of ending the Depression. He argued that when a family received a wage (or salary, or rent, or profit) they spent most of it. What they spent provided income for other people (in shops, factories and transport systems), eg.

Man put to work – earns £100; spends, say £75 ($\frac{3}{4}$ of his income)
Other people earn £75; they spend £56.25 ($\frac{3}{4}$ of their income)
so others earn £56.25 and spend £42.18

and so on. If you carry this example on you will find that the total spent will be £400. And all this from a government expenditure of only £100.

However, the government rejected Keynes' arguments.

Government action in face of the Depression

The political groups, Labour and Conservative as well as Coalition, believed that the government should spend only as much money as it could collect in taxes. By which was meant that the budget had to balance. They also believed that cuts in taxes were a good cure for Depression. They argued that when taxes were cut the lucky taxpayers would spend their money and so create work (as Keynes had proved). But the fact was that in times of depression the lucky taxpayers tended to save their money, not spend it, and so there was less employment.

And since the government collected less in taxes it also cut its spending on such things as roads, houses, bridges and schools. This meant lower incomes for people previously employed by the government and so even less employment for people who might have been given work by their spending. It was, in fact, Keynes in reverse.

In 1932 the government imposed a 10 per cent tariff on nearly all goods imported into the country, in the hope that this would help British industrialists. It was of no use to British exporters. And it was in Britain's export industries that the depression was severest and unemployment was the highest. While there was a general average of unemployment of 23 per cent in August 1932, the figures for some areas were much higher; Jarrow (67 per cent), Merthyr (62 per cent), Maryport (57 per cent) were among towns where there were fewer men at work than were unemployed. The areas which had depended on coal, iron and steel, shipbuilding, textiles, became 'depressed areas' with very high rates of unemployment.

In 1934 the government appointed two Commissioners, one for England and Wales and a second for Scotland. They were supposed to try to persuade industrialists to build new factories in the depressed areas. By 1937 they had had very little success. In that year the depressed areas were renamed as Special Areas — perhaps the change of name was supposed to bring a change in luck. It did not. Only the onset of the Second World War lifted the gloom that hung over Wales, Scotland, the North East and North West.

Palmer's Shipbuilding Yard was opened in 1851; by 1887 it was one of the biggest and most modern in the country. By 1920 it was employing over half the men in Jarrow but by 1932 the yard was at a standstill because there were no orders for new ships. In 1934 the owners of other shipyards bought Palmers and closed it down so that, when trade recovered, there would be less competition for shipbuilding orders. There was little chance of finding work in this town which, claimed its MP, Miss Ellen Wilkinson, 'had been murdered'.

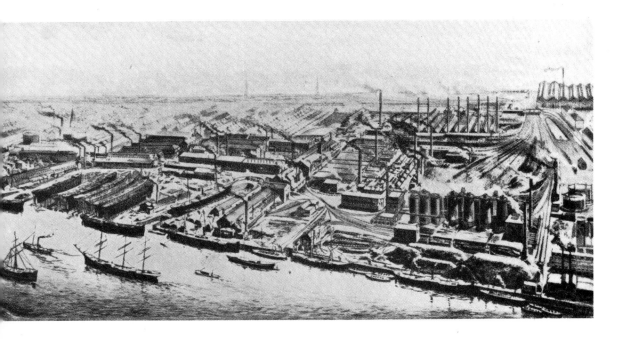

To draw public attention to their desperate situation, unemployed men from Jarrow marched to London where they hoped to see the Prime Minister and others who might have been able to help. Here they were lining up for a meal at Bedford.

1 *From which town had the marchers started out? What was the main industry in that town? Why was there a high level of unemployment there in 1935?*

2 *What did the marchers hope to do when they got to London? Suggest one developing industry which might have used the skills of these skilled workmen. Why were industrialists unwilling to build their new factories in depressed areas?*

Life for the unemployed

In Chapter 22 we will see how the government extended and improved the unemployment insurance scheme so that the families of the unemployed received some income. However, this was a poor substitute for work. Men who had once had a pride in their craft now went through year after year of unemployment. Many hundreds of thousands moved from the depressed areas to the more prosperous areas of the Midlands and the South East (Chapter 23). But millions stayed on in their old homes. Merthyr was once the centre of the world's iron and steel industry. In 1936 over 60 per cent of the men were unemployed.

The unemployed had little money and could only afford a small rent. This meant that they had to live in one or two rooms.

Furniture, clothing, jewellery and household goods such as the 'wireless' had to be pawned before people were able to claim their 'dole' from the Means Test authorities (see p. 232). In their slum homes, even more poorly furnished than they had been in the pre-war days, the unemployed existed on a very poor diet. Most of them gave up any hope or ever working again. However work was finally provided at the end of the 1930s by the need to build tanks, aircraft and ships as part of the re-armament policy. Money was found for this although no money had been found for the building of roads, schools and houses as Keynes had demanded.

On the way to the pawnshop. During the 1930s an increasing number of people were forced to use this method of getting the money needed to buy food.

One of the millions who stood, without hope, at street corners during the depressed 1930s.

213

Documents

a) Life on 'the dole' in the 1930s

The end of this month will make it two years since I worked last. During that period we lived (that is myself, wife and three children) first on 32 shillings a week and since on 29s 3d a week transitional payment.

On the latter scale the family budget works out like this:

	s	d
Rent	11	0
coal (1½ cwt)	2	9
gas (cooking and washing)	1	2
light (electric)	1	0
club subscription (boots, clothing, crockery, bed-clothing etc)	3	0
burial insurance		9
groceries (bread, tea, sugar etc)	6	6
	26	2
balance	3	1
	29	3

The balance has to provide bacon, eggs, milk, meat, cereal, greengroceries etc – in fact, has to buy everything that goes towards making a meal outside of bread, margarine, and a cup of tea, for a family of five all the week.

Just work it out. Multiply a family of five by three meals a day and by seven days a week. The result is 105 individual meals to be provided out of 37 pence! That is less than a halfpenny a meal. This means that we live mostly on tea and toast.

This diet has resulted in recurrent illness. The youngest child has had pneumonia three times since February of last year. She is now suffering from bronchitis, and according to the doctor, is probably developing TB.

The oldest child was in hospital last month with pneumonia. It was out one week and has now gone back again. I myself have only been signed off 'fit' today after an illness lasting a month.

The rent has been missed to meet the extra expenses that always crop up during sickness. And now a registered letter has come from the corporation with one week's notice to quit!

(from Fenner Brockway, *Hungry England*)

b) Surface appearances

The average income of a family on the dole normally averages round about thirty shillings a week. Enormous groups of people, probably at least a third of the whole population of the industrial areas are living at this level.

But they don't necessarily lower their standards by cutting out luxuries and concentrating on necessities; more often it is the other way round. Hence the fact that in a decade of unparalleled depression the consumption of all cheap luxuries has increased. The two things that have probably made the greatest difference of all are the movies and the production of cheap, smart clothes since the war. The youth who leaves school at fourteen and gets a blind-alley job is out of work at twenty, probably for life; but for two pounds ten (£2.50) on the hire purchase system he can buy himself a suit which, for a while and at a little distance, looks as though it had been tailored in Savile Row. The girl can look like a fashion plate at an even lower price. You may have threehalfpence in your pocket and not a prospect in the world, and only the corner of a leaky bedroom to go home to, but in your new clothes you can stand on the street corner, indulging in a private daydream of yourself as Clark Gable or Greta Garbo, which compensates you for a great deal.

You can't get much meat for threepence, but you can get a lot of fish and chips. It is quite likely that fish and chips, art-silk stockings, tinned salmon, cut-price chocolate (five ounce bars for sixpence), the movies, the radio, strong tea and the football pools have between them averted revolution.

(George Orwell, *The Road to Wigan Pier* 1937)

1 *What proportion of the population lived on 'about thirty shillings a week'?*

2 *Why was there a high rate of sickness among the unemployed and their families?*

3 *Look around your town for cinemas built in the 1930s. Make a list of their names. Why did cinema owners give them such glamorous names?*

4 *Who were Clark Gable and Greta Garbo? Why did young people dream of being like them?*

5 *Write a letter from a child in the family where the father is unemployed.*

6 *What evidence is there in these Documents that the years of depression were also years of falling prices. How did this affect (i) people in countries which sold us cotton or chocolate, (ii) British firms trying to sell goods in the countries, (iii) the unemployed, (iv) people in Britain who had a job and a steady wage?*

DISTRESSED AREAS

In 1938 the government's re-armament policy provided some job-opportunities for men who had not worked for, in some cases, ten years.

1 *Why was the British government buying more tanks, aircraft and guns in 1938 than it had done in 1932?*

2 *Why did increased spending on weapons lead to increased employment in the coal, steel and shipbuilding industries? Choose three towns named on p. 206 which benefited from the government's arms spending.*

3 *The government spent more money on arms without putting up taxes. Who had asked governments to do this earlier in the 1930s? On what sorts of things did he want the government to spend money? Why were governments willing to spend money on guns and not houses?*

Questions on Chapter Twenty

1 *Make a list of the reasons why there was less British coal sold in 1935 than in 1913.*

2 *Write a paragraph on the effect of the revaluation of the pound in 1925. Can you work out the effects of a devaluation of the pound (which makes it worth fewer dollars and cents than it had been)?*

3 *Why did the Wall Street Crash lead to unemployment in Britain?*

4 *Write a letter from a foreign banker who wants to get his gold back from the Bank of England in 1931. (Why had he allowed the Bank to borrow his money? Why was he anxious to have it back?)*

5 *Why did the TUC General Council (i) support the coal miners in their opposition to demands for wage cuts, (ii) hope that they might win the battle with the government in April 1926, (iii) call off the General Strike on 12 May 1926?*

6 *How might a policy of slum clearance have helped to lower the level of unemployment? Why did the government do very little extra spending in the 1920s and 1930s?*

Extract

A striker talks

Next May we shall be faced with the greatest crisis and the greatest struggle we have ever known, and we are preparing for it. I don't care a hang for any government, or army or navy. They can come along with their bayonets. Bayonets don't cut coal. We have already beaten, not only the employers, but the strongest government in modern times.

(quoted in W. H. Crook, *The General Strike* 1931)

Chapter 21 New industries and a rising standard of living

New industries

Coal, iron and steel, textiles and shipbuilding – the industries which had once made Britain 'the Workshop of the World' – declined after 1919. Unemployment and depression affected the areas which depended on them (Wales, Scotland, the North-West and North-East). There were, however, other areas and other industries which were booming during the 1920s and 1930s.

In 1920 there were about 200,000 cars on the roads of Britain; by 1939 there were over 2,000,000. Most of these new cars were produced in the continually expanding car factories of Oxford and the Midlands.

In 1918 there were only a handful of aeroplanes in the country and no company operating passenger flights outside Britain. By 1939 there were British airline companies operating regular passenger flights to Africa and Asia, Europe and Australasia, with plans for a service to the U.S.A. Most of the aeroplanes flown by these airline companies were produced in one or other of the factories in the South of England owned by Handley-Page, Sopwith, Saunders-Roe and other British firms. There was a continual increase in the output of artificial silk, electrical goods, food-processing, chemicals and petroleum.

Working on the assembly line at Morris Motors, Cowley, Oxford in 1930. Morris introduced the American-type assembly line system where the workman stays in one place and the work comes to him. The line itself, and many of the tools used by the men were powered by electricity. The men worked in cleaner surroundings and did lighter work than their fathers had done in the older industries.

What was new about them?

Three things should be noted about these new industries. First, they used electricity for power and not coal. This allowed the industrialists to put their factories wherever they pleased. The older industries had been forced to develop near the coalfields from which they got their fuel. The owners of the newer industries, dependent on electricity, had a much wider choice of sites.

Secondly, the new industries were much more scientifically and technologically based than were the older industries in which the physical strength of workmen was so important. The new industries depended much more on their scientists, designers, technologists and technicians than they depended on brawny workmen.

Thirdly, the new industries, unlike the old, sold most of their products in the British home market and not in the foreign, export markets. This meant that the industrialists tended to put their factories as near their largest domestic market (London) as they could. This lowered the costs of sending the product to that market.

Why not go to the older industrial areas?

The owners of the new industries could have built their factories in the old, now depressed, areas. Why did they not do so?

Hoover factory at Perivale, Middlesex. Here an American firm produced vacuum cleaners and washing machines for sale to the prosperous British. Here, as in Cowley, work was lighter and surroundings cleaner. In the 1970s Hoover had its main works at Merthyr, one of the depressed areas of the 1930s. In the 1930s it was allowed to build near London – its main market.

We have already seen that there was a natural attraction of London. London was the largest market with social benefits which attracted the owners and their wives. There were better shops, good theatres and the important social and sporting centres of Wimbledon, Henley, Ascot and Epsom. Many things like this made the sunny, greener South more attractive than the North.

The old industrial areas also carried all the scars of Victorian industrialisation. The slum housing, dirty and now crumbling mills and works and slag heaps, compared most unfavourably with the fresh green fields of Surrey and Middlesex where the new breed of industrialists built their factories.

The older industrial areas also had a history of industrial bitterness. Clashes between rich and poor, industrialists and workers, had led in 1926 to the General Strike. The owners of the new industries wanted to avoid such conflict. They hoped to find less dislike and less industrial strife in the fresh fields of the South-East.

Two nations

And so there was a depressed Britain – the old industrial areas of Wales, Scotland, the North East and North West. At the same time there was a booming Britain – the Midlands, the South and South East. In the nineteenth century Britain's industrial power lay along a line drawn from London through Birmingham to Liverpool. In the 1930s Britain's industrial power lay along a line drawn from Bristol through Oxford to London.

In the older industrial areas, suffering from depression in the 1930s, there was a great deal of nineteenth century housing which lacked almost all the amenities of modern housing – hot water, bathrooms, inside toilets and so on. Industrialists such as Morris and Hoover did not want to build their factories in these depressed and depressing areas.

During the 1920s and 1930s prices of raw materials fell so that houses, cars and clothing became cheaper. Mass production of good quality clothing allowed Burtons and other firms to sell suits for as little as 55 shillings – (£2.75) or, as the 'Sale' ticket shows, for 37 shillings (£1.85).

1 *What imported materials are used in the making of clothes sold in Burtons?*
  Why was there a fall in the prices of these materials in the 1920s and 1930s?
  How did this affect the export of British goods to the countries which produced these raw materials?
2 *Why could working people afford to buy more clothing in the 1920s and 1930s than their fathers could have afforded in pre-1914 Britain?*
3 *Can you name three other multiple stores which opened shops in most towns in the 1920s and 1930s?*

Rising living standards

For people in the booming Britain based on the new industries there was a great improvement in living standards. (At the same time there was an equally drastic fall in living standards in the depressed areas.) For some people the 1930s were 'the good old days' and not 'the depressed years'.

One reason for this improvement in living standards was a huge fall in import prices after 1921. By 1929 prices were about 20 per cent lower than they had been in 1921 and between 1929 and 1933 import prices fell again by about 50 per cent. Wheat, cotton, wool, timber, bacon, eggs, coffee, chocolate, rubber, copper – almost everything tumbled in price. At the same time, the workpeople in booming Britain enjoyed regular employment in the new factories and offices and had stable or even rising wages. If you combine falling prices and rising wages you have the recipé for a rise in living standards. People had money to spend on motor cars (which cost as little as £100 in 1933), household goods such as vacuum cleaners and radios. There was money to spare for holidays. The first of the famous Butlin's holiday camps opened in 1937. There was money to spend on newspapers. The circulation of the daily press went on increasing through the 1920s and 1930s (Chapter 23).

And these popular newspapers helped the prosperous families of booming Britain to spend their new wealth.

Advertisements for cheap clothes, and domestic articles such as furniture as well as electrical appliances, helped to persuade people to buy.

Hire purchase

And if some goods were too expensive to be bought out of the weekly wage packet, there were an increasing number of *Hire Purchase* (HP) companies. The companies were ready to offer the prosperous workpeople the £100 they needed to buy that Ford car or the £25 needed to buy a three-piece suite for the lounge of the new home. People had only to sign a form, promise to pay a few pence a week for two or three years, and they could become the proud owners of cars and furniture. In the depressed areas mothers visited the pawn-shop to hand in their few goods in order to get a few shillings to pay the rent or buy food. In prosperous Britain mothers visited the HP office to hand in a few pence to pay for the luxury goods they were enjoying.

Hire purchase helped provide employment in the factories supplying the goods that were bought on HP as well as in the offices of the HP firms. Without HP the majority of people could not have afforded the goods they bought and the factory owners would not have employed so many people to produce those goods.

Tertiary industries

Agriculture and coal mining are examples of *primary industries*. They are called primary because these industries are concerned with getting something out of nature. You

A typing pool in 1934. The growth of the number of government departments and of large firms such as Hoover provided job-opportunities for better-educated girls. This meant that some families, in London and the South East in particular, had two or three wage earners. This helps to explain the prosperity of these areas.

1 *Why did middle class parents allow their daughters to work in the 1920s and 1930s whereas they would have objected to their working in the nineteenth century?*

2 *Why was there an increased demand for typists and office workers in the 1920s and 1930s?*

might think of some primary products which come from Australia, Malaysia, Zambia, Ghana and the Southern States of the U.S.A.

Primary products such as coal, iron, copper, cotton and wool, are used by industrialists and workmen to manufacture goods such as machines, clothes, and furniture. The manufacturing industries are called secondary industries because they are a second stage in changing a primary product into something else.

Then there are *tertiary industries* which do not produce goods, but help us to get the goods or enjoy them in a fuller way. Or they may provide us with some service which is not essential but enjoyable. An HP firm is one such tertiary firm. By lending money it helps people to get the goods. Shops where the goods are bought, insurance companies, advertising agencies, newspapers, banks, and restaurants are other examples of tertiary industries or firms. There are also other service industries such as hairdressers, and firms which fix the TV or washing machine. These are further examples of tertiary industries.

In an undeveloped nation most people are engaged in primary industries. This was the situation in Britain in the early eighteenth century (Chapters 1 and 2). As a nation becomes more industrialised and employs more of its people in secondary or manufacturing industries (Chapter 2, 3, 4), so it becomes more prosperous and wealthier (Chapters 10–13). Once a nation has reached a certain stage of prosperity it can then afford to spend money on non-essential things and employ people in tertiary industries. It is a sign of a nation's prosperity when the percentage of people employed in tertiary industries rises, and this happened in Britain in the 1930s. Joe Lyons built his famous Corner House. Woolworth's stores opened in almost every High Street. Even the smallest town had two or more cinemas.

Housing

One sign of Britain's growing prosperity in the 1920s and 1930s was the vast increase in the number of houses built. The following table is worth some study:

| | Millions of homes | | |
	Built by local councils	for sale	total
1920–29	1·0	0·5	1·5
1930–39	0·75	2·0	2·75

You will see that local councils built a large number of houses. For these, wage earners paid a rent of between 35p and 75p a week in Birmingham and between 40p and 65p in York. It was only the prosperous workers who could afford

In 1930 William Morris fulfilled one of his ambitions – to produce a car which sold at £100. He could only do this because of (i) falling prices of raw materials (ii) the mass-production methods of the assembly line and (iii) he was confident that he could sell all the cars he produced on the British market.

Joe Lyons was one of the enterprising businessmen who realised that the British people had money to spend on what had once been thought of as luxuries.

The prosperity of Britain in the depressed 1930s was the main reason why Billy Butlin opened his first holiday camp at Skegness in 1936. For many people this was their first chance of a holiday away from home – and at prices they could afford.

A house on one of the many suburban estates built during the 1930s. All the houses on this estate were built for sale. The price was low (£350–450); the building societies provided the money to the houseowner who could afford to buy a car, household goods such as the vacuum cleaner and radio.

these rents. The unemployed and lowly paid were still huddled together in overcrowded slums.

You will also see that councils built fewer houses in the depressed 1930s than they had done in the 1920s. This is very strange at first sight; after all, prices of raw materials were falling in the late 1920s and 1930s. The cost of a council house fell from £440 in 1925 to £320 in 1935. Councils might have been expected to build more at the cheaper price than they did at the dearer one. But, like the national government, councils believed that the best way out of the depression was to cut rates (and taxes). They had less money to spend on things such as houses and roads. They did not accept the ideas put forward by Keynes.

Private housing

In the private sector there was a great increase in the number of houses built for sale in the 1930s. One of the reasons for this was that there was a large number of prosperous people anxious to buy their own homes. There were the workers in the booming industries – over 50 per cent of house purchases in 1936 were made by working class people. There were also the increasing number of people working in the tertiary industries. These were men and women who might have been born to working class parents but who now had middle class jobs in offices, shops, management and so on. They wanted to show that they had emerged from the working class by doing something that their parents had never been able to afford to do – buy their own home.

Building Societies

Most people bought their new homes with the help of the building societies. These had an ever increasing amount of money given to them by investors. If trade in Britain or abroad had been booming, these investors might have given their money to industrialists. But in the 1930s the Building Societies offered a safe and interest-paying investment.

The building societies made it easier for people to borrow from them. First, they lowered their interest rates. Instead of paying 6 per cent a year as in 1932 borrowers only had to pay 4 per cent in 1934 and after. Then, instead of having to pay back the borrowed money in 15 years, as had once been the case, the Societies allowed people to repay them over 20 or 25 years. Building Societies allowed people to borrow 90 per cent of the cost of the new house instead of only 80 per cent as had been the case in the 1920s. Now we can have a look at a table illustrating all these changes:

		1920s	1930s
1	Cost of house	£600	£400
2	Need to put down	£120 (or 20%)	£80 (or 10%)
3	Borrowed	£480 (or 80%)	£320 (or 90%)
4	Interest paid on loan	at 6% £28.80	at 4% £12.80
5	Years of repayment	15	25
6	Annual repayment of money borrowed (line 3 ÷ line 5)	£32	£12.80
7	Total to pay each year (line 4 + line 6)	£60.80	£25.60
8	Weekly payment	£1.15	51p

You will appreciate that it is much easier to repay 51p than £1.15 each week. 51p was about the average rent that had to be paid for a council house. If people had saved £80 or so, they could go in for buying their own homes. And with the help of the many new shops, and the HP companies, they could furnish the home and become part of the prosperous house-owning class of booming Britain.

Documents

a) Old houses and new homes

Wishaw, before 1914, was one of the worst housed towns in Britain. The great majority of its inhabitants lived in one-room houses, 'single-ends' they were called, all set in bleak, dismal rows, and sometimes one row back against another so that no air could circulate through them. Such houses, the worst type of slum, were called 'back-to-back' houses. There was no inside water supply and all water for washing, bathing and cooking had to be carried by the housewife from a single outside tap, which would serve anything from four to sixty houses. There were no inside lavatories, and dry closets stood in brick sheds in the yard facing the windows of the houses. Usually there was neither gas nor electricity.

The dirty nature of the miner's work added to the trials of the housewife attempting to keep a neat and clean home under such conditions. The miners came home covered with the grime of the coal seams. It was a nightly ritual for the housewife to bring water from the outside tap, boil some of it in a kettle on the range and pour it into a tub in the centre of the floor of the one-room dwelling and then help her husband to wash himself, particularly by scrubbing the dirt from his back.

The Town Council acquired a part of a large estate and laid it out as a new housing scheme. The houses themselves varied in size from living-room and two bedrooms, with bathroom and kitchen, to living-room, dining-room and three bedrooms also with bathroom and kitchen. The old slum houses were torn down and new houses erected on the sites.

For the first time the housewife found that she and her husband had a bedroom to themselves while there was a bedroom for the girls and a separate bedroom for the boys. For the first time she found that the house was heated by small convenient fires which did not require much work to keep clean and that water could be heated by the ingenious arrangement of a boiler situated behind the main living-room fire. For the first time both she and the family knew the luxury of a bathroom and of a reasonably well-equipped kitchen. The kitchen usually had a small pantry off it, in which the perishable foods were kept. It had two sinks, one in which to wash clothes before passing them through the wringer to be rinsed in the other. The second, the shallower, was also used for washing-up dishes and beside it was a draining board. Each kitchen had a gas or electric cooker, with an oven for roasts or baking, a grill, a toast-rack, and rings for boiling. Electric points were provided for electric irons and vacuum cleaners. Sometimes cupboards for china and food were built-in.
(G. McAllister, *Houses that are homes*)

1 *Write a letter from the grandmother who has lived in old Wishaw after visiting her daughter now living in the new council house.*

2 *Why would children have been better able to do homework in the new house than in the old?*

3 *Why was there less disease and a lower death rate in the new than in the old districts?*

4 *Give five reasons why life was easier for women in the 1930s than it had been before 1914.*

One of the many council estates built on the outskirts of the older industrial towns and cities. For the workers who could afford the rent, these estates provided a release from the overcrowded and insanitary inner cities and towns. These estates were still too expensive for the less well-off workers.

1 *More people lived in a square mile of slum territory than lived on a square mile of new housing. Why? Why did this result in the outward spread of towns?*

2 *Why did people living on council estates need some method of transport more than did the people living in the inner cities (i) for getting to work and (ii) for doing their shopping? Why did this stop some people moving on to a new estate?*

3 *Why were rents on council estates sometimes higher than rents paid for slum housing in the inner cities? If people could not afford to rent a house in the inner city how might they have been helped to afford to live on the new estate? Why were the new estates occupied mainly by the prosperous workers?*

Questions on Chapter Twenty-one

1 *Read again the first section of this chapter on the growth of the new industries. Most of them sold their products at home. What does this tell you about the prosperity of Britain in the 1920s and 1930s?*

2 *Write a letter from a director of Fords explaining why they have decided to build a factory at Dagenham, Essex, and not at Merthyr.*

3 *Write a letter from a formerly unemployed miner who has left South Wales and found a job on the assembly line in a car factory. (He might write about the cleaniness, lack of danger, wages, his new house, a comparison between the booming area and depressed South Wales.)*

4 *Prices fell in the 1920s and 1930s. Explain how this (i) hurt the producers of primary products overseas, (ii) improved the living standards of many people in Britain.*

5 *'The Age of Prosperity'. Give four reasons why you think this is a good description of the 1920s and 1930s. Would everyone living then have agreed? If not, why not?*

6 *List five reasons why there were more houses bought in the 1930s than had ever been the case before.*

7 *Make a collage of headlines which might have appeared above articles dealing with (i) the £100 Morris car, (ii) the £400 house (iii) the £2 suit, (iv) the opening of a new cinema in your town, (v) the sale of the millionth new car, (iv) the opening of a Butlin's holiday camp.*

Chapter 22

The development of the Welfare State

The Liberals laid the foundations for the modern *Welfare State* between 1908 and 1911 (Chapter 17). Their reforms were pushed through in spite of opposition to their attempts to make life a little better for the less well-off. Some opposed even the modest provision of school meals for poor children. Others accused Lloyd George of being a socialist. The House of Lords had opposed Lloyd George's budgets.

However, during the depressed 1920s and 1930s, Labour, Conservative and Coalition governments built on the foundations that had been laid by the Liberals, and the Welfare State developed.

Unemployment benefit

About three million workers in three trades were covered by the 1911 National Insurance Scheme (Chapter 17). In 1916 the government allowed workers in munitions factories to join the scheme. In 1918 every former member of the armed forces became entitled to 50 weeks of unemployment benefit. This was a major step forward. Under the 1911 Act only insured workmen were to get benefits. In 1918 the government accepted responsibility for giving demobilised ex-servicemen a 'dole', or hand-out, for which they had not paid.

In 1920 a new Act brought over 11 million workers into the Unemployment Insurance Scheme. People earning less than £5 a week, paid into the Insurance Fund. Their employers

Labour Exchanges were first opened in 1909 and originally were meant as places to which the minority of insured workers would go to collect unemployment benefit and to look for work. During the 1930s unemployment benefit and, later, the dole, were paid to unemployed men from a wide variety of occupations.

also paid an amount in for them. They were then entitled to receive a benefit of 75p for a maximun of 15 weeks of unemployment. But agricultural workers, domestic and civil servants, were excluded from this scheme.

In 1921 the government introduced payments for the dependents of unemployed working men. In future an unemployed insured worker would get an extra 25p a week if he were married and 5p for each of his children. This made life a little easier for the families of unemployed men.

Increased costs of insurance

This 1921 scheme had been worked out in the hope that the low level of unemployment in 1919 and 1920 would be the peacetime average. However, this immediate post-war level of only $4\frac{1}{2}$ per cent unemployment was soon proved to be a temporary one. By late 1921 over 10 per cent of working men were out of work. Between 1924 and 1929 the level rarely fell below $12\frac{1}{2}$ per cent and between 1931 and 1933 it stayed at a record level of 23 per cent. The government had failed to keep its wartime promises.

One effect of this high level of unemployment was to wreck the finances of the Insurance Fund. There were more people getting the benefit than had been expected. The government had to pay continually increasing sums into the Fund, and so accept an ever increasing degree of responsibility for the unemployed.

The dole

A second effect of the high level of unemployment was to create problems for the Boards of Guardians (Chapter 7) who were supposed to look after the poor – including the unemployed when their 15 weeks of unemployment benefit had run out. How on earth were the Guardians in Jarrow or Merthyr supposed to manage to look after two-thirds of the populations of these towns? The Government tried to help the Poor Law Guardians. In March 1921 it announced that once a man's right to draw Unemployment Benefit had run out, after 15 weeks, he could then claim uncovenanted benefit (not due to him as a right out of the Insurance Fund) for a further 32 weeks. This new benefit was the 'dole' or hand-out, as distinct from Unemployment Benefit which was due to the workman because he had paid into the Insurance Fund. The government had to set aside £30 million a year to pay for this 'dole'.

The Guardians

However, even after this 32 weeks, millions of men could still not find work in the old, industrial areas where the coal,

YESTERDAY-THE TRENCHES

TO-DAY-UNEMPLOYED

Lloyd George had promised the soldiers 'Homes fit for Heroes'. These Labour Party election posters drew people's attention to the way in which the politicians had failed to live up to their promises even in the 1920s. Unfortunately not even the Labour Party was able to provide solutions to the economic problems. Unemployment was not ended until the war started in 1939.

George Lansbury and the Poplar
Council on their way to gaol.
Lansbury remembered:

* We found our rates going up by
leaps and bounds. We decided that
we would refuse to pay the London
County Council our share of London's
general rates. This saved us several
hundreds of thousands per year. We
were taken to the High Court. The
Judges agreed that we had a good
case, but that the law was against us.
We appealed against the conviction
but lost this and were sent to prison
for six weeks.

While we were in prison the
government decided that the cost of
looking after London's poor was to be
paid for out of rates imposed over the
whole of London. The result of this
was a cut in the rates in Poplar and an
increase in the rates in the prosperous
areas of Westminster and the City
of London.
(Lansbury, *My Work* 1931)

iron and steel, textile and shipbuilding industries were
suffering from the depression. They were then forced to go to
the Boards of Guardians. These collected a Poor Rate from the
ratepayers of their district and used the money to run the
workhouse and to pay poor relief outside the workhouses.
It was a very unfair system. The people in areas where there
was a high level of unemployment had to pay a much higher
Poor Rate than people who lived in more fortunate areas.

The end of the Guardians
At last, in 1929, the government decided to accept the argument that it was unfair to ask local authorities to look after
their unemployed. The Poor Law system was abolished. In
place of the Guardians the government set up Public
Assistance Committees to give out government relief in each
county. This further increased the amount of money which
the government was forced to pay to keep the unemployed.

The May Committee
The government was being forced to accept more responsibility for looking after the unemployed. In 1931 the Labour
government was anxious to balance the Budget and at the
same time to cut taxes. It set up a Committee under Sir
George May to look into what might be done to cut spending.
One of the May Committee's proposals was that there should
be cuts in the wages of government employees such as judges,
teachers and members of the Armed Forces. The Committee
also recommended a 10 per cent cut in the benefit paid to the
unemployed. They argued that, because prices and the cost
of living had fallen, the Unemployment Benefit should also
be cut.

From the painting by Harold Speed.

NO MORE SOCIALIST PROMISES FOR ME, I'M VOTING FOR THE NATIONAL GOVERNMENT

A poster used by the National Government during the General Election held in October 1931. The voters agreed that socialism and increased taxation was not the answer to the problem of unemployment. The National Government won 556 seats while the Labour Party (now without its old leaders) won only 52 seats.

The fall of the Labour government, August 1931

The Chancellor, Philip Snowden, agreed with his civil servants and the majority of bankers and economists who supported the May Committee proposals. Some Labour Ministers wanted the Chancellor to increase taxation as a means of getting the money needed to balance the budget. Snowden rejected this advice. The Cabinet was unable to agree as to what it should do. Ramsay MacDonald, the Prime Minister, went to see King George V who invited him to form a National Government and to see the country through what would be, it was hoped, a short term crisis. Stanley Baldwin, the leader of the Conservative Party, and Herbert Samuel, a leader of the Liberal Party, agreed to become Ministers in this National Government under MacDonald. This government called an election and won a huge majority.

The new government not only cut the benefits paid to the unemployed, but also established the *Means Test*. The Public Assistance Committees would examine not only whether a man was out of work and entitled to a 'dole' but also the financial state of the family as a whole.

Unemployment Assistance

In 1934 the government set up the Unemployment Assistance Board which took over from the Public Assistance Committees. This Board, composed of civil servants, dispensed the £100 million or so which each year the government was now having to pay out in 'dole'. Many old people in post-war Britain have been unwilling to go to the Social Security Offices to claim the money due to them. This is explained by their memory of this Assistance Board with its Means Test. They think that the Social Security Office is modelled on the much hated Unemployment Assistance Board.

Housing

A second field in which the government became increasingly involved was that of providing adequate housing for the working class. Many of the older British towns had thousands of Victorian slums. Lloyd George, in 1918, promised to build 'homes fit for heroes to live in', which would have meant pulling down these old slums and building decent housing. In the Housing Act, 1919, the government agreed to provide money for local councils to build houses to rent to working class familes. This system of government subsidy was extended by other Housing Acts in 1922 and 1923 and estates of many thousands of council houses were built on the outskirts of the older cities and towns.

The government subsidy meant that the council could ask for a lower rent than if it had paid for the whole cost of the house. However, even with this subsidy, the councils were forced to ask for rents which the lowly paid and unemployed could still not afford. In the 1930s, as we have seen (Chapter 21), the government lowered the subsidy so that councils built even fewer houses and in 1939 there were still thousands of families living in inadequate housing.

Health

The Ministry of Health had been set up in 1918. One of the most notable Ministers was Neville Chamberlain. As Minister for Health in the Conservative government (1924–29) he pushed twenty-one laws through Parliament. One of

Unable to find work in their depressed valleys, disliking the humiliations of the Means Test, some Welsh miners formed small groups and sang (and begged) in London's busy streets. Maybe this was a form of self-help of which the Victorians would have approved. Certainly the government seemed unwilling or unable to provide much help to the depressed areas.

these was the first Widows' Pensions Act (1925). Another was a Housing Act aimed at enabling councils to build subsidised housing for letting. It was Chamberlain who abolished the old Poor Law system and the Boards of Guardians and introduced what was meant to be a more humane and generous Unemployment Assistance scheme.

Women

Much of Chamberlain's work was intended to help make life better for women – whether they were expectant mothers, mothers of young children, widows or wives of unemployed workers. Indeed, one of the major features of inter-war Britain was that life became much better for the majority of women. There was a fall in the birth rate, so that most mothers had to deal with only one or two children – their mothers and grandmothers had had to cope with much larger families. In addition to this, housekeeping and shopping became much easier. Labour-saving devices were introduced. More and more food was conveniently packaged and easy to prepare. It was true, as Robert Graves wrote, that 'the prematurely aged wife was coming to be the exception'. (p. 233).

Neville Chamberlain with Hitler in 1938. This is what most people remember about the unfortunate Chamberlain. Few people know that he was a great Minister of Health.

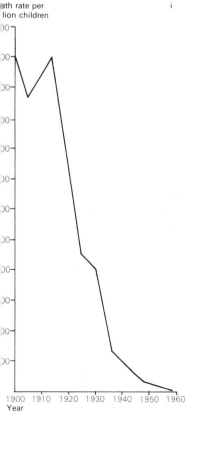

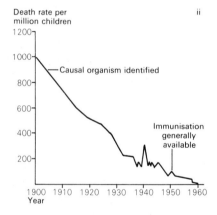

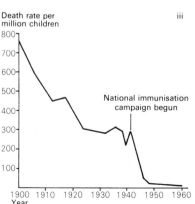

The decline in the rates of (i) infant mortality during the present century (ii) the death rate from whooping cough and (iii) the deaths from diphtheria.

1 *How many infants, per million, died in (i) 1910, (ii) 1920, (iii) 1930 and (iv) 1940?*
2 *How many children, per million, died from (a) whooping cough and (b) diphtheria in (i) 1900, (ii) 1920, (iii) 1930 and (iv) 1940?*
3 *The graphs suggest some reasons for the fall in infant mortality. Name three other reasons for this fall.*

Documents

a) **A well-paid engineer becomes unemployed.** (*This was written in 1937. The Means Test referred to came into force in 1931.*)

After a year of vain efforts I decided to accept any job I could get but I soon found that outside my trade I could get nothing. In the meantime my wife obtained a job as house to house saleswoman, and was able to earn a few shillings to supplement our dole income. It was from this time that the feeling of strain which was beginning to appear in our home life became more marked. Life became more and more strained. There were constant bickerings over money matters. The final blow came when the Means Test was put into operation. Quarrels broke out anew and bitter things were said. Eventually, after the most heartbreaking period of my life, both my wife and son, who had just commenced to earn a few shillings, told me to get out, as I was living on them and taking the food they needed.

I left and took with me a little furniture. I rented an unfurnished bedroom for 4s 6d a week in the house of an unemployed man who had a wife and three children. This happened some fifteen months ago. Since then I have drawn 15s 3d weekly from the dole and have had to sell every bit of furniture I had and try to exist on 8s 0d a week for food. I have never been able to afford coal for a fire. The outlook as far as I am concerned is hopeless. I've given up dreaming of any return to my former life and work, and just hang on hoping something big will happen before I die.

b) **A coal-miner and the Means Test**

It was in June 1927, that I first began to draw unemployment benefit at the rate of £1. 9s. 0d. a week. At that time my eldest boy, who was then fifteen, had not started work as he could not find a job until at last the manager of one colliery told him he would give him a start because he was ashamed to keep turning him away. He is still working at the same colliery his wages being 15 shillings a week, which made our incomes up to £2. 4s. 0d. and enabled us to buy him some clothes. After paying our rent we still had £1. 15s. 0d. a week to live on. Then my second son came out of school and found he could not get work, but he went to the training centre and there eventually got work. His wage was 15 shillings too, so that we had £2. 10s. 0d. allowing for rent.

My unemployment benefit came to an end in March, 1932, when I was disallowed because I had not qualified for the necessary contributory period of thirty weeks. After this I was given a food ticket for 23 shillings a week, which continued until January 1933, when it was stopped because of the Means Test. Before the stoppage our income was over the minimum limit of £2. 17s. 6d. So now we have to depend on the boys and

they have to keep all six of us, including my wife and the two children who are still going to school.

1 *Why, do you think, was it easier for a woman to get a job?*

2 *How did the wife's earnings affect the husband's 'dole'?*

3 *Write a letter from a wife explaining why she quarrelled with her husband.*

4 *When, do you think, did the engineer find 'something big'? (See Chapter 24)*

5 *How many people were there in the family of the unemployed miner? How many were earning in 1933?*

6 *Make a collage of headlines that might have appeared above articles on (i) the Means Test, (ii) husbands leaving home.*

ALLEVIATION'S ARTFUL AID.

c) The caption to this 1921 cartoon showing Lloyd George bringing help to the unemployed (the man in bed) read 'I don't say these hot-water bottles will absolutely cure you, but they should relieve the trouble.'

1 *What part had Lloyd George played in the help given to the unemployed by the 1911 Act?*

2 *Why were there more people out of work in 1921 than there had been in 1920?*

3 *What might have been done to 'absolutely cure you'? Why were governments in the 1920s and the 1930s unwilling to provide that cure? When did they do so?*

4 *What relief was provided by the hot-water bottles?*

5 *Why did this help to the unemployed lead to increased government spending? Why did this lead to a political crisis in 1931?*

Extracts

The unjust Poor Rates

All the council's work in Poplar is hindered because of high rates caused by low rateable values and a poverty-stricken population. Poverty demands big public expenditure, and our low rateable value makes such expenditure the cause of high rates.
(George Lansbury, *My Work* 1931)

Better conditions for women

Most remarkable was the looks of women. The prematurely aged wife was coming to be the exception. Children were fewer; labour-saving devices were introduced; the introduction of stainless cutlery saved an appreciable amount of time; this was only one of a hundred such innovations. Housewives came to count on certain brands of goods; food was sold in the nearest possible stage to table-readiness; the complicated processes of making custard and other puddings were reduced by the use of prepared powders. Cereals, eaten with milk, began to challenge bacon and eggs in prosperous homes, and the bread and margarine of the poor.

Bottled and tinned goods grew more plentiful. Foodstuffs were also gradually standardized; eggs, milk and butter were graded and guaranteed.
(R. Graves and A. Hodge, *The Long Weekend* 1950)

Questions on Chapter Twenty-two

1 *Make a line chart to illustrate the development of the unemployment benefit schemes in the 1920s and 1930s.*

2 *Write a letter from a man who has been out of work for a year in the 1920s, explaining where he gets his money from and what life was like for his family.*

3 *Account for the fall of the Labour government in 1931.*

4 *Why have older people bitter memories of the Unemployment Assistance Board?*

5 *Make a list of ways in which Neville Chamberlain made life better for many people in his years as Minister of Health, 1924—9.*

6 *Why did taxation have to increase as a result of the development of the welfare state? Who might have been opposed to this?*

7 *Write a letter from a Victorian grandmother to her grand-daughter, the mother of a small family in booming Britain of the 1930s.*

Chapter 23   Communications

Electric trams in London, 1912. Electric trams were first used in 1902 and made a great difference to working class people as one remembered:

* When I first went to live in a poor district of South London, our sole communication with London over-the-river was a few erratic horse-omnibuses, and lines of slow-moving, two-horse trams. Here at evening a tired, indignant crowd fought silently for entrance into each successive conveyance; the young and the old were squeezed out and occasionally trampled under. Half an hour afterwards, or perhaps three-quarters, we were deposited near our home. (L. Masterman, *C. F. G. Masterman* 1939)

Horse-drawn traffic

Until the 1890s many people used horse-drawn carriages for travel in town. The very rich owned their own carriage, the middle class might hire a carriage from a livery stable and the lower middle class would catch a hansom cab (a horse drawn taxi). The working class might use a horse-drawn omnibus (these were gradually displaced by the electric trams which were cleaner, quicker and cheaper).

Horse-drawn waggons and carts were used to deliver coal, milk, bread, furniture and the other articles bought in the growing number of large shops. These shops employed thousands of errand boys to deliver smaller goods by bicycle.

The bicycle

Until the 1880s the bicycle had been a heavy and clumsy machine. With its iron frame, solid wheels and lack of springs, it deserved the nickname 'boneshaker'. Even the lighter 'ordinary' or 'pennyfarthing' was not much better. This was produced in 1879 and was lighter (about 49 pounds as against 68 pounds for the 'boneshaker'). But it was very difficult to ride. However in the 1880s the 'safety' bicycle was introduced and by 1897 this had almost completely replaced previous cycles. It had the diamond-shaped frame with which we are still familiar, a lower saddle, wheels of equal size and the pneumatic tyres which had been invented by a Belfast chemist, J. B. Dunlop.

There were a large number of firms producing bicycles, most of them were centred on Coventry where the Coventry Sewing Machine Company had branched out into manufacturing bicycles in 1870. The competition among these firms led to a fall in the price of the bicycle so that it became a popular means of transport. Men went to work on 'bikes'; women went shopping; young men and women took trips out into the countryside. Although the bicycle became less popular after the invention of the motor car and motorcycle or scooter, there are signs that it is coming back into fashion because of the high cost of petrol and of public transport.

The petrol engine

The development of the petrol engine was mainly the work of three Germans. Otto perfected a four stroke compression engine in 1876. He used coal gas for fuel. In 1883 Daimler used petrol in his internal combustion engine and in 1885 Benz used a petrol engine to drive a three-wheeled tricycle. Daimler drove the first motor car in 1887. The first British car was built in 1896 by Lanchester and by 1903 there were over 20,000 motor cars licensed to travel on Britain's roads.

Until 1896 the Red Flag Act (1865) made it necessary for vehicles travelling at more than four miles an hour to have a man waving a red flag walk in front of the speedy vehicle. This Act was abolished in 1896 and a London-Brighton run was made to mark that grant of freedom to the new motorists.

An advertisement for a Daimler car, 1896.

1 *Which class of people bought cars in 1896?*
2 *Why did the advertisers call it 'a horseless carriage'? How far did the designers of these cars try to make it look like the traditional horse-drawn carriage?*
3 *How fast could this car go? Can you suggest why travel in this car must have been uncomfortable?*

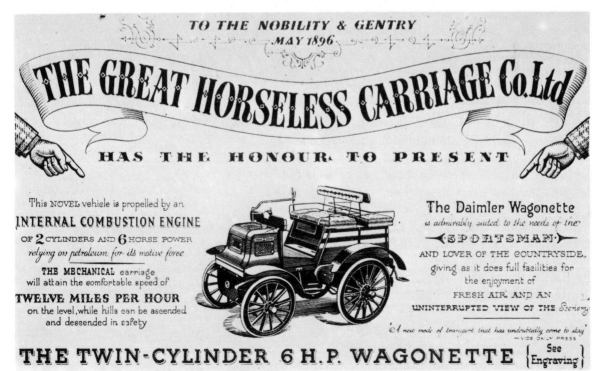

TO THE NOBILITY & GENTRY
MAY 1896

THE GREAT HORSELESS CARRIAGE Co. Ltd

HAS THE HONOUR TO PRESENT

This NOVEL vehicle is propelled by an
INTERNAL COMBUSTION ENGINE
OF 2 CYLINDERS AND 6 HORSE POWER
relying on petroleum for its motive force

THE MECHANICAL carriage
will attain the comfortable speed of
TWELVE MILES PER HOUR
on the level, while hills can be ascended
and descended in safety

The Daimler Wagonette
is admirably suited to the needs of the
◄ SPORTSMAN ►
AND LOVER OF THE COUNTRYSIDE,
giving as it does full facilities for
the enjoyment of
FRESH AIR AND AN
UNINTERRUPTED VIEW OF THE Scenery

'A new mode of transport that has undoubtedly come to stay'
— VIDE DAILY PRESS

THE TWIN-CYLINDER 6 H.P. WAGONETTE {See Engraving}

The cheap car

These first motorists were rich men who could afford to buy the elegant, expensive, hand made motor cars. It was William Morris (later Lord Nuffield), who brought the assembly line method of mass production from the U.S.A. to Britain.

Buying his electrical equipment from Lucas, his tyres from Dunlop, his brakes from Girling, and so on, Morris organised an assembly line along which the practically completed car travelled to the workmen. Each man added one touch to the car such as fixing a door or tightening a wheel until the car was complete. (p. 216).

One result of this mass production method was that Morris and the other manufacturers produced cheaper cars. In 1922 the small family car cost £165; but by 1930 Ford and Austin, as well as Morris, produced cars for £100. It now became possible for even working class people to buy their own cars.

The petrol engine (as well as the similar 'Diesel' engine, perfected in 1892) was also used to power buses and lorries. In 1905 the London General Transport Company replaced its electric trams with the new buses and in the 1920s and 1930s an increasing number of local transport companies followed this example. As cities grew local buses extended their routes into the new suburbs. The 'charabanc' went further afield, to the coast for holidays or to country districts where even railways did not run.

By 1939 hundreds of thousands of people owned a motor-car. Traffic jams were common, particularly during rush hours. Traffic was very heavy at week-ends when townspeople tried to get into the countryside. The approach roads to holiday resorts were crowded during the summer season.

Radio

Marconi, an Italian living in Britain, succeeded in 1899 in sending a message by radio across the Channel to France. In 1901 he transmitted a message from Cornwall to the U.S.A. and by 1912 many shipping firms had incorporated a radio in their vessels. When the sinking *Titanic*'s appeal for help went out it was picked up by many ships, which raced to the scene of the disaster and rescued the survivors.

A number of firms producing wireless sets came together in 1922 to form the British Broadcasting Company to which the Post Office gave permission to send out programmes to the people who owned their sets. In 1927 the government took firmer control of this new method of communication, took it out of the hands of the private companies and formed the British Broadcasting Corporation (BBC).

In 1923 80,000 sets were licensed but by 1939 over 8,900,000 licences were issued so that there was a wireless set in about three-quarters of Britain's homes. It is impossible to estimate the effect that this new communication system had on people in the 1920s and 1930s. Apart from the sheer enjoyment of the many entertainment programmes such as music halls, dance bands and variety shows, there was the process of general education and forming of public tastes. How many people in remote towns and villages would ever have heard the world's great orchestras playing classical music if there had been no BBC? How many would have heard the plays of Bernard Shaw or Ibsen, as well as the less serious plays of J. B. Priestley?

An early schools broadcast.

* The first time I heard the wireless was in Wedmore, Somerset. A couple of men came to give a demonstration to us yokels. The sound was poor. Every now and then something would go wrong; not a very impressive performance. As we left the hall, the older people wagged their heads and declared that nothing would come of it.

Within months aerials were appearing on one house after another, and the first question when you met anyone was: 'Have you got a wireless?' All over the country, as though from nowhere, hordes of young mechanics were available to install a set, to build a set and to attend to repairs.
(Vivian Ogilvie)

1 Why did older people think that 'nothing would come of it'?
2 How quickly did ownership of wireless spread?
What does this tell you about (i) people's standard of living in the 1930s and (ii) the industries in which there was increased employment during the depressed 1930s?
3 How do you think the wireless changed people's habits? What other inventions named in this chapter did as much to alter national habits?

An example of the advertising which national firms used.

The Press and advertising

The development of a cheap, national daily newspaper is linked with the name of William Harmsworth (later Lord Northcliffe). Until the 1880s most newspapers were produced to be sold in their locality. Such papers as the *Liverpool Post*, the *Birmingham Mail*, the *Plymouth Journal* were published and sold in fairly restricted areas.

Northcliffe's great contribution to the development of the daily press was to realise that an increasing number of firms was producing branded goods which were being sold in every town in the country. Some examples are Pear's Soap, Rowntree's Cocoa, Cadbury's Chocolate, Lipton's Tea and Beecham's Pills. These firms advertised their goods on hoardings or in magazines; Northcliffe persuaded them to advertise in his newspaper, the *Daily Mail*. He brought out this paper in 1896, making it look like a portable hoarding or billspace. This horrified the older newspaper owners, who thought that the business of a newspaper was to provide news.

The Daily Mail

Before Northcliffe could persuade the national firms to pay for advertisements in his *Daily Mail*, he had to show them that the advertisement would reach a mass audience. Why should Rowntree pay thousands of pounds for a full-page advertisement in the *Daily Mail* if it was only going to be read by 20,000 or 30,000 readers? Northcliffe promised the people who advertised in his paper that he would sell 300,000 copies each day. None of his rival newspaper proprietors believed him. But he brought out his *Daily Mail* in 1896 and charged only one old halfpenny for it – about one-fifth of a new penny! This made it possible for many thousands of lower middle class and skilled working class people to buy a paper for the first time – they had never been willing to afford the 2p or 3p which the older papers had cost.

But how could Northcliffe persuade them to buy the paper printed in London and rushed by railway to the country's towns and cities? This was his third great contribution to the development of the national press. He insisted that his paper had to be alive and interesting. Headlines were enlarged to catch the reader's eye. Stories were kept short and enlivened with pictures. Items of human interest were included to attract the attention of people who would never have bothered to read a thousand-word article on a law case or a battle.

More readers

His new *Daily Mail* was a great success and by 1900 he was

selling half a million copies. His competitors were forced to follow his example. Lord Beaverbrook took over a failing *Daily Express* and by 1935 this had a daily sale of 2·3 million. At the same time the Labour Party's paper, the *Daily Herald* had 2·0 million readers while the *Daily Mail* (Northcliffe having died in 1922) fell behind with sales of only 1·5 million.

The continual rise in the number of people buying newspapers was a reflection of the continual rise in the nation's living standards. An ever-increasing number of people could afford to pay a penny for a newspaper. It also helps to explain the improvement in the general level of the nation's education. Women read about new foods and clothing materials and were unconsciously educated into better habits than their mothers had had. Campaigns against spitting in the street, or in favour of 'clean hands before meals', were used by newspapers to liven their pages. But they were also a valuable part of educating of the nation into better habits.

The front page of the *Weekly Dispatch* of 31 July 1910. The murderer, Dr Crippen, was among the passengers on the liner *Montrose*. He was recognised by the liner's captain, who sent a wireless message to Scotland Yard. A detective sailed on a fast ship and was waiting at Newfoundland to arrest Crippen when the *Montrose* arrived there. The *Montrose* was one of the few ships fitted with wireless equipment.

1 *Why would Lord Northcliffe have approved of this newspaper's presentation of the news?*
2 *Why is the Marconi firm proud of this particular item of news?*
3 *Why would advertisers have been willing to pay more for advertising space in this paper than in one with a less 'popular' sale and appearance?*

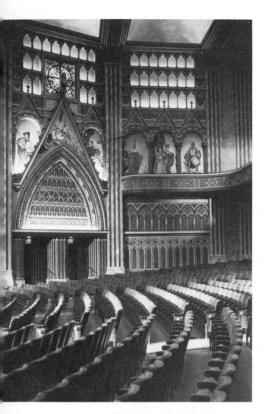

The interior of the Granada Cinema, Tooting, London. This was typical of the thousands of cinemas opened in the 1930s.

The cinema

The rise of the national press was one phenomenon of the 1920s and 1930s. The spread of the habit of cinema-going was another. There had been silent films before 1914 and by 1928 stars such as Chaplin, Mary Pickford and Valentino had become 'pop idols'. These silent films were shown in small 'electric cinemas' which made little attempt to woo the customer. It was considered that the thrill of seeing a moving picture was attraction enough. In 1928 there came the first of the 'talking pictures'. Moving pictures now became even more attractive.

Many companies were formed to produce films. Most of them were based on Hollywood in the U.S.A. Many other firms were formed to build new cinemas in which these films would be shown. In the 1930s cinemas, often seating up to 3,000 people were built in Britain's towns and cities. The cinema owners competed with each other in choosing glamorous names for their new buildings (the Granada, the Alhambra, the Plaza, the Grand, the Majestic) and in furnishing these 'palaces' in the grand style. By 1939 over half the population went once a week, and one-quarter went twice a week, to see films which were intended to entertain but rarely to carry a message. Cinema-going was the great escape route for millions whose daily lives were boring and dull.

Air travel

The American Wright Brothers had made the first flight in a heavier than air machine in 1903 at their base at Kitty Hawk, North Carolina. Bleriot, a Frenchman, had crossed the English Channel in 1909 to win a prize of £1,000 put up by Lord Northcliffe. This was one of the many 'stunts' that Northcliffe used to win the public's attention. Many aircraft were used during the First World War and there was a growing interest in aviation after 1918. In 1919 two former RAF pilots, Alcock and Brown, flew in a converted bomber from Newfoundland to Ireland and became the first to fly non-stop across the Atlantic. In 1919 the world's first passenger service was opened between London and Paris. The fare was £25. This was a luxury which only the rich could afford, and flying in the fragile machines of the time was an experience that only the foolhardy were willing to undertake. In the 1920s a number of aviators such as Alan Cobham, proved that it was possible to fly from Britain to such parts of the world as South Africa, India and Australia. Passenger services were eventually opened up to most parts of the Empire. Imperial Airways (the forerunner of British Airways) was formed to provide the services. Many small firms were engaged in building the aircraft used and by 1939 the aeroplane was much more luxurious, powerful and safe than it had been in 1919. But, there was still no transatlantic service to the U.S.A. This had to wait until wartime requirements forced the aircraft companies to design more powerful engines and stronger aeroplanes.

An Imperial Airways *Heracles* 'plane. This was one of the luxury airliners used on the routes between London and the main cities throughout the Empire in the 1930s.

Documents

a) Aviator Miss Amy Johnson crashes in Burma on record-making flight from London to Australia, 1930.

I ran smack into a monsoon, rain such as I'd never imagined. I was soaked, sitting there in the open cockpit. I came down very low to find my way, following a railway and almost taking the tips off the signal boxes. On the stations I could see Burmese people with umbrellas up. I kept a look-out for the racecourse at Rangoon where I was to land. It was getting very dark and still pouring when I saw a big building and crowds of people waving. Down I went, blinded with rain. Too late I saw mud and goal posts, and realized I was landing on a playing field. In a flash I was in a ditch, the machine on its nose – wings, propeller, undercarriage, all broken. I burst into tears. But I couldn't have crashed in a luckier place; what I had mistaken for a racecourse was the playing field of an engineering college. Students got to work and in two days and nights we rebuilt the plane.

b) Lady Hoare flies with her husband, the Secretary of State for Air, from Croydon to India, December 1926

I remember wondering rather sadly on our bumpy journey to Dijon, the first morning, if it was going to be as rough the whole way, and whether I should get used to it, as I was not, and am not, a perfect sailor. In murky and stormy weather the next afternoon along the Italian coast it ceased to be of great interest whether we arrived in Naples or not. But when we were in the air during the dust storm in the Persian Gulf, which probably was a period of some danger, we were much too interested to be frightened. One of the objects of the flight was propaganda, and my conviction that any ordinary woman could easily do a long-distance flight needed proof.

Two outstanding impressions remain with me. First there is the wonderful interest aroused by the flight, and aroused not only amongst our own people. For the whole way along foreigners and native tribes, veiled women, priests and officials all flocked to visit the machine and to talk to the travellers. The moment the machine landed the barest desert was crowded, and I can remember no landing-ground without the click of many cameras. The other impression is of great kindness and most understanding tact from many and various hosts and hostesses of all nationalities. For instance, the Governor of Malta, the Italian Governor-General at Benghazi, the High Commissioner of Iraq, the British Resident in the Persian Gulf, the officials of the Indo-European Telegraph Co. at Jask, and the Maharajah of Jodhpur, to mention only a few. One and all, from London to Delhi, they gave a delightful background to all the many interests of a unique journey.

1 Read Amy Johnson's account of her flight and suggest two ways in which the modern pilot is better off than she was.

2 What evidence is there that there was no airport in Rangoon in 1930? Can you say why? Is this likely to be true today?

3 Find out more about the careers of Amy Johnson and her husband Jim Mollison.

4 On a map of the world, trace the route taken by the Secretary of State and his wife, in 1926. Write to an airline company (Air India or British Airways) and get a map of the modern route from London to Delhi.

5 How far did the Hoares travel on the first day? Where did they land on the second day? What does this tell you about (i) the speed of the aeroplane, (ii) the fuel capacity of its tanks? Find out how long a modern aeroplane takes to get to France and Italy.

6 Why did the Secretary of State and his wife go on this flight? Find out more about Alan Cobham, another man who tried to make flying popular.

7 Why was there a great interest in the flight in 1926? Would there be the same interest today?

c)

6 LEEDS—NOTTINGHAM—LONDON—PARIS (Daily) L. S. and P.A.

Miles	Airports of			Airports of		
0	LEEDS	dep 11 20 13 40	PARIS	dep	9 30
65	NOTTINGHAM ...	arr 11 50 14 10	HESTON	arr	11 25
		dep 12 0 14 20		dep 9 30 11 45	
175	HESTON	arr 12 55 15 15	NOTTINGHAM. ...	arr 10 25 12 40
		dep 13 25 ...		dep 10 35 12 50	
435	PARIS	arr 15 20 ...	LEEDS	arr 11 5 13 20

‡ Lands at Berck (for Le Touquet) by special arrangement

Distance and Time allowance for conveyance between Airport and Town Terminus

TOWN	AIRPORT	TOWN TERMINUS	Miles	Minutes
LEEDS	Sherburn in Elmet	Corn Exchange ...	12	40
NOTTINGHAM ...	Tollerton ...	Black Boy Hotel ...	2½	30
LONDON	Heston ...	Langham Hotel, Portland Place, W. 1 ...	14	45
PARIS	Le Bourget ...	France—Tourisme, 4-6 Rue de Sèze ...	—	45

FARES

	NOTTINGHAM			LONDON			LE TOUQUET			PARIS		
	Single	Ret.	Ex. Bg.	Single	Ret.	Ex. Bg.	Single	Ret.	Ex. Bg.	Single	Ret.	Ex. Bg.
	s. d.	s. d.	s. d.	s. d.	s. d.	s. d.	s. d.	s. d.	s. d.	s. d.	s. d.	s. d.
LEEDS	18 0	30 0	0 3	42 0	70 0	0 6	84 0	147 0	0 6	105 0	189 0	0 6
NOTTINGH'M ...	...	...	...	25 0	45 0	0 6	70 0	130 0	0 6	90 0	170 0	0 6

Ex. Bag.—Excess Baggage per lb.

1 How far is it from Leeds to Nottingham? What was the average speed of the flight between these cities in 1934?

2 What was the average speed of the flight from Heston (London) to Paris?

3 Why was the time taken to get to and from the airports a deterrent to businessmen who might have thought of flying from London to Leeds?

4 All flying took place in daylight. Why? Why might this deter the London businessman who wanted to visit someone in Nottingham? How might he have travelled to make sure that he got there and back in one day?

1) Lord Nuffield explains his success

The success of Morris Motors happened because we took steps to achieve a continually improving product, and a reduction of cost so that prices could fall. The best way was to get specialists on every separate unit of the job. The work is better and more cheaply done. Even at the present moment, we have contracts running with at least 200 firms for various parts. At Oxford we merely assemble.

The firm that makes only one important part is probably making larger quantities than we should. It is interested in nothing else; it can keep its brains on that unit. We frequently ask contracting firms to do work at prices that they believe to be impossibly low. Usually they have not realised the savings of standardising operations, a continual flow of work.

(Andrews and Brunner, *Life of Lord Nuffield* 1955)

1 Why was a firm such as Girling able to make better quality brakes than Morris might have made in his own works at Oxford?

2 Why were thousands of people able to buy cars in the 1920s and 1930s?

3 Explain how the buying of cars created employment.

4 Why did Morris build his factory in Cowley, Oxford? Why was he, like most other industrialists, unwilling to build his factory in one of the depressed areas?

Questions on Chapter Twenty-three

1 *Read the first section of the Chapter. Can you suggest why (i) travelling through towns was very slow, (ii) Victorian and Edwardian streets were very dirty places, (iii) many working class people walked and never travelled in a bus or cab?*

2 *Why did William Morris not make his own sparking plugs, electric lamps, brakes, and so on? Find out the names of firms which supply nearly all the motorcar firms with these parts. What tertiary industries have grown up as a result of car ownership?*

3 *Why had few people had much chance of hearing any of the world's great orchestras before 1914? Why was this no longer true by 1939?*

4 *Write a letter from someone who has just listened to his first broadcast in the 1920s.*

5 *Ask your local librarian to let you see some nineteenth century newspapers. Make a note of four ways in which they differ from the modern newspaper.*

6 *Why did the development of the railway system help (i) the makers of Pears Soap, (ii) Lord Northcliffe, (iii) trade union leaders such as Ernest Bevin?*

7 *Why did millions of poorly paid and unemployed go to the cinema every week? Why could they afford to do so?*

8 *Find out more about the work of Alexander Graham Bell, the inventor of the telephone.*

Extract

A mobile nation

Buses began to run on new routes: as cities spread out, so the local buses extended their itineraries. The long-distance charabanc challenged the railway for speed and comfort, and made night journeys from the north and west of England to London. The charabanc opened up rural districts which were still almost inaccessible by rail.

The cheap car and the new bus service brought ribbon-building. This meant stringing houses along main roads instead of building them in compact village-like masses. For the tenants, the advantage was obvious; access to the road and an uninterrupted country view from their back windows.

Saturday and Sunday evenings – when cars from London and other big cities were hurrying home in an unbroken stream, trying to overtake one another on tricky, tortuous roads – and the workday rush-hour in Town in foggy weather were the bloodiest times.

(R. Graves and A. Hodge, *The Long Weekend* 1950)

Unit Six   A new society 1939–78

The last forty years have been years of great change. A comparison between the 1930s and 1970s will show this. In part this change was due to the Second World War during which new industries were developed, old industries brought out of the depression and great social reforms either brought in or planned.

The Labour Party won a majority in the House of Commons for the first time in 1945 and built the modern welfare state on foundations that had been laid by the Liberals and Conservatives. In 1951 the Conservative Party came back to power and maintained the modern welfare state – a sign of the growth of the degree of state interference in the nation's life which we now take for granted.

From 1945–70 both the Labour and Conservative governments remembered the high level of unemployment that Britain endured in the 1920s and 1930s. Governments of both Parties tried to carry out policies to ensure full employment (Chapter 26). High wages, full employment, social security benefits and mass production of consumer goods in modernised industries combined to create a new society – in which the majority of the people enjoyed a very high standard of living (Chapter 26). In the later 1950s most writers, and many of their readers, believed that 'there are no poor now' – so great was the contrast between life in the 1950s and life in the 1930s.

However, in the 1960s and 1970s people became less optimistic and they became more fully aware of the many, deep pockets of poverty and hardship that still exist in modern Britain. People also became aware of the two new problems that were the result of the creation of the new affluent society. These were *inflation* (or rising prices) and an almost continual *balance of payments* crisis as Britain bought more of the world's goods than she was able to pay for. The price of full employment was a fall in the value of money and an almost bankrupt Britain. The need for new policies became clearer in the 1970s (Chapter 28).

The demand for labour had been so great that employers welcomed the flood of immigrants which poured into Britain in the 1950s and 1960s. These workers were additions to a labour force which, by the 1960s, included about eight million women workers – about half of them married. Women

"Marvellous! My popularity among the passengers isn't sinking!"

had once had to fight for 'the right to work' (Chapter 18). In the 1960s and 1970s they have achieved that right — at least in most fields. Their modern fight has been for equal pay, equal treatment with male employees doing the same job, and an equal opportunity (Chapter 27).

The new industries of modern Britain need more qualified workpeople than did the old industries of Victorian Britain. One result of this was the growth in the amount of money spent by governments on children's education (Chapter 27). These children also benefited from the development of the welfare state, from many of the products of the new industries (medicines, cheap clothing etc) and from the general rise in the living standards of their parents. But they were also the first to suffer, in the late 1970s, when large-scale unemployment became a serious problem (Chapter 28).

In 1964 the Labour Party won the General Election, largely because the Conservatives seemed to have failed to find answers to Britain's economic problems. Many people hoped that Harold Wilson (on left), George Brown (in centre) and James Callaghan (in doorway marked 'Engine Room') would solve these problems. Unfortunately they did not do so. Indeed they allowed workers to earn even higher wages — which was very popular as the Opinion Polls showed. However the policy was disastrous; the pound became worth less (although not worthless) and Britain had to pay higher prices for all its imports which merely pushed prices up even faster. It seemed, in the 1960s, as if no political party was able to solve Britain's economic problems.

Chapter 24 War and society

In January 1933 Adolf Hitler became Chancellor (or Prime Minister) of Germany. He was popular with the German people and one of his promises was that he would take revenge on the countries which had defeated Germany in the First World War. The leaders of those countries, especially the U.S.A., Britain and France, did not believe that anyone (even Hitler) would want to go to war again after the great sufferings that had been caused by the First World War. Certainly the people of their own countries did not want war. Throughout the 1930s they supported their governments as they gave in to Hitler's demands for more land for Germany and for the Germans to be allowed to have a larger army, navy and air force. Finally, in September 1939, the British and French governments decided that 'enough was enough'. When Hitler invaded Poland, the Allied Powers declared war on Hitler's Germany and the Second World War had begun. It did not end until 1945.

A German U-boat sinking a British merchant ship. Between 1939 and 1945 thousands of ships were sunk and the country suffered because of this loss of scarce shipping, skilled workmen and cargoes.

1 *Explain why the Germans attacked British shipping between 1939 and 1945.*

2 *Why was there an increase in some types of imports during wartime? Why did this, plus the loss of shipping, mean that there was a drop in the level of food imports?*

3 *Why did the government bring in a system of food rationing? How do we 'share out' scarce goods (e.g. Rolls-Royce cars) during peacetime? Why was this not done for scarce food during wartime?*

The First World War had serious effects on the British economy (Chapter 19). The Second World War lasted longer, was fought over a much wider area and was much more destructive of everything, except manpower, than the First World War. It is not surprising that this war had more serious effects than the First World War.

Government control of industry

By 1943 the government controlled three-quarters of the nation's industrial power. It used the products of mines, steelworks, engineering shops and mills for war purposes. One effect of this was that British exports dwindled to almost nothing. Britain lost many markets, particularly in North and South America to which she had once sold many goods in peacetime. Britain had also invested a lot of money abroad. About half these overseas investments had to be sold during the War to help pay for necessary imports.

A general view of the bomb damage in the City of London. This photograph was taken from the top of St Paul's on 3 January 1941. There was similar damage in Liverpool, Manchester, Coventry and many other cities and towns. The Home Secretary's Report after a bomb attack in October 1940 noted:

* London people lost much sleep and suffered anxiety and discomfort, but there was no breakdown, no panic and no mass evacuation, except in the small heavily bombed areas. The effect was one very largely of surprise. After a few days the first horror of the raids wore off and people became adjusted to the new conditions of shelter life. Disorganization was more serious. The complicated network of railways was cut at many places at once. In three weeks, 104 railway bridges were put out of action for periods ranging from a day to a month. Roads were blocked by craters and debris. Thousands of water and gas mains were broken. Telephone exchanges were put out of action and postal deliveries hampered.
(Public Records Office, CAB(67/9) (41/44)

Social effects

Everyone in Britain was affected by the War. Five million people were conscripted into the armed services where members of every social class served side by side. Millions of men and women served in the *Civil Defence* as ambulance workers, firefighters, air-raid wardens and firewatchers. Women of every class queued for food and clothes. The effect of this social mixing, under the stress of war, was to help to remove class distinctions and give people a sense of common purpose.

Social conscience

From early in the War the government imposed a system of rationing for almost all goods. In this way the government ensured that everyone had a share of scarce food and things such as clothes, sweets, tobacco and petrol. For the millions who had lived on the dole until 1939 (Chapter 20), but who now had a job in wartime Britain, there was a chance to buy fruit, meat, butter and eggs. All these were 'luxuries' that they had not known in the depressed years. Many people were determined that if this could be the case in wartime it should be the case in peacetime also.

Evan Roderick Jones, a coal miner in Cryhant, Glamorgan, having Sunday dinner with his family in September 1941. Although food was rationed, the wage-earning miner could afford to eat more food than he could afford during the long period of unemployment.

1 *Why had coal miners been out of work in the 1920s and 1930s?*
2 *Why did many miners manage to get work after 1938?*
  How did this affect the standard of living of the miner and his family?

Evacuation

The government made a decision to *evacuate* children from the crowded industrial cities as soon as possible. The cities were in danger of being bombed and the children would be safer in the suburbs, villages and country towns. Here the government 'dumped' the children onto everyone who had room to spare. The result was the greatest social mixing of the war. Many of these well-to-do people, living in comfortable and large homes. In the first week of September 1939 over one million children were taken from the slums of London and other cities and put into the homes of these, often unwilling, foster parents.

There were many reports of the horror with which the slum children were greeted. Children from places like Stepney had never seen a bath, since there was no bath in nine-tenths of the houses in Stepney. Children from the slums of Glasgow had little idea of using a toilet. They came from an area where there was one toilet between thirty families, few of whom bothered to use the filthy place. Few children knew how to use knives and forks. They had been brought up on bread and margarine, chips and cream buns.

These children were the victims of bad housing, poverty and ignorance. While some people remained hostile to the newcomers, many became convinced that 'something had had to be done'. Some of the demands for social reform came from these middle class homes.

A bombed-out Liverpool family waiting outside a reception centre in 1940. Some children from such families had been evacuated before the bombing started.

The Army and social awareness

At least once a week everyone in the armed forces had to attend a lecture by someone sent by the Army Bureau of Current Affairs. In this way over five million people were educated into social awareness and passed on their changed views to their families and relatives at home.

One of the many classes run by the Army Bureau of Current Affairs. In these classes men and women from different social groups sat together, learned from each other as one former soldier remembered:

* As in all wars, there were phases of violent action punctuated by long periods of boredom and apathy during which people had time to read and argue and discuss. In those days the troops were much concerned with what Britain was going to be like after the war. There was a great deal of discussion going on about war aims. (A. Thompson, *The Day before Yesterday* 1971)

Wartime social reform

The Coalition government was determined to reform post-war British society. It started by instituting major reforms during the war itself. School meals which had once been a hand-out for the poor were made available for every child. This was done partly to allow mothers to go to work and partly to ensure that the young received at least one good meal each day. Every schoolchild received a third of a pint of milk each day. Children under school age were looked after and their mothers could buy cheap milk. The government paid the difference between this price and the normal price. At welfare clinics the government distributed vitamin pills, orange juice and cod liver oil to expectant and nursing

One of the first mothers to draw a Family Allowance, August 1945.

mothers so that their babies were protected from the effects of wartime diet.

These welfare clinics were open to people of all classes. Equally widely available were the services of the Assistance Board which replaced the Unemployment Assistance Board. In wartime Britain it was not only the means-tested poor who went to the Assistance Board; anyone who was bombed out of home or whose husband had died on war service could apply for help.

In 1944 the government passed the Family Allowance Act – which came into operation in August 1945. This Act entitled mothers with more than one child in the family to a Family Allowance payable at the Post Office.

In 1944 the government also passed the Education Act which abolished fee-paying in grammar schools so that for the first time Britain provided 'free secondary education for all'. The government promised to build more universities and colleges and to provide grants for students going on with their education. It also decided that the school leaving age was to be raised to fifteen as soon as possible and to sixteen whenever this could be done.

The Beveridge Report

For most people in wartime Britain the most positive proof that life was going to be better in post-war Britain was the appearance in 1942 of the Beveridge Report. William Beveridge had been a civil servant who had helped Lloyd George and the other radical Liberals. He had been head of the London School of Economics between the Wars and in 1941 the government asked him to head a Commission which would examine the social services.

Beveridge's Report was greeted as a blueprint for the better society which almost everyone looked forward to. People queued at Stationery Offices and bookstalls to buy the Report, while Beveridge himself appeared on thousands of platforms up and down the country, explaining the contents of this bestseller.

Briefly, his Report noted that there were five 'Giant Evils' – Want (or poverty), Disease (or ill health), Ignorance (because of insufficient schooling), Squalor (or inadequate housing) and Idleness (due to unemployment). Beveridge also indicated how each of these 'giants' could be tackled (or 'slain') by government action. His Report called on the government to spend much more on education (which the 1944 Act promised to do). It called for government spending as a means of ensuring full employment (as the 1943 White Paper promised). It asked for the creation of a *National Health Service* in which everyone would get, free, all the medical

William Beveridge. In his Report he wrote:

* Social security must be achieved by cooperation between the state and the individual. The state should offer security for service and contribution. The state organizing security should not stifle incentive, opportunity, responsibility; in establishing a national minimum, it should leave room and encouragement for voluntary action by each individual to provide more than that minimum for himself and his family.
(W. Beveridge, *Social Insurance and Allied Services* 1942)

attention and medicine required. It demanded a vast expansion of council house building, and a new Ministry of National Insurance (created in 1944) to administer the simple insurance scheme by which poverty would be tackled.

Beveridge proposed the abolition of the existing insurance schemes, for health, unemployment and pensions. These involved a number of cards, a number of government departments and separate payments. He proposed that every worker would pay into one Insurance Fund. This Fund would pay out the pensions, unemployment benefits and pay for the expanded Health Service.

While the public greeted this Report with delight, the Coalition government tended to play it down. Churchill talked about 'doing Beveridge when we could afford it' – and many people believed that this might be 'never'. It was the *Daily Mirror* and the Army Bureau of Current Affairs which led the demand that Beveridge's plans should be implemented as soon as the war ended.

A run-down system

During the war about one-third of Britain's homes were damaged or destroyed and factories, ports, bridges and roads had suffered. This damage would have to be made good after the War – so that a good deal of material would have to be imported merely to replace what had been there before. The railway system, coalmining industry, electricity supply system and most of the rest of Britain's industrial capacity had not been properly maintained or repaired so that Britain came out of the war with a run-down industrial system. A great deal of material as well as machinery would have to be imported after the war merely to do, quickly, what ought to have been done during the seven years of war.

Plans for Post-War reconstruction

At the end of the First World War Lloyd George had promised that he would build 'a country fit for heroes to live in'. He had done nothing of the sort. The Second World War Coalition government, led by Winston Churchill, decided that the British people would not be let down a second time. In 1941 a Labour MP, Walter Greenwood, was appointed Minister in charge of planning the reconstruction of post-war Britain. In 1942 the government produced its ideas on this reconstruction in a White Paper which marked a major step forward. The government accepted responsibility for providing decent housing, schools, medical services as well as jobs. In 1943 another White Paper on Full Employment outlined the government's plans for ensuring that there would never again be a repetition of the large-scale unemployment of the 1920s and 1930s.

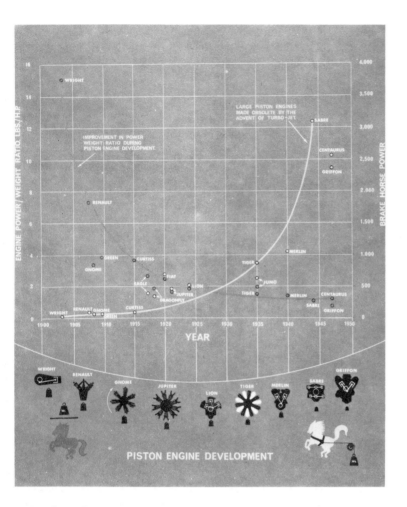

A chart which shows how the piston engine became more efficient and more powerful. Notice the rate of improvement during wartime.

Some benefits

Some economic benefits came out of the war. The government spent a great deal of the nation's money on scientific research and development. Ideas which had been ignored in peacetime were properly financed during the war. Whittle's jet engine, designed in 1936, but ignored by everyone before 1939, was used to power the Meteor, the first jet plane, in 1941. With the invention of the jet, Britain had made a gigantic stride in aviation. Indeed, aviation was a major gainer from the war. In place of the low-powered clumsy machines that flew in 1939 the government paid for the production of powerful engines, huge bombers and speedy fighters. The government also developed improved air-to-air and air-to-ground communication systems which made flying much safer. After the war these new aeroplanes and improved equipment would lead to a much better aviation industry and rapid increases in the numbers of aeroplanes and passengers flying in and out of Britain.

Similar developments took place in many other fields as

scientists were encouraged to experiment so that they might produce new weapons or new ways of manufacturing goods more efficiently. Perhaps the most obvious progress was made in the field of medicine, where penicillin and the miracle sulpha drugs were produced. After the war these drugs and others would allow doctors and surgeons to attack diseases which had previously been major killers.

Election 1945

The war against Germany ended in May 1945, although Japan continued to fight in the Far East. After the rejoicing of V(ictory in) E(urope) Day, Churchill asked Attlee and other Labour members of his government to continue with the Coalition until Japan had been defeated. The Labour leaders were prepared to go along with this demand. They did not fancy fighting an election against the war hero, Churchill. They remembered the Coupon Election in 1918. But the Labour Party was holding its Annual Conference at Brighton in May 1945. Attlee asked the Conference to decide whether

Denis Healey addressing the Labour Party Conference, June 1945. Alfred (later Lord) Robens remembered:

* I do remember very well indeed the numbers of men home on leave who came on to platforms in their uniforms, who were saying they did not want to resume civilian life under the conditions they had had before they went into the services. There's no doubt about this impact of life in the thirties upon these young men.

the Party should remain in the Coalition or come out and be ready to fight the first of the post-war elections.

The Conference decided that the Coalition should be broken up. Parliament was dissolved on June 15, Polling Day was July 5. Because the voting papers of servicemen overseas had to be sent to Britain, the declaration of the result was fixed for July 26. Most people seemed to think that the war hero would lead the Tories to a great victory.

Churchill was followed by huge crowds wherever he appeared during the campaign. People cheered him and seemed to want to thank him for his wartime leadership. But Labour candidates also had their enthusiastic followers.

On July 26 the result was declared. The Labour Party had won 393 out of 639 seats – the greatest electoral victory of all time. Social reform, Beveridge, full employment, reconstruction – life was going to be different.

The war had had a very great effect on the political, social and economic life of the nation and this new House of Commons was the outward sign of these changes.

Churchill received a hero's welcome during the election campaign May–June 1945. The people were saying 'Thank you' for his wartime leadership. But they were going to vote Labour.

Documents

a) Tory and Labour Party Conference, 1945

Although the 1945 Tory Conference had a naturally exalted mood which came from having Winston Churchill as the leader, among the rank and file there was a traditionalist carry-over which seemed to me to be completely out of tune with the times. There were very few new ideas at that conference. There was the great mystique of Churchill; one of my very great memories is seeing Churchill get up, literally with tears streaming from his eyes, to the tune of 'Land of Hope and Glory' and receiving a very great ovation. But the national mood, as personified by Winston Churchill, was certainly not the mood of those people who had been thinking about what Britain would be like after the war and who had ideas as to the political future.

When I went to the Labour Party Conference the thing was very different, there was a different kind of exaltation. You had many soldiers who had come back from the war. Instead of all the white-haired bald-headed pacifists of the past, there was a new breed of Labour supporter. The young Labour officer would once have seemed a contradiction in terms, but here suddenly you had very striking, good-looking young men like Denis Healey, John Freeman, Roy Jenkins, Jim Callaghan coming to the rostrum one after the other – speaking as servicemen who had fought for their country and who had a vision of a new Britain after the war which would be based on socialist principles. Somewhere in the middle you had men like Bevin, a great trade union leader, a man who commanded a big trade union battalion, side by side with Herbert Morrison, a son of the moderate centre, a traditional socialist, yet opposed to extreme leftism. The whole thing of course was presided over by Clem Attlee. Now Clem Attlee himself, though he was a suburban solicitor from Stanmore, a man who had been to a minor public school, a person whose passion was cricket and sherry, here he was – the leader of the party whose interests were soccer and beer, and certainly rather different from the traditional attitudes which Attlee as a middle-class bourgeois represented. The great binding element was a passion for change.

(from A. Thompson, *The Day before Yesterday* 1971)

b) A New MP in the House of Commons, 1945

I had literally never been to the House of Commons before my election. I went into this great chamber and I was sitting down, then the Speaker came in and we had Prayers. Then, before anything could develop, a Welsh miner called Griffiths, a very short vigorous man with blue scars on his nose, got up and started singing 'The Red Flag'. Spontaneously about 300 Labour members all rose up and started singing, or at least trying to sing, 'The Red Flag', because many of the new intake simply

didn't know the words. Most of them knew the tune but they didn't know the words. And there we were – all bellowing away. The Tories on the other side, they looked at us absolutely aghast, they'd seen nothing like it before and to some of them it was as if their fears had been realized and that revolution had arrived, at the Palace of Westminster.

(from A. Thompson, *The Day before Yesterday* 1971)

1 *Why were the Tories 'exalted' to have Churchill as their leader? Why did they believe that he would lead them to a victory in the 1945 Election? (see also Extract 84)*

2 *'People who had been thinking about what Britain would be like after the War'. How had the policies of the Coalition government helped this thinking? What was the significance of the Beveridge Report in this respect?*

f Britain give power to
dslide makes history

E TAKES
SEES KING

ife drives new Premier
to Palace: Dramatic
oves as Potsdam waits

By BILL GREIG

R the first time in history the people of Britain have chosen a Labour ernment with a clear majority over parties.

st night Mrs. Attlee, wearing right red hat, drove her and in a small car to Bucking- Palace. There the King invited Clement Attlee to become e Minister. He accepted.

f an hour earlier a red-eyed Mr. Churchill, ng a cigar and giving the V-sign, had

c) The front page of the *Daily Mirror* on the morning of Labour's 1945 election victory.

3 *Can you explain why so many young officers supported the Labour Party in 1945?*

4 *Find out what positions had been occupied in wartime Britain by: Attlee, Bevin and Morrison. How did this affect (i) Labour Party confidence in their leaders, (ii) the Labour Party's fitness to govern?*

5 *Give four reasons why the Labour Party won the 1945 Election.*

6 *What was the significance of the singing of the 'Red Flag' in the House of Commons in 1945?*

Extracts

Wartime memories

'There was a sense of common purpose that didn't exist in the 30s. The class divisions vanished, or almost vanished; people were employed in very many different ways.

They might be air raid wardens, or dealing with rationing, or this that and the other. It brought them in contact with all kinds of people. They had this sense of common purpose, it gave their lives colour and substance.'

(quoted in *People at War*, BBC, 1971)

Recollections of Christopher Mayhew, Labour candidate in the 1945 election

It was a tremendous crusade, everything was going to be changed. In a strange way, it wasn't only going to be society that was changed, we ourselves were going to be changed. It must sound naive now, and maybe it was only the younger candidates and our younger supporters who felt that, but it was a definite feeling at the time.

Questions on Chapter Twenty-four

1 *Why did government, industrialists and private individuals have to spend a great deal of money on rebuilding in post-war Britain? Why did this affect employment prospects? Why did this rebuilding lead to a rise in the level of imports? How were these paid for?*

2 *Write a series of extracts from a diary kept in wartime Britain in which the author writes about (i) bombing attacks on the towns and cities, (ii) the danger involved, (iii) rationing, (iv) the 'togetherness' of the various social classes.*

3 *Write a letter from a middle class housewife who has been forced to take evacuees from London slums. Write another from one of the children who is living in the countryside, and is in a good home.*

4 *Make a list of (i) reforms, (ii) proposals for future reforms, produced by the wartime Coalition government.*

5 *Why were many families better off in wartime than they had been in the 1930s? How did this experience affect their expectations for the future in post-war Britain?*

6 *Write a paragraph on the Beveridge Report.*

Chapter 25   Industry and the new society

Wartime Lend-Lease

During the war Britain had to cut her exports. To help pay for the imports she needed, Britain sold some of the overseas investments she had made in the nineteenth century. But this did not produce enough money to pay for the munitions and other essential imports. The U.S.A. came to Britain's aid by setting up a system of Lend-Lease. The Americans did not sell goods to the British; they merely loaned them until the war was won. America would not demand payment for goods damaged or destroyed during the war. The British were, in a sense, fighting the war to the last American tank.

The end of the Lend-Lease

This generous arrangement ended as soon as the Labour government had been elected. The American government was not going to help a Socialist government to succeed. From August 1945 war-damaged Britain had to try to earn the money she needed to pay for imports by exporting. And her imports bill after the war would be much larger than it had been in 1938 because she needed very large imports of timber, steel and other items, to rebuild.

The United States loan, 1945

One way of trying to cope with this problem was to cut down on less essential imports. Food imports were held down by continuing the rationing system. Only when the country had recovered after 1950 did this slowly come to an end. The government held down imports of building materials by a system of building licences. These were issued only for the most essential work and post-war Britain continued to carry the scars of wartime bombing until the more prosperous days of the 1950s allowed a relaxation and an increase in imports.

In September 1945 Keynes was sent to the U.S.A. and he got the Americans to lend Britain £1,250 million to pay for the imports needed to help rebuild British industry. It was hoped that this would be enough to get Britain to the point where she could pay her way. Unfortunately there was a sharp rise in prices of raw materials and other goods because the rest of the world was also trying to rebuild after the war. By 1947 all this loan had been spent and Britain was only half-way to the point of recovery.

Ernest Bevin, Clement Attlee and Herbert Morrison, Labour's leaders together, listening to the results of the General Election 1945. Attlee wrote, 'By far the most pressing and dominant item on the agenda was to reconstruct the industry of this country; to redeploy the labour force to enable us to earn our keep in the quite hideous situation which arose from the sudden cut-off of American aid'.

Marshall Aid

Fortunately the American Secretary of State, George C. Marshall, realised that a bankrupt Britain would be the proof that the capitalist system did not work. He proposed that the United States government should give Britain and other war-damaged European countries massive aid.

The signing of Marshall Aid on 7 July 1948. Seated on the left of the picture: Stafford Cripps and Ernest Bevin. Standing on the extreme left a youthful Harold Wilson.

Devaluation

By 1949 British industry had began to recover. Exports were rising and imports held down because of rationing and licensing. But the recovery was not going quickly enough. In September 1949 the Chancellor, Cripps, announced that the pound would be devalued so that British exports would be cheaper and, it was hoped, more would be sold. The pound had been worth $4.03 and a British car costing £400 had sold for $1,612. After September 1949 the pound was only worth $2.80. The same car would now sell at $1,120 and it was hoped more would be sold at the lower price.

Stafford Cripps, Chancellor of the Exchequer, and Harold Wilson, President of the Board of Trade, in the canteen at the Board of Trade in 1947.

Recovery and Korea

By 1950 Britain had recovered. Her exports were twice as large as they had been in 1938 and imports had been held down. Britain was paying her way. Then Britain became involved with the U.S.A., Russians and Chinese in the Korean War (1950–51). This led to an increased demand for materials which the warring countries would need to fight the war. The fear that the war might last a long time pushed up that demand. Prices rose so that Britain had to pay much higher prices for her imports.

The Labour government decided to spend about £1,500 million a year on rearming Britain because of the fear that a Third World War might break out. This increased the government's demand for certain imports and also led to an increase in taxation. This split the Labour government and led to a Conservative victory at the General Election in October 1951. It was the Conservatives who had the benefit of the fall in import prices following the end of the Korean War. They were also able to take advantage of the rise in exports flowing from the new and rebuilt industries developed during the years of shortage and crisis.

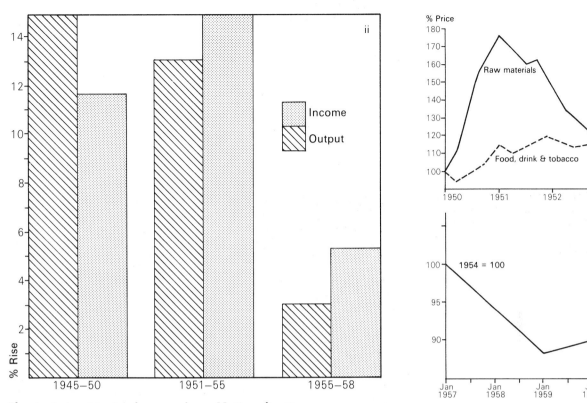

The rise in import prices because of the increase in world demand after the start of the Korean War (i). Britain had to pay more for her imports and obtained relatively less for her exports (ii). After the end of the War import prices fell while prices continued to rise so that Britain obtained more for her output (iii).

Hugh Gaitskell had to produce a budget which allowed for this great increase in expenditure and so put on charges for spectacles and false teeth under the Health Service, partly to raise money and partly, some thought, as a symbol to the country that this was a very tough time. This led to the resignation of Bevan and Wilson and, possibly, to Labour's defeat at the next General Election.

Nationalisation

The Labour government (1945–51) took over large sections of British industry. The Bank of England (1945), the coal industry (1947), the transport system (railways, canals and road haulage), electricity and gas industries as well as iron and steel were taken from private ownership and handed over to public corporations.

One reason for nationalisation was that public ownership enabled the government to control the level of investment in these industries. In future it would be the government that would decide how much would be spent on modernising the railway system, mechanising the nation's coal mines and extending the electricity supply system. This investment, as Keynes had pointed out, would create employment.

Problems of nationalised industries

This use of the nationalised industries has created a problem. Were they supposed to be part of the social welfare system, creating employment by buying equipment during times of depression? Were they to provide cheap fuel, transport and steel to help private companies produce goods more cheaply than if they had charged a 'proper' price? Or were they to be run like any other business, selling their goods at the highest possible price and making the largest possible profit?

This problem has never been solved. Between 1970 and 1974 the Conservative government refused to allow the British Steel Corporation to put up its prices to private industry. The car industry got cheap steel from the nationalised industry and so made high profits from sales of cheap cars. However, the Steel Corporation then had to announce a working loss and the British taxpayer had to hand over hundreds of millions of pounds to this nationalised industry.

The sign of the newly-formed National Coal Board erected on the first day of public ownership in 1947.

The Conservatives and nationalised industries

Under the 1945–51 Labour government the Conservative opposition was too small to prevent nationalisation. When in power (1951–64) the Conservatives denationalised the iron and steel industry but left the rest of the nationalised industries alone. What Attlee called 'the logic of facts' seemed to prevent the Conservatives from handing back coal, electricity, gas and the rest, to private industry.

The Wilson government (1964–70) renationalised the steel industry and the Conservative Heath government (1970–74) did not denationalise it. Nationalisation had come to stay.

Indeed the Conservative government under Harold Macmillan (1956–64), seemed to go halfway to nationalising some industries itself. It forced the many small aircraft building firms to merge into two large firms – Hawker-Siddeley and the British Aircraft Corporation. One small firm, Handley-Page, refused to be driven into merger and tried to 'go it alone', only to become bankrupt and close down.

The Heath government went even further. In 1971 Rolls-Royce announced that it was bankrupt and would have to close down. The government nationalised the aero-engine section of this firm. The Wilson government followed this example in 1976 when it nationalised the bankrupt British Leyland Motor Corporation.

In other sectors of industry there has been a tendency towards merger so that a few firms control large sectors of industry. You can see this at work in the retail trade. Almost every High Street is dominated by the shops of a few, national firms. This is also true of manufacturing industry. Banks have had to follow this example. The financial needs of the larger firms could not be met by the smaller banks and they too have been forced to amalgamate into larger, but fewer, businesses such as the National-Westminster.

Full employment
In the 1930s there were millions of homes which had no wage-earner. After 1945 Britain had such a high demand for workers that millions of homes had two or more wage-earners.

The rebuilding of Britain was one reason for a high demand for labour. The government, through its National Health Service and greater expenditure on education and council-house building, increased that demand. Private industry built new factories and refineries. Nationalised industries modernised and expanded. All this expansion led to a demand for workers.

The wage-earners wanted to buy more goods in the shops with their earnings. This increased the demand for workers in factories producing those goods. Indeed the demand for workers was so high that it led to a campaign to get mothers back to work. By 1977 there were over nine million women at work, six million of whom were married.

Immigration
In this new society it was difficult for employers to get workers for low-paid, dirty or unpleasant jobs. This was particularly true in the South-East and Midlands where there was little unemployment and a great scarcity of workers. Many employers set up agencies in Malta and Cyprus to recruit workers there and in the early 1950s about 20,000 coloured immigrant workers and their families arrived each year from Asia, Africa or the West Indies. In 1960 the boom which had won Mr Macmillan the 1959 Election attracted 58,000 and in 1961 over 136,000 arrived. By 1964 over one million coloured immigrants had settled in Britain.

In 1962 the Conservative government passed the Commonwealth Immigration Act, which limited the number of immigrants allowed into Britain. The Labour government passed an even stricter Act in 1965 but it also passed the Race Relations Act, 1965, to try to prevent the growth of discrimination against the newcomers – and their children who were born in Britain and were British subjects by birth.

Arnold Weinstock of GEC, one of the most successful post-war industrial managers.

The old depressed areas (Development areas)

Because of the constantly increasing demand for more goods, and for more workmen to produce them, employers found that they could not manage in their factories and workshops in the South East and Midlands, to which they had flocked in the depressed 1930s. In post-war Britain they were forced, perhaps unwillingly, to build many of their new factories in those former depressed areas. Employment was created there, and some of the prosperity and affluence enjoyed in the South East and Midlands was brought to these older areas. The government was anxious to persuade employers to undertake such developments. They had, after all, tried to do so in the 1930s. The Town and Country Planning Act (1947) gave the government power to stop industrialists building anywhere they pleased. Until the early 1950s building materials were rationed so that industrialists had to apply for building licences if they wanted to build. The government could persuade the industrialists to build in a depressed area by refusing a licence for materials required for a development in the booming South East but offering one for a building in a depressed area. In this way Hoover were persuaded to build in Merthyr, ICI to build in Pontypool and the North East,

Enoch Powell, then Minister of Health, refused to pay nurses and other health service workers the sort of wages being paid in industry. This was a major cause for the increase in the rate of immigration in the 1960s; the immigrants were willing to do the lowly-paid jobs. Their children, born in Britain, will have higher expectations but the white population may be unwilling to give them the chance they deserve.

* A recent survey of an immigrant area in Birmingham showed a youngster is five times more likely to get a skilled job if he is white than if he is coloured. The chief youth employment officer in another Midlands city put it: 'There is no problem for coloured youngsters at all — provided they realise what their abilities are.' The question that no-one is trying to answer whether this means that if you're black, you're second class. (C. McGlashan in the *Observer*, 25 September 1966)

264

Fords to build in Liverpool and Chrysler to build in Scotland.

With the end of post-war scarcity and the need for building licences, the Board of Trade (now part of the Department of Trade and Industry) controlled industrial development by means of a system of development certificates. Any industrialist who wished to build a factory or workshop more than 5,000 square feet in size – and that is a small development – had to apply to the Board of Trade for a certificate. The Board issued these freely if the application was for a proposal to build in the depressed areas. If, however, the industrialist proposed to build in the more booming areas the Board was less eager to issue a certificate.

A special government department, the Location of Offices Bureau, was created to try to persuade companies to set up their offices in areas outside the crowded South East. This policy was so successful that by 1976 there was a shortage of office jobs in London. This together with the shift of small industrial firms because of city development, meant that there was a rise in the level of unemployment in the inner city – and in inner cities such as Birmingham, Manchester and Liverpool. The government has had to change its attitudes towards office development in London and the Location of Office Bureau is now actively engaged in trying to attract firms back into London as a means of providing work for the people living in inner London.

The government also tried to persuade industrialists to move into development areas by a system of grants and loans. If an employer built in a depressed area he received a grant – not repayable – from the government towards the cost of building, machinery and essential materials. The government built its own factories and let these off at a low rent to industrialists, who were thus saved the cost of building. Loans were available – at low rates of interest – to help the industrialists to build and equip their factories.

The ICI plant in Pontypool. In the 1930s Welsh miners had to beg in London's streets because there was no work for them in the valleys. (p. 230). In post-war Britain, government has used its powers to try to force industrialists to build their new factories in these depressed areas. This plant was begun in April 1945 while the Churchill government was still fighting the war against Hitler.

Documents

a) Toward European Prosperity

Closer economic co-operation began in 1947 with the rebuilding of war-shattered economies. It was stimulated by the Marshall Plan and given practical expression in the Organisation for European Economic Co-operation (O.E.E.C.).

Through the O.E.E.C. great progress was made in getting rid of quota restrictions and barriers between members. Production, consumption and trade in Western Europe have developed rapidly. Its people have reaped the benefits in swiftly rising standards of living.

The O.E.E.C. did not deal effectively with tariff barriers and there was a widespread feeling among its members that this should next be tackled. To abolish tariffs meant the formation either of a Customs Union or a Free Trade Area; the former involves a common external tariff, while the latter enables each country to maintain its individual tariff structure in relation to third countries.

The six signatories of the Rome Treaty looked towards a closely knit European Economic Community, with common economic, financial and social policies, with political federation as its ultimate objective. The U.K. and other members of the O.E.E.C., did not feel able to carry economic cooperation to these lengths. Negotiations towards the formation of a seventeen-country Free Trade Area within the O.E.E.C. collapsed in 1959.

These negotiations showed how much common ground there was in the thinking of a number of countries taking part. In consequence seven of those who were not members of the E.E.C. decided to pursue the aims of removing trade restrictions in a separate group. Their aim has been to keep up the momentum of the search for economic cooperation on a European scale, to build a bridge between them, the E.E.C., and the other members of the O.E.E.C., and to secure the advantage of tariff reductions and quota abolition among themselves, consistent with the movement towards freer world trade.

(The Treasury Information Division, *The European Free Trade Association* 1959)

1 What was 'the Marshall Plan'? How did it help the 'rebuilding of war-shattered economies'?

2 What 'great progress' was made through the O.E.E.C.? What is a quota? Why did the reduction of tariffs lead to increased trade?

3 What benefits did the people of Europe gain from the 'great progress'?

4 *What is a tariff? What two results followed the reduction of tariffs between European countries? How might Britain (i) have gained and (ii) have lost by following this policy of lowering tariffs?*

5 *How would a Customs Union differ from a Free-Trade Area? Why did British links with her Commonwealth make it difficult for Britain to support the plans for creating the E.E.C.?*

6 *What was the hope of the six countries which signed the Treaty of Rome? Name the six countries. Why would 'political federation' lead to Parliament having less power?*

THE CONSUMERS

b) The consumers

1 *How had the war lowered the amount of money Britain received from her overseas investments? Why did this lead to the need for an increase in exports after 1945?*

2 *Why did the government's policy of full employment lead to an increase in some imports? Why would this lead to either (i) increased exports or (ii) balance of payments problems?*

3 *Why did imported goods cost more in 1950 than they had cost in 1939? Why did this lead to the need for an increase in British exports?*

4 *From the answers you have made to questions 1–3 make a summary of the reasons why exports had to rise after 1945.*

5 *What, according to the cartoonist, were some of the problems facing the government's policy of increasing exports?*

6 *Why did the failure to increase exports sufficiently lead to problems for the Chancellor-shopkeeper?*

7 *Governments have had to put limits on (i) wage increases and (ii) government spending to try to help solve the balance of payments problem. How have such policies affected (i) imports and (ii) exports? Why have governments been unwilling to carry on those policies in the years leading to General Elections?*

1 *Read the caption on p. 259. Why did Britain have a balance of payments problem between 1945 and 1950? How was this problem affected by (i) the end of Lend Lease and (ii) Marshall aid?*

2 *Why did the government have to put restrictions on (i) house-building and (ii) food consumption between 1945 and 1950?*

3 *Look at p. 260 and the Fig. on p. 271. Give an account of the problems of re-armament as it might have been given by (i) Gaitskell (ii) Bevan and (iii) the taxpayer.*

4 *Explain why the Labour government nationalised many industries after 1945. Name four of the industries which were nationalised then.*

5 *What is meant by 'devaluation'. What effect does devaluation have on the prices of British imports and British exports.*

6 *Why did import prices (i) rise between 1949 and 1951 and (ii) fall after 1952?*

7 *Why was there a very high level of employment in Britain between 1945 and 1970?*

8 *Why did the British government and other employers welcome immigrant workers into Britain in the 1950s and 1960s? Why did the immigrants want to come to Britain?*

9 *Why were industrialists more willing to build in the depressed areas after 1945 than they had been in the 1930s? How did the government use its powers to influence the industrialists' decisions?*

Extracts

What Marshall Aid prevented

Rations of butter, sugar, cheese and bacon would all have had to be cut by over a third and there would have been less meat and eggs. Cotton goods would have disappeared from the home market, supplies of footwear would have been reduced and tobacco consumption would have been cut by three-quarters. It would have meant even less petrol for private motoring and few films, newspapers and books. Shortage of timber would have meant a further reduction in house building, perhaps to 50,000 a year. Most serious of all, our supplies of raw materials for industry would have been affected, and might have brought unemployment figures up to 1,500,000.
(Board of Trade Journal for 16 October 1948)

The reaction to nationalization

There was also not much real opposition to our nationalisation policy. It was realised on all side that the problem of the coal industry had been shockingly mishandled in the past and that if men were to be got to work in the pits a new start was necessary. Electricity and Gas had already to a large extent passed into public ownership, while the Conservatives had themselves been forced by the logic of facts in 1931 to carry through Morrison's London Transport Bill. Nationalisation of the Bank of England went through with the minimum of opposition. Of all our nationalisation proposals, only Iron and Steel roused much feeling.
(C. Attlee, *As it happened* 1954)

Chapter 26 Social welfare and economic problems

Winston Churchill was leader of the Conservative Opposition after his defeat in the General Election in 1945. In this picture he is shown addressing the Conservative Party Conference in 1947, where, with his friend, Lord Woolton, he started to build up the strength of the defeated Party. One of Woolton's main aims was to make sure that the conservatives should learn to support and not to oppose the social reforms of the Labour government. When they came back to power in 1951 the Conservatives continued the Labour policy of social reform.

The 'social revolution'

Speaking in 1949 to a Conference of Young Conservatives, Robert (later Lord) Boothby, said that Britain had gone through 'the greatest social revolution in its history'. The Labour Party had won its great victory in the General Election, 1945, because so many people had wanted just such a peaceful revolution. Boothby was wrong in at least one respect; the social revolution was not over in 1949. Conservative and Labour governments continued to improve the social security system. He was also wrong in thinking that after 1949 people would be satisfied. There are, even now, continual complaints at the gaps in the social security system.

National Insurance

In his Report, Beveridge proposed a system of National Insurance which, he claimed, would slay the giant evil, Want. James Griffiths, a former Welsh miner, was the Minister of National Insurance in the Attlee government. In 1946 he brought in the Industrial Injuries Act which replaced all the previous and unsatisfactory Workmens' Compensation Acts. In 1948 he introduced the National Insurance Act. National Insurance was compulsory for everyone of working age, except for married women. People paid varying amounts depending on whether they were employed or self-employed. In return for a single payment of 25p a week the worker would be entitled to receive benefit when he was sick or unemployed. He and his wife would also be entitled to a retirement pension and his wife to a widow's pension in the event of the husband's early death. The Act also provided for the payment of maternity benefits before and after the birth of a baby. At the other end of the life-span, a grant would be available to cover funeral expenses. The state became responsible for the welfare of all its people from 'the cradle (and before) to the grave'.

Graduated pensions scheme

As wages increased in the 1950s and 1960s, the benefits due under the Acts of 1946 and 1948 seemed to be too small. This led to increases in the benefits as well as in the weekly payments. In 1961 the Conservative government brought in a graduated pensions scheme. Under the 1946 and 1948 Acts workers paid a simple flat rate into the Insurance Fund.

This is a cartoon by Vicky who came to Britain as a refugee during the 1930s. He was a convinced socialist. He did not believe that Attlee (in hat), Morrison (with glasses), Wilson (with pipe), Gaitskell (between Wilson and Morrison) and the other leaders of the Labour Party were really socialists. They were too concerned merely with winning elections. If this meant that they had to follow Conservative policies they would do so.

This was changed and workers had to pay a percentage of their wages or salaries. In return they received a pension which varied with the size of their contribution. The well-paid got a higher pension than the lower-paid. In 1966 the Labour government applied the same principle to sickness and unemployment benefit.

National Assistance Board (NAB)

The Insurance Acts did not cover everyone. There were the blind, deaf, crippled, deserted or unmarried mothers and the wives of criminals. In 1948 the NAB was set up to look after these people. The Board provides homes for the homeless and for old people. It gives weekly grants to people whose incomes are too small to give them a minimum standard of living. During the 1950s and 1960s retirement pensions failed to increase as rapidly or as often as the cost of living. The majority of people applying to the Board were old age pensioners.

In 1966 this Board and the Ministry of Pensions and National Insurance were replaced by the Ministry of Social Security — as Beveridge had suggested in his Report in 1942.

The National Health Service (NHS)

The first National Insurance scheme had been brought in by one Welshman, Lloyd George, and improved on by a second, James Griffiths. A third Welshman, Aneurin Bevan, was appointed Minister of Health in August 1945. He created the National Health Serivce.

The NHS Act nationalised all the hospitals and provided free medical treatment, including the services of dentists and opticians. It compelled County and County Borough Councils to provide midwives, home-nurses, health visitors, facilities for vaccination and immunisation and an ambulance service. Everyone was free to choose a doctor with whom to register. For the first time there was a 'family doctor' for everyone and not only for those who could afford to pay one whenever they needed his services.

In 1946 it seemed as if the doctors might wreck the scheme. Some of them were frightened that a State Health Service might make them into civil servants, liable to be sent here or there as Ministers decided. Others thought that they might have an official from the Ministry telling them what treatment to give. Very many were afraid that the free system would mean an end to the well-paid system of private practice. The doctors' leaders called for a strike by doctors. They wanted them to refuse to treat patients under the NHS scheme. Bevan fought the doctors for eighteen months. He gave up the idea of paying them a fixed salary and allowed consultants the right to use NHS hospitals and facilities when they were treating private patients. This won the support of the influential leaders of the Royal Colleges of Physicians and Surgeons. They persuaded the mass of doctors to ignore the advice of their own leaders in the British Medical Association. 18,500 of the country's 20,000 doctors joined the scheme and one of the main features of the social revolution had been created in July 1948.

Aneurin Bevan, Minister of Health and Housing in the Attlee government 1945–51. Here he was examining a model of a new residential area.

Bevan is saying to the patient 'Just spots before the eyes. . . . Don't worry, we'll soon cure that!' Some people stood to lose from the introduction of the NHS but they were a minority. An attempt to organise a doctor's strike failed.

Paying for the National Health Service

Bevan thought that the NHS would cost the taxpayers about £140 million a year. However, by 1950 the cost had risen to £350 million. In 1950–51 the Labour government decided to spend about £1,500 million a year on rearmament. To help pay for this and to cut the amount being paid into the NHS, Hugh Gaitskell introduced health charges. Patients had to pay part of the cost of new false teeth and dental treatment. They also had to pay 5p for each prescription handed in at the chemist's and a part of the cost of new spectacles. This led to a political crisis. The Labour government was split over this issue. Since 1951 all governments, Conservative and

"ALL I ASK IS THAT YOU GET IT PROPERLY BALANCED"

The Attlee government created an expensive Welfare State between 1945 and 1950. Then, in 1950, it decided to spend an extra £1,500 million a year on defence. This led to an increase in taxation, a split in the Labour government and a slowing down in the advance of socialism.

An aerial view of Cumbernauld New Town near Glasgow.

Labour, have imposed new charges or increased the level of these first charges.

Housing

In his Report, Beveridge named Squalor as one of the giant evils to be overcome by government action. He wrote about the cramped and squalid conditions in which millions of people lived in Britain's old towns and cities. He showed that schemes for a Health Service and for a better education system would not work unless there was also a State-aided scheme for better housing.

New Towns

In 1944 the Churchill government suggested that fourteen *New Towns* should be built around London. These were not to be merely housing estates from which people travelled to work. They were to live and work in the New Towns.

In 1946 the Labour government passed the New Towns Act which set up ten Development Corporations, each of which was to set up a New Town. The Corporation received money to buy up land required for a town of between 50 and 100,000.

In 1952 the Conservatives passed the Town Development Act which gave government money to smaller towns which agreed to absorb 'overspill' populations from large cities. Bletchley, Aylesbury, Swindon and Basingstoke became overspill towns for taking people out of overcrowded London.

In these New Towns there was a greater mixing of classes than was possible in the older cities and large towns where each class had its own churches, schools, societies and clubs.

The homeless

Millions of people had been made homeless by wartime bombing. Millions more were living in houses which were over a hundred years old in 1945. Many had no bathrooms, no toilets and too little space. Aneurin Bevan, Minister of Health and Housing knew that there was a link between good housing and good health. He wanted to build as many houses as possible. But between 1945 and 1950 the country could import only a limited amount of timber because of the problems over Britain's balance of payments. Some of this timber had to be used to build factories, schools and other essential places. So only 200,000 houses were built between 1945 and 1950. Even so, the total of 1 million new houses was more than any other European country built in this period.

Council housing

Nearly all these houses were built by councils. They were rented by people who could not afford to buy their own homes. Each local council had its Housing Department and people who wanted a *council house* put their names on a waiting list. During 1946 thousands of people in different parts of the country took the law into their own hands. Tired of waiting for a house some put their belongings into old prams or handcarts. They left the one or two rooms where they had been living and set up home in old Army camps. Others took over luxury flats in Westminster and other parts of London. These flats had been occupied by the Services during the war and were waiting for redecoration before being handed back to their owners. The government was forced to help these 'squatters'. 563 Army Camps were made more comfortable and thousands of families helped to move into these temporary homes.

The housing boom 1953–70

Raw material prices fell after 1953 and building costs fell. The government could afford to allow much more timber to be imported because of the improvement in the balance of payments position.

Winston Churchill gave Harold Macmillan the position

A young boy looks out of the window of his house in South East London where he and his parents lived in two rooms. In the other picture on this page the family enjoys the comfort of a council house on one of the GLC's new estates.

of Minister of Housing with the job of building 300,000 new houses a year. Some of these houses were built by councils and were rented by people on the waiting lists. Other houses were built by private builders and were sold to people who could borrow money from a building society. By 1958 over ten million people were living in houses built since 1945. Hundreds of thousands of people were employed in building these houses; many more were employed to make the new furniture and fittings that the proud householders bought to go into their new homes. Here was one reason for the high rate of employment in the 1950s and 1960s.

Inflation, balance of payments and housing

But here also was one reason for inflation – or rising prices. These people were paid to build houses. They had money to

spend on cars. television sets and other goods. Since there were more people with more money chasing after these various goods, the manufacturers and shopkeepers were able to put up their prices. Not all these goods were made in this country. With the increasing prosperity there came an increase in the value of imported goods. German cars, Danish furniture, Japanese transistors and other foreign goods flooded into the British market. This pushed up the level of Britain's import bill. At the same time British manufacturers were able to sell as much as they wanted at home. They did not try to export as much as they might have done. This meant that there was never a great increase in the level of British exports. Here, then, was a second problem because of high employment. Britain was continually trying to spend more than she earned. (p. 266).

Great expectations 1957–60

Because of the high demand for labour, trade unions were able to demand higher wages. Employers were usually willing to pay these because they could get the money back by putting up the prices of their goods. When the country failed to export enough and imported too much, the government 'put on the brakes' by cutting back on the amount of government money spent on building, investment in nationalised industries, and wages for government employees such as teachers and nurses. Then when things improved, the government would take the brakes off and spend more money and so make sure that there was a high rate of employment again.

Harold Macmillan led the Conservatives to victory in the General Election, 1959, on the slogan 'You have never had it so good' and the warning 'Don't let Labour ruin it'.

The beginning of the end 1960–64

Soon after the General Election in 1959 it became clear that the country was once more heading for an economic crisis. Prices were rising too quickly and so were wages. Imports were rising faster than exports so that the country was unable to pay its way and had to borrow from overseas banks to pay for its imports. The United States government, which provided most of the loans to Britain, insisted that Britain join the Common Market.

The Macmillan government was also forced to act at home. It set up the National Economic Development Council (NEDC or Neddy) and the National Incomes Commission (or Nicky). Government ministers, leading employers and trade union representatives sat on Neddy. It was hoped that, together, they could plan Britain's economy in such a way that we would avoid inflation, cut down on our balance of

'Well, gentlemen, I think we all fought a good fight . . .'

Trog, in the *Spectator*, showed Mr Macmillan with 'members' of his 'Cabinet' on the day after the General Election, 1959. The satisfied buyers of the consumer goods shown here had voted for Tory Freedom and had rejected Gaitskell's demand for 'More Socialism'.

Signs in cartoon: CONSERVATIVE FREEDOM WORKS; LIFE IS BETTER WITH THE CONSERVATIVES DON'T LET LABOUR RUIN IT; PLANNED ECONOMY; SIGNPOST FOR THE SIXTIES; LAB '61

By 1961 Macmillan and his Chancellor, Selwyn Lloyd, had been forced to end the boom which had helped them with the 1959 election. Here Selwyn Lloyd was trying to hitch a lift from Harold Wilson, the leader of the Labour Opposition who had, in his pocket, the plans for bringing Britain out of a depression – he hoped.

payments' deficits and still manage to maintain a high level of employment.

Nicky was to advise the government on what wage increases the country could afford. Macmillan and his Chancellor, Selwyn Lloyd, hoped that once they had explained the position to trade unionists these would accept a lower level of wage increases than they had got used to. In 1961 there was a wage freeze during which the government tried to forbid employers to pay any increases at all. But this meant that people had less money to spend on goods in the shops, so that there was unemployment in the industries which had supplied these goods. This made the government unpopular. Just before the General Election 1964, Macmillan resigned.

The new government, under Sir Alec Douglas Home, tried to win back popular support by allowing higher wage increases, spending more money on investment and so making more jobs. But the result was, inevitably, a rise in the rate of inflation and a huge deficit on the balance of payments.

The Labour government under Harold Wilson tried to deal with these problems by adopting Selwyn Lloyd's policies of holding down wages and trying to plan the economy. By 1970 this government had succeeded in putting right the balance of payments. Britain was exporting more and importing less than it had been doing. Labour's supporters in the trade unions agreed to hold down wage demands for 1967 and 1968. But in 1969 the Wilson government was forced to give up its policy of holding down wages, because it wanted to win popular approval in the General Election in 1970.

There was a free-for-all in wages during 1969 and 1970; some unions got wage increases of 25 per cent (or one quarter) – others increased their wages by as much as $33\frac{1}{3}$ per cent (or one third). It is not surprising that by the time of the Election in 1970 inflation was once again getting out of hand. The Heath government came to power promising to 'Reduce Prices at a Stroke'. It couldn't and it didn't, as we shall see in Chapter 28.

Documents

a) A united Europe, a world power

I think what mattered to Macmillan, he's often said it, was the way in which the old world, Europe, would adapt itself to the new conditions, and he used to compare it to the ancient world, with Rome as America, and Greece as Europe. You could have a whole series of nation states, if you like, the Greek city states in modern guise, or you could build the new Constantinople in Europe allied to the great empire of the United States. But at the same time with its own life, and its own power, and I think he certainly saw the E.E.C. as a way towards something new of that kind.

(Sir Philip de Zulueta, 1971)

b) E.F.T.A. — a threat to European Unity

I think that from the start the idea of the Free Trade Area was a device directed against the Common Market. It excluded agriculture, it included only industrial products, and it was directed towards providing a split between Germany and France. France was interested in agricultural problems; Germany didn't like it, especially Dr Erhardt who didn't like any commitment on agriculture. I think it was engineered to destroy the Common Market and replace it by something which would exclude agriculture, and which would not have had the institutional arrangements for which the E.E.C. was the model. On the British side, there was the idea that they should build something which would be the Common Market without agriculture, without institutions; this was the aim of the Free Trade Agreement, which failed. They hoped probably that the Community would go in that direction.

(Etienne Hirsch)

c) General de Gaulle versus Britain

There had been a slight coldness between Britain and France towards the end of 1958, so immediately after the General Election in 1959 I went on a special visit to Paris to see if I could promote better relations again. General de Gaulle said, 'I would like you very much to come into the E.E.C., but you cannot come in from your point of view unless you bring your Commonwealth with you. We cannot have you in, if you bring your Commonwealth with you, so I'm afraid there can be no agreement.

(Selwyn Lloyd)

d) A special relationship with the U.S.A.

I thought it was very important that Britain played its role in Europe because it seemed to me that this was the only way that a soundly built structure could ever be erected in Europe, a political structure which would avoid all the destructive rivalries of the past. Therefore I felt that one had to look at the British nuclear relationship which was very heavily dependent on the United States, that the renewal and the extension of this relationship was bound to impair Britain's ability to play the role in Europe, which seemed to me to be a very desirable one. So that looking at it in those terms, from the point of view of what American policy should be, it seemed to me that we ought to discourage the extension of the nuclear deterrent into succeeding decades — which of course, is what we didn't do at Nassau. The effect of the decision at Nassau with regard to Polaris was to ensure that Britain would continue to be a nuclear power into the seventies and perhaps even into the eighties and I think that this is obviously one of the elements which resulted in de Gaulle's decision, on 14 January 1963, to deny British entry.

(George Ball, ex-American Secretary of Defence)

1 *From Documents (a) and (b) draw up a list of reasons why Britain wanted to 'enter Europe'.*

2 *Which countries were in E.E.C. in 1960? Which countries were in E.F.T.A. in 1960?*

3 *From Document (b) draw up a list showing the differences between E.E.C. and E.F.T.A. Why did Britain help to form E.F.T.A. and not join E.E.C.?*

4 *From Documents (b), (c) and (d) show why France was opposed to Britain's application to join E.E.C in 1961–2.*

5 *When did Britain join E.E.C.? Who was Prime Minister? What position had he held in 1961–2?*

6 *Arrange a debate on: 'Britain has gained by entering the E.E.C.'.*

"Naturally, Britain and U.S. must reaffirm their intention to arrange their domestic affairs so as to maintain confidence in their currencies"

I.M.F.

OLIVER

1 What is the I.M.F.?

2 Britain had received Marshall Aid in 1947. From which two new sources was Britain receiving loans in 1961 when this cartoon was drawn?

3 Look at the quotation in the left-hand corner. Do you think that countries which lend money to Britain have a right to tell Britain how to run her domestic policies? Why?

4 How might the government be able to 'arrange (her) domestic affairs' as the lenders demanded?

5 If the government failed to 'arrange (its) affairs' properly, what request might Britain have to make to the I.M.F. and the European lenders?

6 Why did Britain need even more aid from foreign lenders in 1974–6 than she had done in 1961?

1 Make out a list of reasons for the high level of employment between 1945 and 1970. (See also Chapters 24/25.)

2 How far do you agree with the claim made by Robert Boothby in 1949 (p. 268)? On what did he base his claims? Show that the Conservatives followed Labour's policies after 1951.

3 What criticisms would you make of the social security system to-day?

4 Why did the government bring in the graduated insurance scheme in 1961? How far did that differ from the scheme brought in in 1946 (p. 268)? Which do you think is the better scheme? Why?

5 Explain the fears of the doctors in 1946–7. How did Bevan overcome their opposition?

6 Explain the victory of the Conservatives in the General Elections of 1951 and 1959.

7 Why did the post-war governments build New Towns? Explain the differences between the New Towns and large suburban council estates?

8 Why was there a shortage of housing after 1945? How far was this problem dealt with by (i) Bevan and (ii) Macmillan?

9 What evidence is there that the economic crisis which affected Britain in the 1970s had its origins in the early 1960s?

Extract

Inflationary conditions
But the challenge to our intelligence remains, though the difficulties with which we must wrestle are almost precisely the reverse of those that beset us in the thirties. An overstrained economy with constant anxiety about the 'balance of payments,' shortage of labour, and an inflation that has generated a new insecurity. These are the problems with which contemporary statesmen must concern themselves.
(Harold Macmillan, *Winds of Change* 1966)

Chapter 27   Women and children

Many British women had gained a great deal from the economic and social changes of the 1930s. There were more job opportunities for women of all backgrounds and all qualifications (or none). Because of the spread of knowledge of birth control, most married women had smaller families than their mothers and grandmothers had had. As a result they were healthier. The production of household gadgets coupled with the larger income of many British families enabled many women to run their homes and have time to do a job.

The War 1939–45
Women played a more active part in the nation's life during the Second World War (1939–45) than they had played in the First. They served in the armed forces, worked in munitions factories and took the place of conscripted men in offices, shops, schools and factories. After 1945 they did not have to give up their newly-won economic freedom as so many of their mothers had been forced to do in 1919, when trade unions, politicians, school managers or office controllers united to get women back into their homes to make way for the returning soldiers.

Full employment
The main reason for the greater job opportunities for women in post-war Britain has been the constantly high demand for workpeople in the affluent society. Employers have been

During the Second World War, women – single and married – played their part as workers and members of the armed services. After the War the role of women in society had to change because of their experience during the war. They were not prepared to be second-class citizens.

In the nineteenth century most jobs were dirty and needed physical strength. This changed during the inter-war period. Since 1945 there has been an even greater change. Now there are millions of women working in clean surroundings in shops, offices, factories, and x-ray departments such as this. Many of these jobs call for skills and educational qualifications so that women have to be given more educational opportunities.

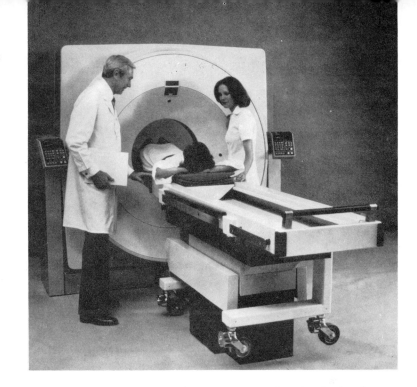

forced to turn to women to make up for the lack of men workers. Women have been asked and allowed to do all sorts of jobs from traditional women's work such as teaching, to traditionally male jobs such as driving heavy lorries, buses and piloting civil aircraft. For most women, as for most men, work has been made easier. Science and technology have united to take the dirt out of many jobs.

The need for physically strong workpeople has decreased. For women, as for men workers, many jobs are now light and pleasant. Many married women, therefore, have been able, easily, to combine the role of worker with that of housewife. Their grandmothers in Victorian Britain were worn out with trying to cope with these two roles. In post-war Britain this has not been the case.

Education for girls

One result of the increasing job opportunities for women has been a changed attitude towards the question of educating girls. We have seen that Edwardian parents considered it important to educate their boys but less important to consider the education of their girls. In post-war Britain few parents have denied their daughters equality of opportunity with their sons. They have had to think about the lives that these girls were going to lead. Most of them will get married, and marry at an earlier age than their mothers or grandmothers. They will tend to have only two or three children.

Most of these women have their children before they are twenty-five. By the time they are thirty years of age the

Girls in a secondary school. During the nineteenth century only a few girls from rich families went to secondary schools. Since 1945 girls have had the same chances as boys in secondary schools – a sign of their 'liberation' and of the needs of British industry for more and better qualified workpeople.

youngest child is in school. They live in modern, easily-run homes, using the vacuum cleaners and washing machines, refrigerators and food mixers which modern industry produces. The result is that running a home is even easier than it had been in the 1930s. And what are these modern women to do after the age of thirty? They can expect to live until they are well over seventy so that they have a long period of life facing them when their children have gone to school. It has become increasingly clear that a majority of married women wish to take up some sort of job. Some do for economic reasons. Their families badly need the extra income. Many, however, go to work, they say, for social reasons.

Barriers to women's progress

There are still a number of obstacles facing women. Medical schools and universities admit a smaller proportion of girls than boys. Employers are still reluctant to release girls for day-release classes at technical colleges. Many people in positions of authority still believe that women have fewer rights than men. In many cases a woman applying for a job will stand less chance of getting the job than a man of equal qualifications.

Barriers to advancement go up early. A striking example is the provision for science teaching. A survey in 1961 showed that if the standard laid down for boys' schools were extended to girls' schools, only 13 per cent of girls' schools would pass.

This seems a strange state of affairs. So does the fact that only 8 per cent of the girls eligible for the day-release scheme are in fact enrolled, compared with 33 per cent of the boys.

But in spite of these drawbacks women have made great strides down the road to equality since 1945. The Equal Pay Act (1969) made it illegal, after 1975, for employers not to pay equal wages for equal work. This Act was piloted through Parliament by Barbara Castle, a leading Minister in the Wilson government (1964–70) and one of a number of prominent lady politicians of recent years.

Children at school

Most children who have grown up in post-war Britain have known only affluence. Born into families enjoying high or, at least regular incomes, they have lived in modern or modernised homes equipped with a variety of gadgets and comfortable furniture. Their parents have realised the value of education. And these concerned parents have been able to afford to allow their children to have a longer time at school than was the case before the war.

Children's appearance

Manufacturers have produced a greater variety of good, but cheap, clothing for children of all ages. Their prosperous parents have been able to afford these 'luxuries' and firms such as 'Ladybird' and 'Mothercare' have flourished in post-war Britain. These lucky children have been well clothed. They have also been well fed. They have received the benefits of the National Health Service and have been altogether healthier than children before the war.

Margaret Thatcher and Shirley Williams. Their positions are both a tribute to their ability and to the improvement in the position of women in British society. The suffragettes had not fought in vain.

A modern kitchen. With a smaller family and modern gadgets making it easier to run a home, married women have found it easy to be both mothers and workers.

One indication of this improvement has been the decline in the death rate among children. This has been called 'the key to the national well being'. In the disease-ridden Manchester of the 1840s about 35 per cent of children died before reaching the age of five. They were born into over-crowded, dirty homes. Brought up by parents suffering in dire poverty, these children were easy prey to any and every disease. Their deaths were a proof that all was not for the best in self-help Britain. The decline in that death rate in the later part of the nineteenth century was one proof that social life of the country was improving. The rapid fall in that death rate in post-war Britain is the proof that the majority of the British people enjoy a high standard of living. The virtual disappearance of many former killer diseases such as diphtheria, tuberculosis and scarlet fever, is an indication both of medical progress and general living standards.

More education

We have seen that one aspect of British history during the last two hundred years has been the shift of emphasis from primary industry (such as agriculture), to the secondary (or manufacturing) industries and, more recently, to tertiary industries. We have also seen that both secondary and tertiary industries require workpeople who are better qualified than their fathers and grandfathers had been. W. E. Forster had realised this in 1870 (Chapter 13) and we have seen that Britain's failure to develop her educational system was one of the reasons for her decline from greatness. One aspect of British history since 1945 has been the effort to make British industry more able to compete with the modern industries of the U.S.A., Germany and Japan. The 1944 Education Act was a step in that direction.

Many proposals in this Act have still not been carried out. In particular, Britain still does not have the nursery schools that this Act promised. But most of the Act has been put into effect. Britain has an educational system of free primary schools for children up to the age of eleven, followed by free secondary school for all older children. The 1944 Act intro-duced the system of grants which makes it possible for any boy or girl of sufficient ability to go from school to college or university.

The 'eleven plus'

One side effect of the 1944 Act was the spread of the 'eleven-plus'. This was an examination by which clever working class children had won places into the fee-paying secondary (grammar) schools after 1907. After 1945, middle class children were forced to sit this examination which has been used to pick out the children who would benefit from the academic education provided in the grammar schools where 'O' Level and 'A' Level examinations are taken as qualifications for entrance to jobs, colleges or universities.

The eleven-plus examination came under increasing attack throughout the 1950s and 1960s. One study showed that over one-third of all Welsh children went on to grammar schools, while only 15 per cent of Surrey children did so. The reason for this difference was not that Welsh children are on average over twice as clever as Surrey children, but that there happened to be a large number of old grammar schools in Wales. In Wales and in Surrey (and everywhere else) the eleven-plus examination was used to fill the empty desks in the local grammar schools, however many there were.

Comprehensive schools

Reports of the differences in the percentages of eleven-plus 'passes' in Wales and Surrey suggested that there was a large number of clever children not going to grammar schools in Surrey (and other such places). This was a waste of talent which the country could not afford. Even more disturbing was a survey carried out by J. W. B. Douglas. He studied the educational performance of every child born in a week of March 1946. His survey showed that children of middle-

A comprehensive school – a sign of educational development and British wealth. A poorer country could not afford such a 'luxury' nor allow its children to remain at study until they were 16 or 18.

class parents (in general people who had themselves had a grammar school education or better) had an advantage over working class children of equal intelligence.

Other surveys showed that the eleven-plus examination was not in fact picking the right children. Out of every twenty children picked by the grammar school, six or seven turned out to be unsuited and kept out six or seven of the remaining eighty who should have been admitted. One proof of the ability of 'the failures' was the growth in the number of children in secondary modern (non-grammar) schools who were passing the GCE examination.

These were the main arguments used by people who opposed the eleven-plus examination system. They proposed a variety of secondary schools systems which would do away with selection at the age of eleven. Some areas followed the Leicester Plan of junior and senior high schools. Others started sixth form colleges. The most controversial were the large, all-in comprehensive schools, such as those established by the London County Council. The first, Kidbrooke, was opened in 1954 with 1,700 girls. The *News Chronicle* called it 'A Palace of Learning', the *Evening Standard*, 'A Sausage Machine'.

Part of Imperial College, London, one of the world's leading institutions for technological education.

Colleges of Technology

The government has played a more active part in the nation's education. In the 1950s a good deal of attention was paid to the development of the Colleges of Advanced Technology. Lord Woolton was the Cabinet Minister responsible for this in 1954.

In the 1960s a number of new universities were opened, a great expansion took place in the number of people attending Teacher Training Colleges (renamed Colleges of Education) and Technical Colleges. In 1973 the government finally carried through one of the promises of the 1944 Act by raising the school-leaving age to sixteen. Britain had taken another step along the road to giving her children a chance similar to that enjoyed by children in most other industrialised countries.

Documents

a) Why must the British spend more on children's education? 1959

More recently, however, the emphasis has come back to education as an investment. There are perhaps two special reasons for this. The first is the new doctrine that the nation can control its own economic development. And secondly, there is the new emphasis placed upon the belief that the prosperity, and even the safety, of the nation depend on 'keeping up in the economic race'. The need to invest in education has been seen most clearly in the technological field; but it does not require much imagination for the argument to be extended to other educational spheres. Today, it seems to us that education is generally thought to be a 'nation-building' investment fully as much as part of the welfare state.

b) Percentage Distribution of 'Ability' among 5,940 National Service Recruits to the Army who left School at Various Ages

Among the families of manual workers it is still the exception for a child to stay at school after he is legally free to go, so that the available resources of men (and presumably also of women) of high 'ability' are not fully used by the present system. The Table makes it clear, that, among National Service men entering the Army, while nine-tenths of those in the top 10 per cent in ability stayed at school voluntarily for at least one year more than they had to, over four-tenths of them (42 per cent) left by 16.

	School-leaving age		
Ability Group	15 or less	16	17 or more
1	9	33	58
2	65	22	13
3	94	4	2
4	98	2	—
5	98	2	—
6 (lowest)	97	3	—
All Groups	77	12	11

1 *Was Crowther right (Document (a)) in thinking that it was a 'new' idea to link education with economic progress?*

2 *Find out which Colleges of Technology, Colleges of Advanced Technology, Polytechnics or Universities have been opened in your area since 1959.*

3 *Look at the Table at the end of Document (b). Can you suggest reasons why 42 per cent of the children in ability group 1 left school before they reached the age of 16?*

4 *Arrange a debate on the motion 'That the school-leaving age should not have been raised to sixteen'.*

Extracts

Smaller families

Ferdinand Zweig made a survey among married workers in five factories in different parts of the country. His findings illustrate that modern families are small families:

Number of families with Numbers of Children

	0	1–2	3	4 or more	Total
Sheffield	24	93	22	11	150
Workington	13	54	11	11	89
Vauxhall	20	64	15	8	107
Dunlop	13	55	18	20	106
Standard	17	53	15	11	96
	87	319	81	61	548

Working women

Would these married women have preferred to stay at home rather than to go out to work? The big majority, that is, forty-two out of sixty-seven, answered this question in the negative. They were very outspoken on this point, saying, 'I would rather be here – the mind is occupied': 'I am not keen on house work, housework does not satisfy me': 'Nothing to do at home'.

Companionship was again and again referred to as the great incentive. 'You can have a laugh here. It is good to be with others.'
(Zweig)

Sex discrimination

Miss Hess, Principal of the Studley Agricultural College for Women, was once an applicant for a headship of an important farming institute. She was told that she had the experience and qualifications needed, and could undoubtedly to the job, but did she realise that 50 per cent of their students were men? Miss Hess asked: 'And what sex are the other 50 per cent?'

Questions on Chapter Twenty-seven

Ambitious parents

It seems clear that most families can now support their children throughout a longer school education than would formerly have been practicable. This is a consequence of earlier marriage, earlier child-bearing within marriage, smaller families, longer expectation of life and more opportunities of paid employment for married women.

(Report of Government Committee on Education 1958)

The way things were

I can remember as a child being haunted by the beggers in the streets, the crossing-sweepers who held out their tattered caps for pennies, the children in rags, fluttering like feathers when the wind blew through them, the down-and-outs sleeping out under the arches or on the benches in the parks with an old newspaper for cover.

(Lady Violet Bonham Carter)

1 *List four reasons why the modern mother finds it easier to combine her two roles of mother and worker.*

2 *Explain why employers in post-war Britain were anxious to recruit women workers whereas employers in Britain in the 1920s and 1930s did not do so.*

3 *Write a letter in which Lord Woolton (p. 287) explains to the Prime Minister, Winston Churchill, why Britain had to expand its educational service.*

4 *Write a letter from the mother of a modern family explaining why she wishes to get a job.*

5 *Do you think that girls have the same educational opportunities as boys? Give some examples of inequality from the text and from your own research.*

6 *Do you think that children from poorer homes have the same educational opportunities as do children with better-off parents? Why? How could the government help reduce this inequality?*

7 *Make a collage of headlines which might have appeared above articles dealing with (i) the abolition of fee-paying grammar schools (1944), (ii) the opening of the first London Comprehensive School (iii) local opposition to the introduction of a comprehensive system of education (iv) the opening of the first College of Advanced Technology.*

Chapter 28   From crisis to opportunity

A new start 1970–72

In 1957 Macmillan told the British that they had 'never had it so good'. Until 1974 they believed it was possible to have it even better. They wanted a higher standard of living although they also wanted a shorter working week. They refused to listen to warnings about inflation. They wanted to buy foreign imports, although they were not producing enough to be able to pay for the goods.

In the 1970 General Election Edward Heath led the Conservatives to victory. He seemed to be determined to put things right. His Chancellor, Anthony Barber, reduced the level of income tax and company taxation. This meant that people had more money to spend. Heath hoped that they would 'buy British' and so help British companies to buy the new machinery needed to make British firms more able to compete with modernised foreign firms.

Because the government collected less taxation Heath decided that his government would also spend less. People were forced to pay more for some of the things they had once received either free or cheaply from the government. There were price increases for school meals, dental treatment, medicines and other welfare services.

The government also announced that, unlike the Labour government, it would not give money to firms which were

A Garland cartoon of 31 March 1972. From left to right: Sir Alec Douglas Home (Foreign Secretary), Lord Carrington (Minister for Defence), John Davies (Industry and Trade), Robert Carr (Minister for Employment) and William Whitelaw (Chief Whip). They are trying to plug leaks in the dyke marked Tory Policies. After only two years, the policies which the Heath government had hoped to put into practice had been shown to be either unworkable or unacceptable.

unable to make their own way. In future, the 'lame ducks' would be allowed to die off. This would save the government the money it might have spent on subsidising unprofitable firms and industries.

Anthony Barber encouraged industrialists to plan the buying of new machines and the building of new factories. One way in which he did this was by greatly increasing the supply of money. Since there was plenty of money available, it was hoped that firms would take the chance of modernising their factories and plants.

Finally, the Heath government passed the Industrial Relations Act which was intended to limit the power of the trade unions and their leaders. It was unions, said the Heath government, which had been mainly responsible for the high wages, low output and general backwardness of British industry. The Act tried to make it more difficult for unions to call strikes.

Heath and the unions

But the policies were failures. The trade unionists of the 1970s had grown used to a high standard of living and to full employment. They were not going to allow a government to bring to an end their way of life. One group of workers at the Upper Clyde Shipyards refused to accept the 'lame ducks' policy and they forced the government to change its mind. The yard, and their jobs, were saved by a government subsidy.

The rise in the money supply between 1971 and 1976 (see above).

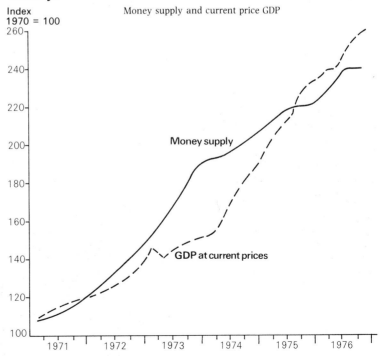

261

A photograph taken on 16 June 1971 outside 10 Downing Street, where these leaders of the Upper Clyde shipyard workers went to see Mr Heath. They had refused to accept the government's decision to close down the yard – as part of the government's policy of not helping 'lame ducks'. Jimmy Reid (second from left) and James Airlie (on Reid's left) were the spokesmen. The workers forced the government to change its mind. Aid was given to the yard which is now prosperous and busy.

In 1972 and again in 1974 the Heath government tried to stop the miners' union getting the pay increases they demanded. Since the mines were owned by the government this brought the miners' union and the government into conflict. In 1972 the government climbed down when the miners went on strike. Again, in 1973–4, the government at first refused to pay the increase demanded. The miners then went on strike. There was no coal being sent to the generating stations and the country had to put up with weeks of electricity cuts. This period is now remembered as 'the three day week' because of the regulation which closed factories, offices and shops for two working days each week to try to save electricity.

Heath had a large majority in the House of Commons in February 1974. But he called a General Election during the miners' strike and the three day week. Perhaps he hoped to win a larger majority although that would not have solved the miners' strike. Perhaps, as he has said, 'the problem . . . is insoluble' and he hoped that, somehow, an Election would help solve the insoluble. His defeat in the 1974 Election is sometimes blamed on the miners.

Oil prices

The problems facing this country and the Heath government were made worse in 1972–3 by the Oil Producing and Exporting Countries (OPEC). The OPEC countries got together and pushed up the price of their oil. Britain, and other industrialised countries, had to pay four times as much for oil at the end of 1973 as they had been paying at the start of 1972.

Some people felt the effect of the price increase through the petrol pump where the price of petrol shot up to over 80p a gallon. More important was the effect of the increased price on those firms which use oil as a raw material. The petrochemical industry takes the oil and turns it into paint, plastics, fibres and animal foodstuffs. The prices of all these products had to go up once the price of oil increased.

So there was a great increase in prices. But even more serious was the effect on the country's economy of the great increase in the payments made to the OPEC countries. In the past these had taken, say, £500 million from Britain to pay for the oil. Now they were taking, say, £2,000 million. This meant that Britain had £1,500 million less to spend on other imports. Other countries suffered in the same way. Each country therefore tried to cut its other imports so that it could afford to pay the increased price for the oil. This meant that Britain and other exporting countries were able to sell less of their goods. Unemployment rose as a result of this drop in exports.

Unemployment also rose because of the effect of the increased prices people had to pay for petrol and oil-based products in Britain. If we have to pay say £20 a week for our petrol instead of only £5, then we have £15 less to spend on other goods in the shops.

One of Britain's many large petro-chemical plants where oil is changed into a variety of products from paint to plastics, from clothing fibres to animal feeding stuffs.

Inflation 1972–7

Anthony Barber had increased the amount of money in the country and this encouraged some people to borrow from the banks. Their spending of this borrowed money helped to push up the prices of goods — because there was no increase in the supply of goods to equal the increase in the supply of money. Some employers agreed to union demands for higher wages — and got their money back by putting up the prices of their products.

On top of the Barber-led inflation came the effects of the increase in oil prices which pushed up the rate of inflation. And to add to the misery there was a great increase in the price of wheat and other foodstuffs because in 1972–3 the U.S.A. government sold most of their crop to Russia which had had a series of very poor harvests. When the sugar crop failed in Cuba and the coffee crop failed in Brazil the prices of these foodstuffs went up four and five times. By 1976 the annual rate of price increases was over 30 per cent. This meant that goods which would have cost £100 at the start of the year were costing £130 by the end of the year.

Changes in prices and wages between 1972 and 1978. Notice the high rise in the prices of imports (food, oil, raw materials) and the resulting rise in retail prices of the goods we buy in the shops. At first, wage rates rose even more rapidly. The Callaghan–Healey policy (1975–78) was to try to bring down the levels of prices and wages. Notice that wage rates fell more rapidly than did prices. Hence there was a fall in living standards in 1976 and 1977 – the price British people had to pay for the too-easy way in which they had lived in the past.

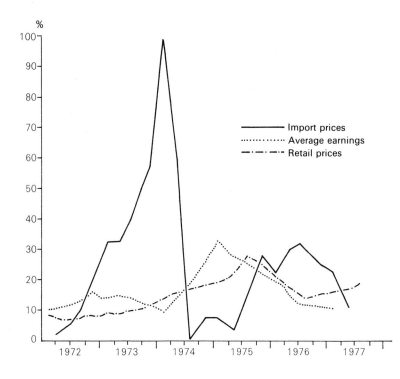

Balance of payments

These great increases in the prices of British imports (oil, wheat, sugar, coffee and so on) meant that by 1975 Britain was spending more than she earned. This was not a new development. We had been living like this in 1947 when Marshall Aid helped us out of our troubles. We were in this position in 1961 when Selwyn Lloyd was Chancellor. In 1964 we had to borrow £800 million from foreign bankers to pay for the imports which our exports were unable to pay for.

But in the 1970s the difference between what we earned (by exports) and spent (on imports) was about £2,000 million a year. The failure of the Heath government to deal with the miners in 1974 gave some people the idea that the country was ungovernable and was heading for a breakdown. The failure of the country to pay its own way led other people to think that Britain was going to become bankrupt. Those foreigners who had British pounds (OPEC countries, shipping firms and so on), tried to get rid of them. But few people wanted to buy them. And when few people want an article which a lot of people want to sell the price drops. This happened to the pound.

And this fall made matters even worse, as the following example shows. Suppose that a bag of coffee costs $100. When the £ = $2.50 we have to pay £40 for that bag of coffee. But if the £ falls to $2.00 then we have to pay £50. And if it falls to $1.50 then we have to pay almost £70. The

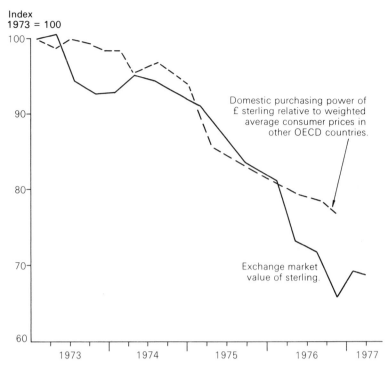

Index
1973 = 100

Domestic purchasing power of
£ sterling relative to weighted
average consumer prices in
other OECD countries.

Exchange market
value of sterling.

The fall in the value of the pound 1973–1978. Notice that as more money was printed foreigners put a lower value on British money. The result of this was that our imports cost us more.

falling value of the pound drove up import prices – which were already being pushed up by the effects of the increases in the prices of oil, wheat, sugar and coffee.

Wage increases

Union leaders saw prices rising sharply so they demanded huge pay increases. They did this to make sure their members were able to buy as much at the end of the year as they had been buying at the start of the year. Since prices were rising by about 30 per cent, so wages rose by 30 per cent – for those people whose unions could force employers to pay such increases.

But this was something that could not be allowed to go on. If wage rates went up by 30 per cent in one year, employers would have to put up their prices to try to get that money back. The result would be that inflation would go on rising in the following year. This would lead to unions demanding maybe 40 per cent wage increases and so on until we were getting 100 per cent pay increases. But the standard of living would not have been rising at all because we would have been paying higher prices for the same quantity of goods.

Wages policies

So the government had to step in and try to bring down both prices and the size of wage increases. The Heath government (1970–74) introduced a *wages policy* in 1972–3. Since the

The level of unemployment in manufacturing industry 1970–76. This unemployment was due to
(i) a drop in the level of world trade as countries tried to cope with the increase in oil prices.
(ii) the failure of British firms to modernise. There was another large number of people who lost their jobs when the government cut down on its spending.

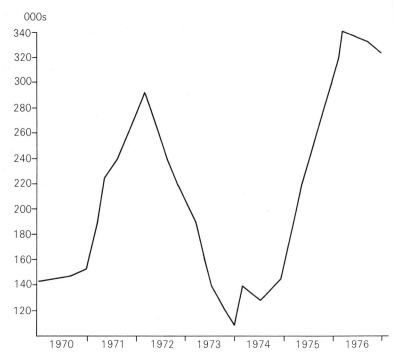

government employed about 6,000,000 people it could have some direct control over the wages paid to a larger section of the working population (doctors and nurses, teachers and civil servants and so on). It could only encourage other employers to try to limit wage increases.

The Labour government, which took over power in 1974, took a tougher line. It got together with the leaders of the trade unions and arranged a policy which these leaders agreed to follow. In 1975–6 no one was to receive more than £4 a week and in 1976–7 no more than 6 per cent increase in pay. In 1977–8, pay increases were limited to 10 per cent.

One effect of this limiting of wages has been a fall in living standards since prices have risen more than wages. The dizzy days of 'never had it so good' appear to have gone. The majority of people seem to have accepted this, although unwillingly.

Another effect of this policy has been to increase the level of unemployment. Since prices remain high we have to spend a larger fraction of our wages on essential, but expensive goods, such as food, fuel and so on. This leaves us less to spend on other things. This means that some firms cannot sell their products and have to dismiss some of their workpeople.

Government cuts
In order to pay for her imports Britain had to borrow money from foreign bankers. As in 1961 the bankers insisted that

the government had to take steps to cut down imports and increase exports so that the country would, once again be paying its way.

One part of the policy which had to be followed led to cuts in the amount of money that the government spent on public welfare. Since the government spent less on building, investment, defence, teachers' salaries and so on, there was unemployment in some industries and for some teachers. The unemployed had less to spend than they had while they were working. They bought fewer goods – and so there was another increase in the number of people dismissed in other firms.

Economists and other advisers to the government believed that the increased level of unemployment would have an effect on wage levels. They believed that the workers would be so frightened of losing their jobs that they would accept lower wage increases than they might have expected and demanded when employment levels were higher.

However, in fact, this did not happen. There was a rise in unemployment. There was a cut back in the level of production – so that the economy was said to be stagnant, or standing still. But unions went on demanding very high wages and employers kept on putting up their prices, so that inflation continued to be a major problem. This caused the economists and other writers to bring out a new word. 'Stagflation' was defined as the situation in which the economy was not expanding and yet, contrary to older theories, prices continued to rise.

Our oil

The 1970s was really a dismal decade when unemployment rose, standards of living fell and the country had to borrow vast sums of money from foreign bankers. But in 1978 it was possible to see that, for a time at least, there would be some hope of improvement.

Britain had now got its own oil-producing areas, mainly in the North Sea. This meant that, already, we had to import much less oil than we had to import in the past. So the imports side of the balance of payments dropped. And it would drop still further when we provided all our own oil. Indeed we would be able to sell oil to other countries so that the export side of the balance of payments would rise. Britain would be well able to pay her way. This would be a very great change from the 1960s and early 1970s.

This would allow the governments of the future to go ahead with plans for industrial and social expansion at home. The increased money spent on development would again

(Opposite) One of Britain's North Sea oil rigs, the symbol of the chance that Britain has to make itself, once again, prosperous and modern.

lead to increases in imports as in the past. But this time such increases would not lead to balance of payments crisis.

The government would collect huge sums of money (£2,000 million in 1978 and £5,000 million a year in and after 1981) from the oil companies which produced the oil in the British oil fields. This would enable the government to cut taxes, spend more on industrial development and on social welfare. The days of cutting appeared to be over.

But to finish on a note of caution. The oil will not last for ever and Britain has to prepare itself so that it can pay its way when the oil runs out in about forty years time. There is a danger that we may spend the money unwisely — as a man would who sold his house and furniture in the summer only to freeze to death during the winter. It is to be hoped that we will be wiser in the 1980s than we were during the falsely-glamorous days of the fifties and swinging sixties. Some people believed then that Britain's economic prosperity was safe because, for a while, British singers (such as the Beatles) and fashion-designers (such as Mary Quant) seemed to lead the world of pop music and teenage fashion. It is to be hoped that the prosperity which we hope to get from our oil will prove to have firmer foundations than the short-lived and false prosperity which was based on a few teenage idols.

The children to whom the uncertain future belongs. Here they are raising funds for Shelter — one example of young people caring for the less fortunate members of our society.

"THE HANDSOME PRINCE BEGAN CUTTING AWAY AT THE BRANCHES THAT HAD GROWN UP ROUND SLEEPING BEAUTY!"

a) Denis Healey, the Chancellor of the Exchequer (1974–8) had to cut down on the amount of money spent by the government in 1976 and 1977. This meant that there had to be 'cuts' in the spending of various ministries. This led to unemployment in the firms which would have been supplying goods to the armed services, schools, health service and so on.

1 Why did the cuts made by Denis Healey lead to
   (i) larger classes in schools (ii) unemployment in the Barber to blame for these cuts?

2 How had governments used the nationalised industries and public services to create employment since 1945?

3 Why did the cuts made by Denis Healey lead to (i) larger classes in schools (ii) unemployment in the road-building industry (iii) longer waiting lists at British hospitals?

4 Which groups of people might have welcomed the cuts made by Denis Healey? Why?

1 What was the main economic problem facing Britain in 1961?

2 How did the Heath government try to improve Britain's economic position between 1970 and 1972? How did the government help (i) the taxpayer and (ii) industrialists?

3 Explain why the government increased the money supply in 1972–3? Why did this lead to an increase in the prices of (i) houses and (ii) food?

4 Why did foreigners put a low value on British money in 1966 and after 1973? How does the fall in the value of the pound lead to increased prices for British imports? How does this affect the cost of living in Britain?

5 Make a summary of the reasons for the high rate of inflation from which Britain suffered between 1973 and 1977. How did governments try to deal with this problem?

6 Why does North Sea oil offer Britain a chance to (i) solve its balance of payments problem (ii) increase the amount of money spent on social welfare and (iii) cut the level of taxation?

Glossary

Act of Parliament Most of the laws which control our lives are the result of Acts passed by Parliament. Before a proposal (or bill) becomes an act it is discussed by both Houses of Parliament on three separate occasions. If the majority of members of the House of Commons (M.P.s) vote to approve the proposal (or bill) on these three occasions, it is then presented to the Queen (or King) for signing. After this signing, the former bill becomes an Act and forms part of the law of the country.

Anaesthetic You may have had an anaesthetic given by a dentist. It is a drug or gas used either to make a person unconscious or to affect part of the body so that a person will not feel the pain of an operation.

Aqueduct This comes from the Latin words for water (aqua) and to lead (ducere). An aqueduct is a man-made channel usually of brick or stone, which builders constructed when they wanted to take a canal across a valley.

Balance of payments The balance of payments is the difference between all money going out of the country, through trade or investment, and all money coming in. The result will be favourable (or in surplus) when the country takes in more money than it pays out. It will be unfavourable (or in deficit) when the country pays out more than it takes in.

Bessemer converter Until 1856 steel making was slow and an expensive business. Benjamin Huntsman had developed the crucible method around 1740, but it only produced small quantities of costly steel. In 1856 Henry Bessemer invented his 'converter'. In this process, air was blasted through molten pig iron, burning out the carbon and other impurities. Then fero-manganese (containing carbon) was added to the purified iron and the result was a purer form of steel. The Bessemer process changed pig iron into steel in less time than the crucible method. The result was a fall in the price of steel from 1856 when it replaced iron – in railway tracks, ships, bridges, machinery and a thousand other things.

Card (as in carding wool) The card was an oblong board in which rows of teeth were set. In the domestic system the carder prepared the wool for the spinner by pulling them through the wool until each strand lay parallel with every other strand. Crompton and Arkwright each invented a carding machine. In these steam driven machines, the teeth were embedded in large cylinders or rollers which could deal with large quantities of wool.

Cast Iron Cast iron took its name from the moulds (or casts) into which the molten iron was poured after it had been smelted in the furness. It was very rigid and was suitable for use in such forms of building as railway stations, unlike wrought iron. But cast iron was very brittle because it contained many impurities. This meant that it could be easily smashed by a hammer and could not be used if it was going to be exposed to sudden strain.

Charter This is a written grant of certain rights usually given by a King or by Parliament. Charters have been granted to townspeople to allow them to set up a Corporate Borough and to groups of people wishing to set up societies, schools, institutes (such as the Institute of Civil Engineers) or trading companies such as the East India Company.

Chartist Movement The Chartists were the men who in the 1830's and 1840's wanted wide scale reform of the Parliamentary and electoral systems. In 1838 William Lovatt published the first People's Charter; in 1839 the Chartists presented their demands to Parliament – which were rejected and again in 1842 and 1848.

Civil Defence is an organisation for dealing with the effects of possible disasters, either natural or as a result of war.

A Civil Servant is anyone who works for any government department. Today there are many thousands employed in the Civil Service, a sign that the government plays a large part in the economic and social life of the country.

A Coalition is the temporary joining of two or more political parties to form a Government.

Common Land still exists in some places, such as Wimbledon Common. There use to be large areas of such common land where people were free to collect their timber or to graze animals, but most common land was closed during the eighteenth century by land owners.

Conscription This takes place where every man between certain ages is forced to enter the army, navy or air force, unless he is doing a job which the Government considers to be of 'national importance' – such as coal mining.

A Constituency is the area of a county or a borough which is represented by a Member of Parliament. Each of us lives in a Parliamentary Constituency.

Corn Laws were passed in 1815 to prevent the importing of foreign wheat if the price of British wheat was lower than £4 per quarter (28 lbs). These laws were passed by a Parliament controlled by land owners and farmers. Working people and employers opposed these laws which kept the price of bread higher than it might have been. The repeal of these laws in 1846 was a sign that the land owners and farmers no longer controlled Parliament and that the middle-class employers began to use the political power which they had been given by the 1832 Reform Act.

A Corporate Borough is a town which has been given a Charter which allows the people to elect a Council (or Corporation).

Council Houses are built by and owned by a Local Council (or Corporation). Normally the rent is less than that in private houses. The Government and the Local Council make up the difference. This enables less well off people to rent a house.

The Crucible method of steel making was developed by Benjamin Huntsman (a clock maker) who moved to Sheffield in 1740. He wanted better quality steel to use as springs in his clocks and watches. Poor quality steel was heated in crucible (or clay pots). The result was a high quality steel. But the process was very slow and expensive, and could only be used to produce small quantities.

Death Duties were the taxes which had to be paid before an heir took the property left by its former owner. They were first imposed in 1894. Anyone inheriting £1,000,000 had to pay 8% (or £80,000) to the Government; people inheriting £50,000 had to pay only 4% and people inheriting a small sum paid nothing. In 1909 Lloyd-George increased these duties by one-third and later Chancellors increased them very heavily.

Devaluation is the reduction in the value of a country's money when compared to the value of the money in other countries. The number of francs, for example, for which we can get for each pound will fall if our Government devalues the pound. The Government devalued the pound in 1949 and again in 1967.

Enclosure was the process by which the farmer's separate strips in different open fields were exchanged for a single compact farm surrounded (or enclosed) by a wall, hedge or fence. The same applied when the Common was divided into separate farms. Enclosure took place mainly in the eighteenth century. Those who wanted to enclose the village land had to get Parliament to pass an Act.

Evacuation On the outbreak of war in 1939 the Government arranged for the city children to be taken to safer homes outside the cities where the danger from bombing was much smaller. This was known as the Evacuation.

Free Trade During the nineteenth century British manufacturers argued that goods should be sold free of import taxes, anywhere in the world. Because Britain was the first country to industrialise, manufacturers were not afraid of foreign competition. Free trade seemed a good idea. By the end of the nineteenth century other countries had become industrialised and their manufacturers were able to produce goods of a better quality and at a lower price than British manufacturers could manage. This led to the demand for a British tax, or tariff, on foreign goods. Free trade only worked when Britain led the world.

A Franchise is the right to vote at (parliamentary) elections.

A Fuller When cloth was first woven on the loom, it looked something like a piece of knitting; it had little

'body'. It had then to be thickened and made stronger by soaking it in a mixture of water and a special chemical called fuller's earth. The Fuller was originally the man who stamped the cloth in this mixture.

General Enclosure Act In 1801 the Government decided that Parliament was spending a great deal of time on separate enclosure acts. So Parliament was asked to pass the *General Enclosure Act*. Those people who wanted to enclose land could then use the powers of that Act and did not have to get their own separate Act of Parliament.

A Guild was originally a society to which the workers in a particular craft (such as cloth makers, carpenters and goldsmiths) belonged. Each member paid a weekly fee and in return he would get a weekly payment if he were unemployed, sick or injured and unable to work. After his death the Guild would look after his widow and children. The Guild's Officers also supervised the work of their members, to make sure that they only made high quality articles and so maintained the good name of the craft. Modern trade unions are like guilds, but do not concern themselves with the quality of work.

Hire Purchase People who cannot afford to pay for what they want in cash can borrow the money from a finance house, which pays the shopkeeper for the article (such as a car) and collects a weekly or monthly payment from the buyer (or purchaser) who does not own the goods until he has made the final payment. Until then, although he is using the article, he is hiring it. If he fails to make a payment the finance house may take the goods from him.

Home Rule This stands for the wish of many Irish people to be separated from Great Britain. They wanted to have a Parliament of their own in Dublin which would enable them to rule themselves.

The House of Lords is one of the two Houses of Parliament. Until 1912 the House of Lords had the same powers as the House of Commons. But since the passing of the Parliament Act of 1912, the Lords has been less important than the House of Commons.

Improvement Commissioners were groups of men who had become dissatisfied with conditions in their town. They persuaded Parliament to pass a separate Act which gave them certain powers in their own town, such as forcing builders to put drains in their houses. Each improvement act also allowed the Commisioners to collect a rate from the householders in their district to help pay for the work they carried out.

Innoculation is the method of making it difficult for people to catch a disease by giving them a vaccine (or weak form of the disease). The body is able to deal with this weak form and learns to make the antibodies to fight the disease.

Income Tax is a tax on a person's income. It was imposed as a temporary tax in 1798 to help pay for the French Revolutionary wars. This tax was abolished in 1815, but brought back again in 1842 by Sir

Robert Peel. He, and later Prime Ministers, hoped that the tax would be abolished one day. In fact it has been steadily increased.

The Independent Labour Party (I.L.P.) was formed by Keir Hardy in 1893. The aim of the I.L.P. was the election of a group of working men to be Members of Parliament which would be separate from or independent of the two existing parties – Liberal and Conservative. This aim was only achieved when the I.L.P. won the support of the Trade Union Congress in 1899.

An Industrialist is a man who owns a manufacturing firm. Most firms began with one man or one family providing the money to build a factory, mill or workshop. But few big companies nowadays are owned by one man or one family.

Inflation To most people inflation means rising prices, whereas it really refers to an increased amount of money in circulation which leads to rising prices.

A Joint Stock Company Almost all firms and businesses started with one man or family. But some industries and businesses needed more money than any single person or family could provide for. To provide the money the public were invited to buy stock (or a share) in the firm (or company). People could buy one share or thousands; their share of the firms profits were varied with the number of shares they bought. The railway industry provides an early example of such a company.

A Journeyman The word comes from a French word *jour* meaning day. In the original guilds when a boy completed his apprenticeship, he was allowed to go to work as skilled worker or journeyman, for any master craftsman and to ask for a day's wages for a day's work. In time, he could become a master craftsman, if he could make a piece of work which the Guild's Officers agreed was good enough to be called a 'masterpiece'.

Labour Exchanges were offices set up in every town after 1908 to enable unemployed workers to seek employment. After the 1911 Insurance Act unemployment benefit was paid out of the Labour Exchanges to those entitled to receive it.

Local Education Authorities (L.E.A.'s) Before 1902 the majority of the country schools were run be either one of the voluntary societies, or by a locally elected school board. In 1902 Parliament passed an Act which handed the work of running the schools to Borough Councils and County Councils. Since the 1944 Education Act County Councils are the only L.E.A.s which run primary, secondary, and further education.

Magistrates are people appointed by the Government to administer the Law in a particular district. Until the eighteenth century they had to do many jobs, which, today, we expect councils and other authorities to do.

The Means Test Whenever a person applied for unemployment relief or dole to the Unemployment Assistance Boards, the income and possessions (that is the 'means' of the whole family) were taken into account.

Mild Steel contains a small percentage (about 0.1– 0.2%) of carbon. It is a strong, tough metal which is suitable for the making of pipes, beams and car bodies. But it cannot be 'tempered' or hardened so that it cannot be used to make drills of chisels, etc.

The National Health Service (N.H.S.) was set up in 1946 and gives every person the right to the services of a doctor, dentist and optician; the right to treatment in hospital or, when needed, to a midwife or health visitor as well as the right to all medicines and drugs that are prescribed. At first these services were to be provided without the patient making any immediate payment. However since 1950 various Governments have made patients pay for some of the services when they receive them.

Navvy is a shortened form of the word 'navigator'. He was one of the men who built the canals in the eighteenth century.

New Towns The New Towns Act of 1946 allowed for the planning of 15 new towns, of which 8 were to be built around London. They were not supposed to be suburbs but complete communities where people would not only live but also work and shop.

Open Fields In 1700 the land around most villages in the south and east of England was divided into four huge fields. One of these was the Common. The other three fields were divided into strips, each about one acre in size. Every farmer had one or more of these strips in each of the three fields.

Open Hearth Furnace In 1866 a German William Siemen, living in England passed pre-heated air and coal gas over a shallow bath of molten pig iron in his open hearth furnace. This method was an improvement on Bessemer's converter.

Pig Iron was produced by melting iron ore in a furnace. This liquid metal was poured into an oblong mould called a 'pig'. This iron was hard and brittle. Pig iron needed reheating to be turned into wrought iron.

Primary Industry One of man's first (or primary) needs is food and raw materials with which to make goods. Agriculture, fishing and mining are examples of primary industries.

The Privy Council was originally the advisers chosen by the King or Queen to adise him (privately). The modern Privy Council has less power and consists mainly of present and former members of Parliament.

Rates are the rates imposed by the local council which go to pay for schools, refuse collection, libraries, etc. A government office (the Rating Officer) puts a value (the rateable value) on each property in the district and charges rates accordingly.

Rotary Steam Engine In 1781 James Watt, who had done much to improve the steam engine, invented a system of levers and cogs which converted the up and down movement of the piston to a circular movement. This meant that the steam engine could be used to drive machinery.

The Rotation of Crops This is a system of growing different crops in a regular order to keep the soil fertile. During the seventeenth century farmers discovered that clover and other grasses put nitrogen back into the soil, while, at the same time, providing summer food for the cattle and sheep. They also started to plant turnips which the animals ate (in the fields) during the winter. A typical four crop cycle (or rotation) of crops would have been: wheat, barley, turnips, and clover or rye grass. There was no longer any need to let land lie 'farrow' (unused) in order to regain fertility.

A Royal Commission is a committee set up by the Government, acting in the name of the King or Queen (hence the 'Royal'). At different times commisions have been set up to examine problems (such as public health) or institutions (such as schools) or a system (such as the Poor Law). The commissions have been set up to examine problems writes this down in a report which is presented to the Government. Normally the commission will suggest what new act ought to be passed to make things better.

Social Hierarchy The word hierarchy has come to mean any arrangement (of people or things) where there is grading. A social hierarchy is a grading of people according to their position in society. In pre-industrial villages there was a fairly clear division of the people into different groups with the Squire of the Manor at the top and the squatters and beggars at the bottom.

Social Mobility In industrialised countries it is fairly simple for people to move from one social grade or class to another. A son or daughter of working class families may easily become a doctor, lawyer or engineer and so become a member of the middle classes. This is known as social mobility.

The Spinning Jenny In 1768 James Hargreaves invented a machine which spun eight threads of wool at the same time, and so speeding up the spinning process. He called it a Jenny, because that was his wife's name.

Squatters In the eighteenth century squatters were people with no legal right to any land. They lived by the common where they kept a few animals and some vegetables. They lost their patches and their huts when the common was enclosed.

After 1945 the word was used to describe homeless people who broke into other people's empty homes and lived there. They too have no legal right to the house in which they were living.

The Stock Exchange Here 'stock' means a certificate which the Government gives to people who lend money. Originally the stock exchange was a building where people who owned such stock could sell it to other people who had money and wanted to buy stock. Today it is also the place where people who have shares in joint stock companies can sell their shares when they wish to do so.

Subsidy This normally means the payment of money by the Government (or a local authority) to keep down the cost of something.

Suffragetes were women who campaigned to try to get Government to change the voting laws so that women would have the same voting rights as men.

Tariff Reform A Tariff normally means a tax or duty which has to be paid on imports. By 1850 Britain had adopted a policy of free trade. Other countries kept tariffs on imports into their countries. British goods going to, say, Germany or the U.S.A. became more expensive than they should have been. Meanwhile foreign goods could come into Britain without paying any tariff. In the 1880s there were demands that Britain should have a tariff system against foreign goods. In 1903 Joseph Chamberlain resigned from the cabinet to lead a nationwide campaign to try to win support for his reform policy.

The tenter was a wooden frame on which the cloth was stretched after it had been treated by the fuller (see). It was attached to the frame by a series of tenter hooks. Even today we talk of 'being on tenterhooks' as meaning being kept in a state of anxious suspense.

Tertiary industry Tertiary industries are those where people provide a service rather than produce goods. Such people are teachers, doctors, policemen, barbers and so on. These people do not work in either primary or secondary industry. They are said to be in a third grade – or tertiary industry.

The Trade Union Congress (TUC) A congress is a meeting or a coming together. Until 1868 the various trade unions had little contact with one another. In 1868 the leaders of the Salford trades council invited leaders of other trades council to come to a meeting. Since then there has been an annual coming together of the leaders of the nation's trade unions. The modern TUC is now a permanent organisation of officials which work for the unions which meet at the annual conference.

Turnpikes A turnpike is a barrier on a road where travellers have to pay a charge (or *toll*) In the eighteenth century the builders of new roads put up many such toll-gates to get the money to pay for their new road.

Wages Policy describes the attempts by government to control the level of pay settlements.

The Welfare State This is used by most people to describe the growth since 1908 of government departments and services to look after the old, sick, and unemployed.

Wrought Iron Wrought iron was iron which blacksmiths and others could work – or shape, into tools, horseshoes, gates and so on. It was the earliest form of iron produced in Britain.

Index

Acknowledgements

The publishers would like to thank the following for their permission to use copyright material:

Aerofilms p. 116, p. 224; Batsford p. 8 above, p. 20, p. 58, p. 72; City of Birmingham p. 107 above and below; Bishopsgate Institute p. 76; Bodleian Library p. 52; British Airways p. 241; British Broadcasting Corporation p. 237; British Leyland p. 221; British Library p. 8 below, p. 92 below, p. 108; British Oxygen p. 293; British Petroleum p. 298; Cadbury Schweppes p. 148; Carlisle Tool Board p. 47; Conservative Party Library p. 283 above; Cyfartha Castle Museum p. 54; Daily Express p. 215; Darlington Museum p. 40; Dudley Library p. 61, p. 150; EMI Ltd p. 281; Mary Evans p. 90; J Garland p. 30 below; General Electric Company Ltd p. 263; Glasgow Art Gallery p. 173; Henry Grant p. 282, p. 285; Greater London Council p. 117, p. 135; Guildhall p. 50; Hertfordshire Library Services p. 121 above; Hoover Ltd p. 217; Illustrated London News p. 3, p. 106; Imperial Chemical Industries p. 265; Imperial College p. 286; Imperial War Museum p. 192, p. 193, p. 194, p. 195, p. 196, p. 246, p. 250 above, p. 280; Institute of Mechanical Engineers p. 95; Journeyman Press p. 166; Keystone Press p. 251, p. 259 below, p. 260, p. 268, p. 292; King's College Medical School p. 123 above; Labour Party Library p. 227 above and below, p. 259 above, p. 283 centre; John Laing p. 42 below; Leeds Museum of Education p. 128; Leicestershire Museums p. 11, p. 53; London Express News p. 210, p. 245, p. 264, p. 266, p. 211 below, p. 276, p. 279; London Transport Executive p. 234; University of London (Goldsmith's Library) p. 50 below; Manchester Public Library p. 4, p. 24, p. 28, p. 30 above, p. 81; Mansell Collection p. 7, p. 23, p. 67, p. 70, p. 75, p. 77, p. 79, p. 82, p. 85, p. 86, p. 88, p. 91, p. 103, p. 104, p. 113, p. 118, p. 120, p. 127 below, p. 130, p. 131, p. 156, p. 158, p. 159 above and below, p. 163, p. 175 above, p. 176, p. 177 below, p. 182, p. 189, p. 212 below; Marconi p. 239; Museum of London p. 190; Museum of Rural Life p. 13, p. 141; National Coal Board p. 262; National Library of Wales p. 38; National Monuments Record p. 56; Crown Copyright, National Railway Museum, York p. 39, p. 41; National Trust p. 6; Newcastle Central Library p. 211; New Statesman p. 269, p. 290; Oxford University Press p. 19 above and below, p. 36; Penny Magazine p. 9; Popperfoto p. 183 above, p. 205, p. 247, p. 248, p. 255; Punch p. 44, p. 59, p. 60, p. 89, p. 92 above, p. 109, p. 154, p. 171, p. 174, p. 177 below, p. 184 above and below, p. 201, p. 232; Radio Times Hulton Picture Library p. 5, p. 12, p. 14, p. 16, p. 17, p. 18, p. 22, p. 25 above, p. 27 above, p. 28, p. 32, p. 33 below, p. 51, p. 68, p. 69, p. 71, p. 74, p. 78, p. 80, p. 87, p. 105, p. 110, p. 111 above, p. 112, p. 126 above, p. 129, p. 133, p. 139, p. 143, p. 145, p. 146, p. 147, p. 157, p. 164 above and below, p. 168, p. 172, p. 175 below, p. 179, p. 179 above and below, p. 180, p. 186, p. 187, p. 188, p. 197, p. 198, p. 199, p. 200, p. 208, p. 209, p. 212 above, p. 213 above and below, p. 216, p. 218, p. 222 above and below, p. 226, p. 228, p. 229, p. 230, p. 231, p. 235, p. 236, p. 238, p. 240, p. 250 below, p. 254, p. 270; H. Roger-Viollet p. 122; Royal Commission on Ancient and Historical Monuments p. 27 below; St Thomas's Hospital p. 123 below; Salvation Army p. 160; Science Museum p. 25 below, p. 34, p. 35, p. 42 below, p. 83, p. 96, p. 153, p. 253; Senate House Library p. 125; Sheffield City Library p. 97; Spectator p. 295; Syndication International p. 256, p. 271 above; John Topham p. 127 above; Trades Union Congress p. 95, p. 99, p. 100, p. 101, p. 102, p. 165, p. 202; Waterways Museum p. 37 above; Worcester Library p. 48; Wrighton International p. 283 below; York Library p. 33 above.

The cover illustration is '*Omnibus life in London*' by William Maw Egley.